1,666,017

students worldwide took the ACT in 2012

781

of those received a perfect score of 36*

1

of those 781 students has authored a full-length ACT prep book

Maria Filsinger

didn't get a 36 the first time she took the ACT. Acing the test, however, was a goal she was determined to achieve, as she had her heart set on attending Stanford University and wanted to do everything in her power to create the strongest application possible. After researching the test and using the test-taking strategies described in this book, Maria took the ACT in March of her junior year and scored what fewer than .05% of high school students in America did that year: a perfect 36.

Maria's 36 helped take her academic success to the next level: she became a 2012 United States Presidential Scholar, won a National Merit Scholarship, and was accepted by Stanford University. With thousands of dollars in additional academic scholarships and generous financial aid, Maria was able to achieve her longtime dream of attending Stanford, where she is currently pursuing a degree in Bioengineering. Eventually, she hopes to get M.D. and Ph.D. degrees and become a research scientist at a top university.

Maria wrote *ACT 36 in Just 7 Steps* to help students from all parts of the country and all backgrounds achieve their ACT and college goals. She hopes that by attaining higher ACT scores, these students can gain access to greater college and career opportunities.

*From the ACT 2012 Graduating Class Report.

ACT 36
in JUST 7 STEPS

ACT 36

36

in JUST 7 STEPS

Maria Filsinger

Shaan Patel

New York Chicago San Francisco Athens London Madrid
Mexico City Milan New Delhi Singapore Sydney Toronto

3 4 5 6 7 8 9 10   QFR/QFR   1 0 9 8 7 6 5 4

ISBN   978-0-07-181441-6
MHID   0-07-181441-8

e-ISBN   978-0-07-181442-3
e-MHID   0-07-181442-6

Library of Congress Control Number: 2013930082

ACT is a registered trademark of ACT, Inc., which was not involved in the production of, and does not endorse, this product.

McGraw-Hill Education products are available at special quantity discounts to use as premiums and sales promotions or for use in corporate training programs. To contact a representative, please visit the Contact Us pages at www.mhprofessional.com.

This book is printed on acid-free paper.

Contents

2 Prepare for ACT Math 89

7 Review the ACT practice exam 325

Reminders for exam day 351

Acknowledgments

I warmly thank everyone who has helped me along the epic journey of writing this book—especially Shaan, for sending me that fateful e-mail; my two loving parents, for being the most amazing and self-sacrificing parents in the world; my brother, Gabriel, for always being there for me at any hour of the day or night; and all of my friends, for never wavering in their encouragement of this sometimes-crazy endeavor.

I also extend my gratitude to all of the teachers who have inspired and encouraged me from the first days of kindergarten through my last days of high school. I consider the quality of my education one of the greatest and most valuable gifts in my life, one that was given selflessly by the incredible educators that I've had the pleasure to learn from. Thank you for sharing with me a love of learning that I will carry with me for the rest of my life.

I could not have done it without all of your help.

Learn how to study for the ACT

Dear ACT Exam Taker,

Hi! Welcome to *ACT 36 in Just 7 Steps*, the only full-length ACT preparation manual written by a student who achieved a perfect 36 on the ACT. This book presents a practical, focused approach to preparing for the ACT and will help you be successful on exam day, just like I was!

Who am I? I'm a student who achieved a score of 36 on the ACT when I took it during my junior year, was admitted to Stanford University, won thousands of dollars in scholarships, and was awarded academic honors such as National Merit Finalist and Scholarship Winner, AP National Scholar, IB Diploma Student, and 2012 Presidential Scholar.

But who am I *really*? In real life, I'm no different from you. I'm a teenager who loves to hang out with my friends, procrastinate, spend time on Facebook, and pursue my favorite sport—horseback riding. I attended a public school in Minnesota, grew up on a farm with horses and chickens in the backyard, and never knew much about the ACT until well into high school.

However, succeeding academically has always been extremely important to me, and with my eyes set on attending a top university, I knew that doing well on the ACT was a necessity, not an option. For that reason, I set myself up for success by using the same strategies that I'll relay to you in the coming pages. Just like me, you can use these tips and tricks to drastically improve your ACT score.

So who am I *now*? I'm an excited 19-year-old who just finished her freshman year of college. But for the purposes of the next few hundred pages, I'm your personal ACT expert and tutor. I'll share all my best strategies with you so that you too can succeed on this important exam.

Thorough ACT preparation is not easy, and it takes time to get accustomed to the strategies that will ultimately make you successful. When getting ready to take the ACT, I had to balance test preparation with AP and IB courses, an intense athletic competition and training schedule, a job, extracurricular activities, and volunteer work. It wasn't easy. But looking back, I know it was worth it. My best advice to you is to not shrink away from working hard now—not only with regard to the ACT exam, but with regard to high school in general—for I promise that your hard work will pay off, whether it is with scholarships, acceptance to prestigious universities, or exclusive opportunities. Most of all, I wish you the best of luck with your ACT preparation. I will be with you every step of the way on your journey to achieving a perfect 36.

Sincerely,

Maria Filsinger

ACT 36 exam taker and your personal ACT tutor

Four key principles

These key principles are the foundation of successful ACT preparation. They allowed me to raise my score significantly, and by following these principles, you too can turn *ordinary* ACT prep into *perfect* ACT prep!

Principle 1 · *Learn 36 Strategies*

36 Strategies are my tips and tricks for a variety of question types on the ACT exam. I developed these strategies by carefully reworking each ACT question to uncover which strategies and thought processes had allowed me to achieve my 36.

Principle 2 · *Study 36 Examples*

36 Examples show how my *36 Strategies* work on the various ACT question types. Through these examples, you will experience firsthand how mastering my strategies can lead to success on questions across all sections of the ACT.

Principle 3 · *Complete 36 Practice Problem Sets*

To help you test your mastery of my strategies, the discussion of each question type is followed by *36 Practice Problem Sets.* The best way to master the strategies and raise your score is to solve real ACT questions. Completing each set of practice problems will help you put the strategies to work for you.

Principle 4 · *Concentrate on 36 Review*

One of the most important (and most overlooked) principles in successful ACT prep is review. Working practice problems without reviewing the questions you answered incorrectly will do little to improve your performance. Review can pinpoint the areas you need to work on and identify problems that you can fix. *36 Review*—the careful examination of *36 Strategies, 36 Examples,* and *36 Practice Problem Sets* that you have worked—is the key to locating weak points in your ACT performance.

The ACT: the basics

There are several important facts that everyone should know before taking the ACT.

What is the ACT?

The ACT is a standardized college entrance examination; it is produced by American College Testing, Inc. (ACT) and required by many U.S. colleges and universities. The first ACT exam was administered in 1959, and the exam has been rapidly growing in popularity over the last few decades, so much so that in 2011, more students took the ACT than took the SAT.

The exam comprises four subjects: English, Mathematics, Reading, and Science, with an optional Writing test. Each of the four required sections is worth 36 points, while the maximum score on the Writing test is 12. The scores are averaged for a composite score of 1 to 36.

Why does the ACT exist?

Whose idea was it to force high school students to take this exam in the first place? The driving force behind standardized testing was the lack of opportunity for students whose families and geographical areas hadn't taken advantage of higher education. Aiming to level the playing field, the ACT created an exam by which all students could be measured against one standard instead of against the widely varying standards of high schools and regions. The ACT provides information that a student's grade point average (GPA) may not, especially due to the grade inflation that results in artificially high GPAs for students at some schools, compared to the grades at other schools where a 4.0 GPA is virtually unheard of. The ACT also reveals a student's critical thinking ability, which may not be reflected in the GPA of a student who is incredibly intelligent but lacks the drive or work ethic to perform well on assignments and tests.

What are the differences between the ACT and the SAT?

Some colleges require ACT scores from applicants, some require SAT scores, and some accept either. Find out which exam is required by the colleges you're planning to apply to. If you're interested in a school that accepts the results of either exam, you may want to take both the ACT and the SAT to find out which exam you score better on. In fact, you can take a practice exam for each—and not have to pay the fees.

There is a general feeling that the SAT is "trickier" than the ACT and that the ACT is fairer and more straightforward. The ACT tends to be more time-sensitive than the SAT, so ACT exam takers may have to rush to finish a section within the time allowed. The SAT Verbal sections focus more on vocabulary than their ACT counterparts, and the ACT Math section includes trigonometry, while the SAT doesn't. Both exams include an essay, although the essay is optional on the ACT. The SAT essay is the very first part of the exam, while the ACT essay comes last—a benefit, I believe, because you are warmed up and ready to go instead of starting cold. The ACT includes a Science section; the SAT does not.

Ultimately, you won't know which exam you'll perform better on until you take them. To see which exam better fits your test-taking style and gives you better scores, take both.

What is the format of the ACT?

The ACT contains four or five sections:

- ◂ English
- ◂ Mathematics
- ◂ Reading
- ◂ Science
- ◂ Writing (optional)

All sections count toward your score—there is no "variable" section, as on the SAT, that will not be counted. *Every one of your answers matters.*

How many questions are there on the ACT?

The total number of questions on the ACT, excluding the Writing test, is 215.

◂ English	75 questions (36 points)
◂ Mathematics	60 questions (36 points)
◂ Reading	40 questions (36 points)
◂ Science	40 questions (36 points)
◂ Writing (optional)	1 essay (12 points)

How long does the exam take?

The entire testing process takes about three hours, or three and a half hours if you take the ACT with Writing.

◂ English	45 minutes
◂ Mathematics	60 minutes
◂ Reading	35 minutes
◂ Science	35 minutes
◂ Writing (optional)	30 minutes

There are short breaks between sections, when you can sharpen your pencils, drink from your water bottle, and stretch. A snack/restroom break is usually provided after the first two sections, when you can use the restroom, refill your water bottle, and energize with a quick snack.

How is the exam scored?

The number of correct answers in each section is tallied to obtain the *raw score.* (No points are subtracted for incorrect answers—so it's important to answer every question, even if you guess.) The raw score is then converted into a *scaled score* of 1 to 36. The scaled score accounts for differences in the difficulty of the exam from one testing session to another. ACT statisticians use an elaborate system to compensate for slightly harder and slightly easier exams. Their goal is to make scaled scores across several exams reflect the same level of difficulty.

ACT will report your scaled scores, as well as a *percentile ranking* for each. The percentile ranking tells you how your performance on the exam compared to that of all the other students who took the same exam. A percentile ranking of 76 percent indicates that you scored better on the exam than 75 percent of the people who took it, and lower than 23 percent.

ACT will also report your *subscores*. In the English, Mathematics, and Reading sections, there are subscores for subsections:

- ◄ English (1–36)
    - Usage/mechanics (1–18)
    - Rhetorical skills (1–18)
- ◄ Mathematics (1–36)
    - Pre-algebra and elementary algebra (1–18)
    - Intermediate algebra and coordinate geometry (1–18)
    - Plane geometry and trigonometry (1–18)
- ◄ Reading (1–36)
    - Social science/Natural science (1–18)
    - Prose fiction/Humanities (1–18)
- ◄ Science (1–36)—no subscores

While college admissions offices rarely consider your subscores, or even your scores by section—they focus primarily on your composite score—subscores can be useful in determining your strong and weak subject areas. After you've taken the ACT exam once, these subscores identify where you need the most improvement, allowing you to study in a focused and efficient manner.

If you take the ACT with Writing (I'll discuss the pros and cons later), you will receive two additional scores: (1) a scaled score of 1 to 36 that combines your performance on the essay and the English section, and (2) your Writing subscore of 2 to 12, which represents the combined scores of two readers of your essay, each of whom has scored your essay on a scale of 1 to 6. Neither of these additional scores contributes to your composite score.

The average score on the ACT is about 20, with 90 percent of scores falling between 17 and 23. To attain the average score of 20, you need to answer about half of the questions correctly. On other tests, answering half the questions incorrectly might be terrible, but because of the ACT's inherent difficulty, 50 percent merits an average score. In many high school classes, 75 percent is equivalent to a C, but 75 percent on the ACT yields a score of about 26—a quite respectable score that ranks at the 90th percentile, meaning that you scored better than 89% of all students who took the ACT.

To achieve a perfect 36 score, you don't have to answer every question correctly. When I got my 36, I answered two questions wrong, one in Mathematics and one in English. When my composite score was calculated, however, it rounded to 36.

How often is the ACT administered?

In most parts of the United States, the ACT is offered six times a year, in September, October, December, February, April, and June. The February date is not offered in New York State. The testing usually begins at 8 o'clock on a Saturday morning. To find the specific dates, visit the ACT's official website at ACT.org.

How much does it cost?

In Summer 2013, the ACT costs $36.50 without the Writing test and $52.50 with it; the fees vary slightly from year to year.* The Writing test costs extra, because the ACT pays two readers to read and score your essay. The $36.50 testing fee includes a score report for you, your high school, and up to four colleges. If you are absent on exam day or switch to the ACT with no Writing before testing begins, the extra $16 for the Writing test is refundable on written request.

There are additional fees for late registration, standby testing, international testing, test date changes, test center changes, sending a score report to additional colleges, telephone reregistration, and the Test Information Release (TIR) service—more about the TIR later.

If you can't afford to pay for the ACT, ask your school counselor for an ACT fee waiver form; you can't contact the ACT directly about a fee waiver. Visit ACT.org to see if you qualify. A waiver covers only the basic registration fee, not the additional fees described in the preceding paragraph. Furthermore, the fee waiver applies to a single registration only, whether or not you take the exam on that day.

How do I register?

You should register about a month in advance of the exam date in order to avoid paying a late-registration fee. Visit ACT.org, create a personal account, and register online. You can access your exam scores from your personal account.

Standby testing is available if you miss the registration deadline. Besides the additional fee of $45, you aren't guaranteed a seat or an exam booklet—seats are available on a first-come, first-served basis, and the morning can become very stressful. The deadline to register for standby testing is 12 noon (Central time) on the Tuesday before the Saturday of testing.

How important is the ACT?

Answers to this question differ widely, depending on whom you ask. When making admissions decisions, colleges take into account standardized test scores, especially the ACT. Scoring well on the ACT tells these institutions that you are able to analyze data, draw conclusions, make predictions, and solve

---

*All fees reported in this chapter are current as of Summer 2013.

problems. While many colleges insist that they don't use ACT scores as a cutoff in the admissions process, the truth is that standardized testing is one of the quickest and easiest ways for colleges, especially those with thousands of applicants, to sort their applicants. Barring extraordinary circumstances, applicants with a score below a certain point may be rejected by certain colleges.

Of course, your ACT score is just one part of your college admissions package. Your high school grades, teacher recommendations, extracurricular activities and achievements, and admissions essays, as well as volunteer and community service, all play a role in the admissions process. A perfect score of 36 doesn't guarantee admission to a particular school, just as a low score doesn't mean certain rejection. Admissions offices look at the whole individual, not just the test scores—but why not make the ACT a strong point of your application rather than a weakness? It is, after all, the area in which you can improve most easily in a short period of time. Working hard to prepare for the ACT and achieving a strong score can help you make up for weaknesses in your application that can't be addressed in a limited time frame.

The ACT is important. It's not the be-all and end-all of your college application, but it plays a significant role in the admissions process.

How many times should I take the ACT?

This is a hotly debated topic. Most students take the ACT once or twice, once during their junior year and again during their senior year. Most colleges won't know how many times you take the ACT, since they'll see only your best score, the one you choose to send. Keep in mind, however, that some schools, such as Stanford University, require you to send all of your scores. I took the ACT three times: once in eighth grade for practice, and twice in my junior year. My recommendation is to take the exam not less than twice but not more than four times. Statistically, most students score better on the ACT the second time; taking it again won't hurt and probably will help, especially if you practice on your weak areas before taking the exam again. Don't take the ACT more than four times— the mental energy, effort, and time spent preparing for and taking the exam would be better applied to other aspects of the college application process.

How is the ACT reported?

The ACT sends out score reports one at a time. There is no cumulative ACT report that contains the scores from all the times you've taken the exam. Be sure you know which colleges require your scores every time you take the exam.

You can send your scores to colleges in two ways:

- On testing day, you can select up to four colleges to send your scores to; the cost of sending these scores is included in the registration fee.
- You can have your scores sent after you've seen them. Keep in mind, however, that this costs $12 per report per test date per college. For

example, if you wanted to send your scores from two ACT exams because you scored better on Mathematics and Science as a junior but better on English and Reading as a senior, the cost to send those reports to one college would be $24.

Here's my recommendation: if you know that you're applying to a college that requires you to send all your scores from all your exam dates, send your score reports to that school as part of your registration; in all other circumstances, wait until you see your scores before deciding which to send. You would be balancing the additional cost against the disadvantage of not knowing what your scores are (and, therefore, what colleges would see).

If you decide to send scores before you take the exam, you need to know which colleges you are applying to and look up their codes online. A list of colleges with codes is available on exam day, but it is easier to know the codes in advance to avoid last-minute confusion.

What is the TIR?

The Test Information Release (TIR) is an optional service that includes, for a fee of $19, a list of your answers, a copy of the multiple-choice questions that you answered, the answer key, and scoring instructions. If you took the Writing test, you'll also get a copy of the writing prompt, the scoring rubric, and your score. You can order the TIR when you register for the ACT exam, but it is only available for certain exam dates listed on ACT.org and does not include any international or special exam dates. You can also order the TIR up to three months after your exam date—after you have received your scores. For an additional fee, you can order a photocopy of your answer document, which includes your essay if you took the Writing test.

TIR materials, if ordered on testing day, are normally sent about four weeks after you receive your score report; you probably won't receive the TIR materials before the registration deadline for the next exam date or early enough to be able to use them before the next exam. For example, if you order the TIR when you take the ACT exam in September, it wouldn't make sense to take the exam again until December; this would give you sufficient time to use the TIR materials to prepare for the next exam.

I highly recommend ordering the TIR when you take the ACT exam the first time: you'll know which questions you struggled with and why, and can review what mistakes you made and how you made them. Analyzing your answers can help you avoid making similar mistakes the second time around.

Should I take the ACT Writing test?

Many colleges require or recommend that applicants take the optional Writing test. Visit ACT.org/aap/writing to determine if the institutions you are interested in require the Writing test. If you're not sure which schools you'll be applying to, I recommend taking the ACT with Writing—just in case.

Some schools use Writing scores to determine course placement, as well as to aid in the admissions process.

What is the PLAN?

The PLAN is a preliminary ACT exam offered by the same company and exam writers that produce the ACT exam. In many high schools, all freshmen and sophomores are encouraged to take the PLAN, and I highly recommend taking advantage of this opportunity.

Your scores on the PLAN will help you prepare for the actual ACT, and will indicate which sections will be most challenging for you. The PLAN can also help students decide which courses to take in their junior and senior years, as well as provide insight into potential career paths. For more information, visit ACT.org/planstudent.

What about special circumstances?

Students with disabilities or learning disorders may request special test-taking conditions. If you have a diagnosis from a qualified professional, you may be granted an alternate test format or more time to complete the exam. For more information, visit actstudent.org/regist/disab/.

The truth about the ACT

Your performance on the ACT measures only one thing: how well you perform on the ACT. It is not a measure of your intelligence, nor does it indicate how prepared you are for college. Of course, being intelligent and taking rigorous courses in high school will help you score well on the ACT, but at the end of the day, it's just a test, and no single test can accurately reveal your intelligence or academic promise.

If your current ACT score is low, don't be discouraged. The ACT tests very specific subject matter, some of which you may not have been taught. The purpose of this book is to prepare you to score well on the ACT, and I'm sure you will find that much of the information in this book wasn't covered in your high school courses.

Essential materials

You'll need the following materials before you begin your ACT exam prep:

- ◂ **This book.** *ACT 36 in Just 7 Steps* will be your guide throughout the process and will provide helpful tips and tricks for effective ACT preparation.

- ◂ **A 36 Review notebook.** Buy a notebook with at least 150 pages, divided into five sections. As you prepare for the ACT, you'll use this notebook to take notes on questions and areas you're struggling with, to prepare for your essay, to create your own test-taking methods, and more. Label the five sections as follows:

  1. English
  2. Mathematics
  3. Reading
  4. Science
  5. Writing

- ◂ **ACT practice exams.** Practice is essential, and you will need to work a lot of ACT practice questions. This book provides hundreds of ACT practice questions, but you'll need more than that! You can buy a book of ACT practice exams, or you can find free exams online. You will need at least 10 ACT practice exams.

- ◂ **ACT's Question of the Day.** Take advantage of the ACT Question of the Day, posted daily at ACT.org/qotd.

- ◂ **Pencils, eraser, watch, and calculator.** Since you will use these materials on exam day, you should use them as you prepare. Even though you may have a timer on your phone, it's better to time yourself with a watch: you can wear a watch on exam day, but you can't use your phone. Also, practice with the calculator that you'll use on exam day.

- ◂ **Self-motivation.** This is the tool that will help you meet your ACT goals. No one or nothing can magically raise your score without your putting in the effort. Good preparation isn't easy; it takes energy and hard work. There will be times when you want to give up, times when you wonder how all this effort is ever going to pay off. I can give you strategies and techniques to improve your score on the ACT, but it's up to you to put them to use.

  What drives you to study for the ACT? The motivation to succeed should come from you, not from your parents, friends, or teachers. When I was preparing for the ACT, I knew that in order to be accepted by a school like Stanford, I was going to need a high score on the ACT, and I wasn't going to let a poor or average score stand in the way of my dream. Discover what motivates you, and remind yourself of this as you study. Is it a school you want to get into? A scholarship you want to get? A program you want to be a part of? Whatever it is, never lose sight of your goal when you're preparing.

On the first page of your 36 Review notebook, write what motivates you. As you use your notebook during test preparation, look at that page frequently and recall what inspires you to keep working, keep studying, keep preparing.

If you really apply yourself, you'll exceed even your own expectations. When I was working hard in high school, and pushing myself harder and harder, I kept my goals before me. On your hardest days, remember that all your hard work will pay off.

General ACT preparation

Most ACT prep books tell you *what* you need to study for the ACT, but not *how* to study. This book is different. *How* you study for the ACT is just as important as—if not more important than—*what* you study.

If two students have access to the same study materials, why does one student score higher than the other? The answer lies in how each student applies the information, and that is what this book will teach you to do. As you study, keep this in mind: "Practice doesn't make perfect. Perfect practice makes perfect." This book will help you achieve the perfect practice that will make acing the ACT possible.

Many students pass through high school without ever learning to study properly. Studying is a key life skill that requires a lot of practice, and you have to practice studying to be good at it. In this section, I'll share the techniques and strategies that helped me achieve a perfect score on the ACT. My method may not be the only way to achieve a 36—certainly, others have aced the exam using other methods—but my method worked for me, and you don't have to be a genius or a 4.0 student for my strategies to work for you.

Take a diagnostic exam

Take at least one full-length ACT practice exam before you begin your test preparation. This will provide clues about your strongest and weakest areas. Simulate exam conditions as much as possible: make sure you have a quiet, undisturbed place; time yourself; and take the whole exam in one sitting. After the exam, fill in the following chart:

Exam 1

Number of questions incorrect/Total number of questions

English
  Usage/mechanics
    Punctuation _____/10
    Grammar/usage _____/12
    Sentence structure _____/18
  Rhetorical skills
    Strategy _____/12
    Organization _____/11
    Style _____/12
Mathematics
  Pre-algebra and elementary algebra _____/24
  Intermediate algebra and coordinate geometry _____/18
  Plane geometry _____/14
  Trigonometry _____/4
Reading
  Prose fiction _____/10
  Social science _____/10
  Humanities _____/10
  Natural science _____/10
Science
  Data representation _____/15
  Research summaries _____/18
  Conflicting viewpoints _____/7
Writing
  Essay _____/12

If you're not sure of the category to which a question belongs, refer to its corresponding section in this book. Your goal throughout ACT preparation should be to significantly decrease your "Number of questions incorrect." Once you've identified your weakest areas, you can focus on them and study more efficiently and effectively for the ACT.

Work together: 36 Practice and 36 Review

The two pillars of successful ACT preparation are practice and review. The seven steps below outline how *36 Practice* and *36 Review* work together:

---

1 · Learn 36 Strategies
2 · Complete an ACT practice section
3 · Score your ACT practice section
4 · Check questions you answered correctly
5 · Check questions you answered incorrectly
6 · Complete your 36 Review
7 · Repeat steps 1 to 6

Step 1 ⁀ *Learn 36 Strategies*

Learn this book's strategies for an ACT subject area that gives you trouble.

Step 2 ⁀ *Complete an ACT practice section*

Practice on a section that contains questions related to the weak area.

Step 3 ⁀ *Score your ACT practice section*

Score the section to discover how you performed.

Step 4 ⁀ *Check questions you answered correctly*

Check that you understand the technique or strategy behind each question that you answered correctly. Make sure that you could repeat the way you solved that problem if you were confronted with a similar problem in the future. This process shouldn't take more than 10 or 20 seconds per question. If your answer was just a lucky guess, enter the problem under "Problems to review" in the appropriate section of your 36 Review notebook.

Step 5 ⁀ *Check questions you answered incorrectly*

Enter these problems under "Problems to review" in the appropriate section of your 36 Review notebook. For future reference, note the exam, section, page number, and question number of each problem. Write the main part of the question, as well as the key to solving the problem that you missed earlier. If you can't figure out why your answer was incorrect, mark it for later review.

You don't have to enter every single problem that you answered incorrectly—just the ones that are hardest for you. Limit yourself to no more than seven entries per practice section.

Step 6 ⚹ *Complete your 36 Review*

Once a week, review your English, Mathematics, Reading, and Science "Problems to review." In this way, you will maintain your familiarity with the problems that are hardest for you. If you can't solve some problems, seek help from a parent, friend, or teacher.

Step 7 ⚹ *Repeat steps 1 to 6*

Repeat this process for another ACT subject area that gives you trouble. Review the *36 Strategies* at least twice to make sure you really understand them. Take all the practice sections of one ACT exam before moving on to another exam; you will then be able to fill in the following charts to track your progress.

Exam 2

Number of questions incorrect/Total number of questions

English
    Usage/mechanics
        Punctuation   _____/10
        Grammar/usage   _____/12
        Sentence structure   _____/18
    Rhetorical skills
        Strategy   _____/12
        Organization   _____/11
        Style   _____/12
Mathematics
    Pre-algebra and elementary algebra   _____/24
    Intermediate algebra and coordinate geometry   _____/18
    Plane geometry   _____/14
    Trigonometry   _____/4
Reading
    Prose fiction   _____/10
    Social science   _____/10
    Humanities   _____/10
    Natural science   _____/10
Science
    Data representation   _____/15
    Research summaries   _____/18
    Conflicting viewpoints   _____/7
Writing
    Essay   _____/12

Exam 3

Number of questions incorrect/Total number of questions

English
    Usage/mechanics
        Punctuation   _____/10
        Grammar/usage   _____/12
        Sentence structure   _____/18
    Rhetorical skills
        Strategy   _____/12
        Organization   _____/11
        Style   _____/12
Mathematics
    Pre-algebra and elementary algebra   _____/24
    Intermediate algebra and coordinate geometry   _____/18
    Plane geometry   _____/14
    Trigonometry   _____/4
Reading
    Prose fiction   _____/10
    Social science   _____/10
    Humanities   _____/10
    Natural science   _____/10
Science
    Data representation   _____/15
    Research summaries   _____/18
    Conflicting viewpoints   _____/7
Writing
    Essay   _____/12

Exam 4

Number of questions incorrect/Total number of questions

English
  Usage/mechanics
    Punctuation   _____/10
    Grammar/usage   _____/12
    Sentence structure   _____/18
  Rhetorical skills
    Strategy   _____/12
    Organization   _____/11
    Style   _____/12
Mathematics
  Pre-algebra and elementary algebra   _____/24
  Intermediate algebra and coordinate geometry   _____/18
  Plane geometry   _____/14
  Trigonometry   _____/4
Reading
  Prose fiction   _____/10
  Social science   _____/10
  Humanities   _____/10
  Natural science   _____/10
Science
  Data representation   _____/15
  Research summaries   _____/18
  Conflicting viewpoints   _____/7
Writing
  Essay   _____/12

Exam 5

Number of questions incorrect/Total number of questions

English
    Usage/mechanics
        Punctuation   _____/10
        Grammar/usage   _____/12
        Sentence structure   _____/18
    Rhetorical skills
        Strategy   _____/12
        Organization   _____/11
        Style   _____/12
Mathematics
    Pre-algebra and elementary algebra   _____/24
    Intermediate algebra and coordinate geometry   _____/18
    Plane geometry   _____/14
    Trigonometry   _____/4
Reading
    Prose fiction   _____/10
    Social science   _____/10
    Humanities   _____/10
    Natural science   _____/10
Science
    Data representation   _____/15
    Research summaries   _____/18
    Conflicting viewpoints   _____/7
Writing
    Essay   _____/12

Exam 6

Number of questions incorrect/Total number of questions

English
    Usage/mechanics
        Punctuation   _____/10
        Grammar/usage   _____/12
        Sentence structure   _____/18
    Rhetorical skills
        Strategy   _____/12
        Organization   _____/11
        Style   _____/12
Mathematics
    Pre-algebra and elementary algebra   _____/24
    Intermediate algebra and coordinate geometry   _____/18
    Plane geometry   _____/14
    Trigonometry   _____/4
Reading
    Prose fiction   _____/10
    Social science   _____/10
    Humanities   _____/10
    Natural science   _____/10
Science
    Data representation   _____/15
    Research summaries   _____/18
    Conflicting viewpoints   _____/7
Writing
    Essay   _____/12

Exam 7

Number of questions incorrect/Total number of questions

English
  Usage/mechanics
    Punctuation ———/10
    Grammar/usage ———/12
    Sentence structure ———/18
  Rhetorical skills
    Strategy ———/12
    Organization ———/11
    Style ———/12
Mathematics
  Pre-algebra and elementary algebra ———/24
  Intermediate algebra and coordinate geometry ———/18
  Plane geometry ———/14
  Trigonometry ———/4
Reading
  Prose fiction ———/10
  Social science ———/10
  Humanities ———/10
  Natural science ———/10
Science
  Data representation ———/15
  Research summaries ———/18
  Conflicting viewpoints ———/7
Writing
  Essay ———/12

Exam 8

Number of questions incorrect/Total number of questions

English
  Usage/mechanics
    Punctuation _____/10
    Grammar/usage _____/12
    Sentence structure _____/18
  Rhetorical skills
    Strategy _____/12
    Organization _____/11
    Style _____/12
Mathematics
  Pre-algebra and elementary algebra _____/24
  Intermediate algebra and coordinate geometry _____/18
  Plane geometry _____/14
  Trigonometry _____/4
Reading
  Prose fiction _____/10
  Social science _____/10
  Humanities _____/10
  Natural science _____/10
Science
  Data representation _____/15
  Research summaries _____/18
  Conflicting viewpoints _____/7
Writing
  Essay _____/12

Exam 9

Number of questions incorrect/Total number of questions

English
  Usage/mechanics
    Punctuation   _____ /10
    Grammar/usage   _____ /12
    Sentence structure   _____ /18
  Rhetorical skills
    Strategy   _____ /12
    Organization   _____ /11
    Style   _____ /12
Mathematics
  Pre-algebra and elementary algebra   _____ /24
  Intermediate algebra and coordinate geometry   _____ /18
  Plane geometry   _____ /14
  Trigonometry   _____ /4
Reading
  Prose fiction   _____ /10
  Social science   _____ /10
  Humanities   _____ /10
  Natural science   _____ /10
Science
  Data representation   _____ /15
  Research summaries   _____ /18
  Conflicting viewpoints   _____ /7
Writing
  Essay   _____ /12

Exam 10

Number of questions incorrect/Total number of questions

English
  Usage/mechanics
    Punctuation _____/10
    Grammar/usage _____/12
    Sentence structure _____/18
  Rhetorical skills
    Strategy _____/12
    Organization _____/11
    Style _____/12
Mathematics
  Pre-algebra and elementary algebra _____/24
  Intermediate algebra and coordinate geometry _____/18
  Plane geometry _____/14
  Trigonometry _____/4
Reading
  Prose fiction _____/10
  Social science _____/10
  Humanities _____/10
  Natural science _____/10
Science
  Data representation _____/15
  Research summaries _____/18
  Conflicting viewpoints _____/7
Writing
  Essay _____/12

Final ACT practice exam
Number of questions incorrect/Total number of questions
....

English
   Usage/mechanics
      Punctuation   _____/10
      Grammar/usage   _____/12
      Sentence structure   _____/18
   Rhetorical skills
      Strategy   _____/12
      Organization   _____/11
      Style   _____/12
Mathematics
   Pre-algebra and elementary algebra   _____/24
   Intermediate algebra and coordinate geometry   _____/18
   Plane geometry   _____/14
   Trigonometry   _____/4
Reading
   Prose fiction   _____/10
   Social science   _____/10
   Humanities   _____/10
   Natural science   _____/10
Science
   Data representation   _____/15
   Research summaries   _____/18
   Conflicting viewpoints   _____/7
Writing
   Essay   _____/12

The goal of this seven-step plan is to take full-length ACT exams in manageable chunks of 20 to 30 minutes. Keep in mind that this is a time-consuming process, and working through steps 1 to 6 may take several hours. You can break the process up by performing steps in multiple sessions.

When to prepare

Finding time to prepare for the ACT can be difficult. Balancing several hours of test prep a week with school, sports, extracurricular activities, work, and family obligations can be quite a feat. It is crucial, however, that you add ACT prep to your list of activities and make sure that it is a top priority. Don't tell yourself that you'll study for the ACT in your "spare time"—if you're like me, you won't have any spare time, as hobbies, sports, and activities rapidly expand to fill all your waking hours. Schedule ACT study time just like you would schedule any other activity. Make your test prep a necessity rather than an optional activity; this will ensure that it actually gets done.

During the school year It can be especially difficult during the school year to find several hours a week for test prep. Here's a good way to fit it in:

- Prep for the ACT for a total of 4 to 8 hours a week.
- Prep for the ACT at least 4 days a week.
- An ACT prep session should last no less than 30 minutes and no more than 2 hours.

During the summer It's much easier to focus on test prep during the summer. The temptation of spending time outdoors and with friends can be hard to resist, so be sure to stay disciplined:

- Prep for the ACT a total of 8 to 15 hours a week.
- Prep for the ACT at least 5 days a week.
- An ACT prep session should last no less than 30 minutes and no more than 3 hours.

Squeeze it in You can turn small chunks of time throughout the day into significant progress. Do you have five minutes waiting for a friend to meet you? Ten minutes waiting for a meeting to start? Fifteen minutes waiting in the car to pick up a sibling or parent? All of these chunks of time can add up, and taking advantage of otherwise wasted time can give you an edge in prepping for the exam. Here's how:

- Review the ACT Question of the Day on your smartphone or laptop.
- Complete a portion of an ACT practice section.
- Outline a response to a sample ACT Writing prompt.

The 36 six-phase schedule

Use this handy schedule to plan your ACT preparation. It's divided into phases rather than weeks, so that you can shrink or expand it to fill the time you have for prepping.

No matter how much time you have to get ready for the ACT, this phase schedule can work for you. Even if you pick up this book with only six weeks before the exam, you can work through one phase a week. If you get this book in June, with an exam date in September, you have three months to prepare—15 days for each phase.

Using this six-phase schedule, you'll study all the steps of the book, complete the *36 Practice Exam*, and complete 10 additional ACT practice exams. You won't be overwhelmed if you stick to the schedule and perform one phase at a time.

Phase 1

- [ ] Complete the ACT diagnostic exam (Exam 1) in a single, timed sitting.
- [ ] Study **General ACT preparation** and **Step 1 · Prepare for ACT English**.
- [ ] Complete each section of ACT practice exam 2.
- [ ] Review each question in exams 1 and 2, and write problems for review, questions, and keys in your 36 Review notebook.
- [ ] Review your 36 Review notebook.

Phase 2

- [ ] Complete ACT practice exam 3 in a single, timed sitting.
- [ ] Study **Step 2 · Prepare for ACT Math**.
- [ ] Complete each section of ACT practice exam 4.
- [ ] Review ACT practice exams 3 and 4.
- [ ] Review your 36 Review notebook.

Phase 3

- [ ] Complete ACT practice exam 5 in a single, timed sitting.
- [ ] Study **Step 3 · Prepare for ACT Reading**.
- [ ] Complete each section of ACT practice exam 6.
- [ ] Review ACT practice exams 5 and 6.
- [ ] Review your 36 Review notebook.

Phase 4

- [ ] Complete ACT practice exam 7 in a single, timed sitting.
- [ ] Study **Step 4 · Prepare for ACT Science**.
- [ ] Complete each section of ACT practice exam 8.
- [ ] Review ACT practice exams 7 and 8.
- [ ] Review your 36 Review notebook.

Phase 5

- [ ] Complete ACT practice exam 9 in a single, timed sitting.
- [ ] Study **Step 5 · Prepare for ACT Writing**.*
- [ ] Complete each section of ACT practice exam 10.
- [ ] Review ACT practice exams 9 and 10.
- [ ] Review your 36 Review notebook.

---

*If you won't be taking the optional ACT Writing test, spend this time reviewing the chapter on the section that you're least confident about.

Phase 6

☐ Complete the final ACT practice exam at the end of this book in a single, timed sitting.

☐ Review the final ACT practice exam, using the solutions at the end of this book.

☐ Review the areas you had trouble with in the English, Math, Reading, and Science chapters of this book.

☐ Review your 36 Review notebook.

You don't learn anything new in Phase 6. The light preparation during this phase will keep your mind fresh and ready for exam day.

If you've completed the schedule above and taken the ACT, but are dissatisfied with your score, repeat the schedule and retake the exam. All you will need is new ACT practice exams.

Notice the major theme of the schedule: review, review, review. You're constantly reviewing previous questions, areas you've completed, and your 36 Review notebook, which will fill up with personal test-taking insights and hints. Although this sounds repetitive and even boring, it's crucial to review material to make sure that you fully understand it by exam day.

A word of caution—don't let the review get in the way of efficiency! If there's a section you score well on (say, Science), you can skim or even skip the review of that chapter and spend the time you've saved on improving performance in your weak areas.

A consistent schedule

A regular schedule helps you stay on track with your ACT prep—and not procrastinate, as most of us are more than happy to do. Set aside particular days and times of the day for study, and respect those times. Slow and steady preparation is the best way to accomplish your ACT goals.

Where to prepare

Effective ACT preparation requires focus and concentration; your living room, with the television blaring and a younger sibling running and yelling, isn't an ideal location. I recommend studying at the local library. Libraries typically have quiet, comfortable study spaces free from distractions. This may sound more boring and isolated than studying at home or with friends, but it has strong advantages. If you've never studied at a library before, you may be skeptical. Try this: spend two hours of ACT prep at home, then two hours at a library, and compare how much you accomplished in the two venues. You will be amazed at how much more productive you can be in a quiet, isolated place.

If a library isn't accessible, find a location that has these features:

◄ **Quiet.** When you're trying to learn an ACT concept, you don't need background noise that keeps you from focusing.

◄ **Plenty of work space.** Every time you have an ACT prep session, you're going to need this book, your 36 Review notebook, and several ACT practice exams. A large desk area will provide ample space to spread out your materials.

◄ **Away from home.** A friend drops by, your mom asks you to do chores, your younger siblings are yelling, or you decide to take a break that turns into a two-hour nap—these are just some of the distractions that keep you from working effectively at home.

◄ **Away from friends.** Studying with friends can be fun, and you may have a friend with whom you study well. ACT prep, however, is a process best undertaken alone. Friends can cause you to become distracted, lose focus, and waste time that you can't afford to lose as you prepare for this critical exam.

◄ **Away from technology.** With the increasing popularity of smart-phones, as well as addictive social media sites like Facebook and Twit-ter, staying focused while studying is harder than ever. While studying for the ACT, stay away from your laptop, smartphone, iPad—anything with Internet access. The ACT is a paper-and-pencil, written exam, and you simply don't need technology to assist you.

I recommend putting your phone in silent mode and placing it out of sight, or even turning it off completely. You can take a break every hour or so for a snack, texting, and Facebook/Twitter time. I also rec-ommend that you don't listen to music while you study. Some students claim that it helps them study or that they are more productive when listening to music, but test prep requires a lot of concentration—and music, especially music with lyrics, can be a huge distraction.

What to memorize

In a sea of overwhelming test-preparation requirements, there is good news! The amount of material that you actually need to memorize in order to do well on the ACT is quite small. With the exception of a few key rules and equations, you won't be doing any memorization during your ACT preparation. Unlike many of the tests you take in high school, the ACT doesn't test rote memoriza-tion—it tests how well you think and solve problems.

Physical and mental health

What is this—a self-help book? In a way, it is. I can't emphasize enough the importance of physical and mental health when approaching the ACT. Regular exercise has been proven to enhance memorization and studying. When you improve your physical health, your mental health improves, too. Exercise is one activity where music is acceptable, even beneficial. If the isolation of indoor studying has you feeling cooped up, lace up your running shoes and grab your iPod!

Eating healthy can also help you perform better. A healthy diet increases energy and makes it easier to focus, and it beats the crash of sugar and caffeine highs.

General 36 Strategies

Throughout this book, you'll encounter *36 Strategies*—the building blocks for success on the ACT. Many of these strategies are subject-specific, but there are five general strategies that will help you at every step of your preparation.

---

1 · Practice how to take the ACT
2 · Write it all down
3 · Bubble one page at a time
4 · Skip and return
5 · Always guess—always

General 36 Strategy 1 ⚊ *Practice how to take the ACT*

This strategy seems obvious, but many people invest their time and money in a test-preparation program like this one and don't change *how* they approach the exam. They may read the book and pick up a few tips along the way, but they don't "buy into" the strategies presented. It is crucial to apply the strategies provided in this book in your everyday practice, and not just save them for exam day. It is the hours of practice using the strategies that will allow you to use them effectively when it really counts.

Don't be afraid to change your test-taking habits; trust in the strategies in this book, even if they are different from your ordinary approach. They should be different! A test-prep book wouldn't help at all if it advised you to prepare for a test as you always have.

General 36 Strategy 2 ⚊ *Write it all down*

Write it all down in your exam booklet. *All* of it. Some test takers leave their exam booklets as clean as if the booklets had just come out of their packaging. They read the questions *without* underlining key information, check the answer choices without using their pencil to eliminate some, and go straight to bubbling in the answer sheet. They're making a huge mistake!

Writing in the exam booklet gives you an extraordinary advantage: it allows you to "think" with your pencil as well as with your mind. When you read a question, underline words or phrases that contain the most important information. When you review the answer choices, strike through the ones you know are incorrect, and circle the correct answer. This takes only a few seconds, and it will save you time when returning to skipped questions. Of course, you should make sure that none of your marks blocks out answer choices that you may need to revisit.

Many test takers don't write in their exam booklets, because they were forbidden to do so by teachers who were saving the booklets for next year's class. Holding all this information in your head makes a test much harder than it needs to be. Writing in the exam booklet organizes your thinking and helps you focus on the most critical parts of questions and answers.

When you close the ACT exam booklet after three hours of testing, it should be covered with squiggles, jottings, circles, and other marks.

General 36 Strategy 3 ⁄ *Bubble one page at a time*

You can save a lot of time by circling your answer selections for all problems on a page, then bubbling in your selections on the answer sheet for all the problems at once. This strategy has several advantages:

- ◄ You will save time. Flipping back and forth between your exam booklet and answer sheet wastes valuable seconds.
- ◄ Especially in the Reading and Science sections, this strategy helps you focus on the set of questions on each page as a whole, rather than on each individual question.
- ◄ The satisfaction of bubbling in a full page of answers (usually for four or five questions) gives you a confidence boost every time.

General 36 Strategy 4 ⁄ *Skip and return*

On a timed test like the ACT, saving a minute on a question here and there can lead to big gains over the course of the exam. For this reason, it's crucial that you skip every question that you don't know how to answer.

Many students stare at a difficult question for a few seconds; confused, they read and reread the question, staring blankly at it with the hope that an answer will magically appear; and they try different approaches without success. By the time they guess or move on to the next question, not only have they wasted valuable time, but they've taken a blow to their confidence that may affect their performance on other, easier questions.

You—the savvy, prepared ACT student—will use a different strategy. You will *immediately* skip a question that meets any of the following conditions:

- ◄ You can't figure out what the question is asking.
- ◄ The question confuses you.
- ◄ You can't eliminate more than one of the answer choices.

Skipping a question after spending only a few seconds on it can be scary, but it will help you immensely in managing your time. If you have the willpower to skip a confusing question immediately, you've done the hardest part of this strategy: the skipping. When you reach the end of the section and return to the questions you've skipped, you're likely to find that some of them make sense almost instantly! You've given your brain a fresh start that increases your chances of solving the problem.

Even if you still can't figure out some skipped problems, you're better off than if you had wasted time on them and not finished the section—perhaps not getting to questions that you could have answered in a few seconds.

When in doubt, skip. You can return to the question later.

General 36 Strategy 5 ⌐ *Always guess—always*

The ACT does not penalize you for guessing incorrectly. *Always* guess. If you can't figure out a problem at once, use the skip-and-return strategy. If you return to the problem and are still stumped, guess. Chances are, you'll guess correctly at least some of the time, and that will boost your score.

Extra tips and tricks

- ◄ Don't let previous answer choices influence your answer choice for the question you're working on. Just because your last five answers were C doesn't mean that the correct answer to the current question isn't C.
- ◄ When marking the exam booklet, don't cross out parts of questions or answers so that you can't read them. If you return to a question and realize that you read it wrong, you can read the answer choices again— if you haven't aggressively crossed some of them out. Cross out the answer letter rather than the answer itself.
- ◄ Don't be frustrated by days when your study sessions seem to accomplish little. Your efficiency will fluctuate—some days will be better than others.
- ◄ While you're studying, take breaks and eat snacks. Take a break every hour or so; snacks will ensure that your brain and body aren't running on empty.

Prepare for ACT English

ACT English, the first section of the exam, is designed to measure your ability to understand, interpret, and use the English language as a tool of communication and expression. Yet—like the other sections—the ACT English section measures only how well you perform on the ACT English section.

One of the joys of standardized testing is that it's predictable—and the English section doesn't deviate from the pattern. Fortunately, the ACT company is very open about exactly what the English test focuses on, and we can home in on those areas during our preparation. Knowing what's going to be tested and how it's going to be tested, it's hard for you to go wrong once you've studied and memorized the English 36 strategies!

Stats

Time allowed	45 minutes
Number of questions	75 questions
Time allowed per question	36 seconds

The English section contains five passages, each of which is accompanied by about 15 questions. In practice and on the actual test, you should aim to complete each passage in a little less than 9 minutes, leaving a few moments at the end to make sure you've bubbled correctly and haven't made any glaring errors.

First, we'll explore the five English 36 strategies, and then launch into a detailed study of each of the six subsections of the English test.

⊡ Breaking down ACT English

"Six elements of effective writing are included in the English Test: punctuation, grammar and usage, sentence structure, strategy, organization, and style. The questions covering punctuation, grammar, and sentence structure make up the Usage/Mechanics subscore. The questions covering strategy, organization, and style make up the Rhetorical Skills subscore."
—ACT.org

English 36 Strategies

1 · Say it out loud (well, not really)
2 · Eliminate choices you know are wrong
3 · Don't forget about "NO CHANGE" and "DELETE"
4 · Shorter is sweeter
5 · Read and answer as you go

English 36 Strategy 1 ⚲ *Say it out loud (well, not really)*

One of the most effective strategies for success in ACT English is "reading aloud" in your head. If the answer is not immediately obvious from reading the underlined part of the passage (sometimes it is!), try reading the passage in your head, first with no change and then with each of the answer choices. A lot of the time, one answer choice will "sound right" while the others "sound wrong"—and this is a time to trust your instincts. Throughout high school, you've encountered correct English grammar and usage far more often than incorrect language. This is especially true if you read a lot, because most authors use correct English, and correct English begins to "sound right" to your ears. If you are confident that one choice sounds far better than the others, go ahead and bubble in that answer and move on. You've saved valuable seconds, which you can apply to other, more difficult questions. Try this strategy in the following example:

English 36 example

On sunny days, I like to sit by the

<u>calm. Tranquil</u> lake and watch the fish
     1

swimming beneath the shimmering

surface.

1. **A.** NO CHANGE
   B. calm tranquil
   C. calm, tranquil
   D. calm, tranquil.

Reading the sentence fragment by itself first, with no change, probably doesn't sound right to you, and it shouldn't! A long pause between calm and tranquil just sounds wrong. If you read aloud answer choice B, the words "calm" and "tranquil" seem mashed together—too close to sound right. It's only when you get to choice C that the sentence reads smoothly, as it should. A quick check of choice D, which introduces an unnatural pause between "tranquil" and "lake," confirms that the correct choice is C.

Be sure to read the sentence as it is, without allowing yourself to make mental corrections. Remember to "read" a long pause for a period, and a short pause for a comma. Our brains are very smart and often correct what we are reading; make sure that you read the sentence as it's written.

Don't worry if you couldn't tell the difference in how the choices in the example sounded, or if they all sounded just fine to you—the goal of this chapter is to give you the rules with which you can differentiate correct and incorrect English; being able to differentiate the two subconsciously is an added bonus.

English 36 Strategy 2 ⟋ *Eliminate choices you know are wrong*

It helps that some answer choices in ACT English are very obviously wrong. The test is written so that even the most incompetent readers and writers (perhaps those who speak another language at home and only understand enough English to get by) can still answer some questions correctly. Thus, you'll be able to immediately rule out quite a few choices, because they don't make any sense. If you're lucky, you'll be able to eliminate all but one choice for a particular question. If a choice sounds downright absurd, contains a clear grammatical error, or is completely unrelated to the passage, promptly cross out the letter corresponding to that choice. Even if you can't isolate the correct choice and are forced to guess, you're 25 percent closer to guessing the correct choice with each incorrect choice you eliminate.

English 36 example

The cute lab puppies

<u>were barking and rolling</u> around
        2

in excitement as Anna and I walked

to the door.

2. **F.** NO CHANGE
   G. they were barking and rolling
   H. were barking, and rolling
   J. did bark and did roll

After reading through choices G, H, and J in this example, you were probably able to eliminate all of them, leaving the "NO CHANGE" choice as the only possible answer. After quickly confirming that the sentence does indeed sound fine as it is, you could quickly circle choice F and move on.

English 36 Strategy 3 ⟋ *Don't forget about "NO CHANGE" and "DELETE"*

Most questions in ACT English offer "NO CHANGE" as an answer choice. Many first-time test takers think that since there are choices for changing a passage, it should probably be changed, and they instinctively shy away from selecting "NO CHANGE." This is a serious error that could lead to many lost points on the ACT exam, because recent estimates show that "NO CHANGE" is the correct answer choice more than 25 percent of the time. "NO CHANGE" is just as likely—if not *more* likely—to be the correct choice. ACT English emphasizes the value of being short and succinct in writing, so if the other answer choices are long and the underlined segment is short, "NO CHANGE" is most likely the correct answer.

Many ACT English questions offer "DELETE the underlined portion" as a choice. "DELETE" means that you would remove the underlined words and let the sentence stand without them. Here's an example:

English 36 example

After the battle, the winning army took control of the city and the general wedded the city's young and beautiful princess—she was truly pretty.
₃

3. **A.** NO CHANGE
   B. , and she was truly pretty.
   C. —pretty as she was.
   D. DELETE the underlined portion.

As you can see, "DELETE" is a particularly attractive choice when the underlined segment restates an idea that was expressed earlier in the passage; in this case, "truly pretty" restates "beautiful." ACT English avoids redundancy like the plague, so if the underlined segment looks redundant or repetitive in any way, chances are "DELETE" is the best answer choice. In fact, "DELETE," if offered as a choice, is even more likely to be the correct answer choice than "NO CHANGE"—it is the correct answer more than half of the time! When you're stuck on a question that offers "DELETE" as a choice and you need to guess, make sure that the sentence makes grammatical sense without the underlined segment; if it does, choose "DELETE" as your answer.

English 36 Strategy 4 ⸱ *Shorter is sweeter*

ACT English generally favors short, concise answers. Think about which answer choice says the most in the fewest words; chances are, that's the correct answer! From a purely statistical standpoint, the shortest answer choice has been shown to be correct on about half of all ACT English questions. If you've zipped through the English section, automatically choosing the shortest answer choice for each question, you would score a 15—without reading a single question! Obviously, you don't want a 15, but the key idea here is that the shortest answers are right about half the time, which makes them fairly good bets when you find yourself guessing.

How many questions on the ACT test your ability to find and eliminate repetitiveness and verbosity? Quite a few, actually: about a third of the English test consists of questions that require you to scout for redundancy and relevance.

Sometimes, it's hard for students to keep in mind that longer isn't always better, especially since many English teachers reward length and the use of big, complicated sentences. Nevertheless, it is imperative to remember that *this is not the case* in ACT English. Length for the sake of length is to be avoided, and the short, clean answer will almost always be the one you're looking for.

Here's an example of the "short is sweet" strategy at work:

English 36 example

After the loss, my coach patted us all

on the back, reminding us that there are

no true wins without <u>losing games too.</u>
   4

4. **F.** NO CHANGE
   G. losing a few games.
   H. losing games, as well.
   J. losses.

See how choice J expresses the same idea as the other choices but is able to do it in a single word rather than in a whole phrase? That is the kind of brevity that the ACT likes on the English section. Keep this in mind as you work through the test; bigger is *not* better!

English 36 Strategy 5 ⁄ *Read and answer as you go*

This is more of a technique than a strategy, and it has to do with how you move from passage to passage on the test. Unlike in other sections, you shouldn't look at ACT English questions before reading the passage, and you shouldn't read the whole passage before moving on to the questions. Instead, you should answer each question as it comes up in the passage. The reason is this: an overall understanding of the passage, in addition to attention to the questions, is necessary to answer questions that appear at the end of the passage and reference the passage as a whole. Don't skip sentences because they don't have underlined segments—you might need that information to answer later questions. Read the whole passage completely so that you have a good sense of its organization and style; you may need to answer questions about these points later.

Categories

The questions on the English section of the ACT are of two types: usage/mechanics and rhetorical skills.

	NO. OF QUESTIONS	PERCENT OF TOTAL
Usage/mechanics		
Punctuation	10	13%
Grammar/usage	12	16%
Sentence structure	18	24%
Rhetorical skills		
Strategy	12	16%
Organization	11	15%
Style	12	16%

As we work through each of these subsections, we'll focus on strategies that will help you identify which of the answer choices is correct.

Chances are, some (hopefully, many!) of the subsections will seem more like common sense than anything else. You don't need to revisit these sections after reading them once. However, be sure to mark the sections that are difficult or unfamiliar to you, and revisit those until you are sure that you understand the strategies. Use this handy chart to help you organize your ACT English prep:

TOPIC	COMMON SENSE	KINDA MAKES SENSE	WHOA ... WHAT?
Usage/mechanics			
Punctuation			
The comma	☐	☐	☐
The dash	☐	☐	☐
The colon	☐	☐	☐
The semicolon	☐	☐	☐
The apostrophe	☐	☐	☐
Grammar/usage			
Pronouns	☐	☐	☐
Subject-verb agreement	☐	☐	☐
Verb tense	☐	☐	☐
Parallel structure	☐	☐	☐
Adjectives and adverbs	☐	☐	☐
Idioms	☐	☐	☐
Double trouble	☐	☐	☐
Sentence structure	☐	☐	☐
Rhetorical skills			
Strategy	☐	☐	☐
Organization	☐	☐	☐
Style	☐	☐	☐

Usage/mechanics (53%)

Punctuation

The ACT English section tests your understanding of the correct use of several marks of punctuation: the comma, dash, colon, semicolon, and apostrophe.

The comma

We'll expand our discussion of the comma in the SENTENCE STRUCTURE section of this chapter, but let's start with the *Big Five* comma uses. (Of course, the comma has many more uses, but discussing them wouldn't help you on the test.)

1. **To separate elements in a series**

This is the most basic use of the comma and the one you've probably seen most often. It looks like this:

> I went shopping and bought milk, eggs, and cheese.
> My sister Ann loves to run, to skate, and to swim in the pool.

In these cases, the comma is used to set apart each item in the list from the other items. While there is some debate on the topic, the ACT adheres to the rule that there *should* be a comma after the second-to-last item in the list before the conjunction (in the first example above, "milk [COMMA] eggs [COMMA] and cheese" versus "milk [COMMA] eggs and cheese," which gives the impression that the eggs and cheese are combined in some way).

Here's an example of an ACT question that tests this kind of comma usage:

English 36 example

The <u>wet soggy and dejected-looking</u> puppy shook itself by the door,
₅

splattering the white carpet with

a shower of mud and grime.

5. **A.** NO CHANGE
   B. wet, soggy and dejected-looking
   C. wet, soggy, and dejected-looking,
   D. wet, soggy, and dejected-looking

Choice D is the correct answer, because it has commas where they should be (separating the three items in the list) and doesn't have commas where they shouldn't be (after the last item in the list, as in choice C).

2. **Before a conjunction, to connect two clauses**

A comma is used before a conjunction like "and," "or," "but," "for," "nor," "yet," and "so."

> He'll eat cherries, but not strawberries.
> Sarah ran into traffic on the way to work, so she was late for her meeting.

See how the comma creates a pause before the conjunction? Let's see how this might be tested on the ACT English section:

English 36 example

The policeman shouted at the criminal

to <u>stop yet, the man</u> kept running.
₆

6. **F.** NO CHANGE
   G. stop, yet the man
   H. stop yet the man
   J. stop, yet the man,

The comma should be placed directly before the conjunction, so choice G is the correct answer. Reading each choice aloud in your head, you should be able to identify why choices F, H, and J are incorrect.

A common mistake is to place the comma after the conjunction instead of before it (in the example above, as the sentence was originally written). When speaking naturally, we sometimes insert a short pause after the conjunction, but in formal written English, there is no comma after the conjunction—only before.

3. **To set off introductory words and phrases**

This is another very common use of the comma. It looks like this:

Before running, I laced up my shoes tightly.
Being the feminist that I am, I joined in my community's annual March for Equality.

In these examples, the comma tells the reader that there is a separation between the introductory idea and the rest of the sentence. It creates a pause that allows the sentence to make sense when spoken aloud. Here's an example of a question testing your knowledge of this type of comma:

English 36 example

Looking back, I watched my parents

7

slowly disappear into the crowd, feeling

the sting of unwelcome tears in my

eyes.

7. A. NO CHANGE
B. Looking, back I watched
C. Looking back I watched
D. Looking back, I, watched

It's important to be able to identify the introductory word or phrase so that you know where to place the comma. If, for example, you looked at the sentence above and decided that "Looking" was the introductory phrase without realizing that "back" is part of that idea, you would mistakenly place the comma after "Looking," as in choice B. However, if you carefully examine the sentence and recognize that "Looking back" is the introductory phrase, you know that the correct place for the comma is between that phrase and the rest of the sentence, as originally written, so choice A is correct.

4. **To set off nonessential or parenthetical phrases and clauses**

If you don't know what "nonessential" or "parenthetical" phrases and clauses are, don't worry! While these terms may seem long and incomprehensible, they simply refer to phrases and clauses that can be removed from the sentence without changing the meaning of the sentence in a significant way. For example:

My mother, who is a cook, made a delicious dinner for my birthday.

In this sentence, the clause "who is a cook" could be removed from the sentence without changing the key idea (that Mom made dinner). Here's another example:

My hobby, collecting stamps, has become more of an obsession this
summer.

Here, "collecting stamps" is the parenthetical (unnecessary) element.

In these cases, the comma tells the reader that the phrase or clause set off is "added information" that pertains to a subject that's already been mentioned. Here's a question that tests your knowledge of this comma use:

English 36 example

The most expensive item at the

<u>auction, an exquisite Taiwanese painting was</u>
8
bid on by over forty bidders!

8. **F.** NO CHANGE
   G. auction, an exquisite Taiwanese, painting was
   H. auction an exquisite Taiwanese painting was
   J. auction, an exquisite Taiwanese painting, was

The key is to correctly identify the parenthetical phrase. In this sentence, you should identify the parenthetical phrase as "an exquisite Taiwanese painting"—an extra bit of information telling us what the most expensive item at the auction was. Once you've correctly identified the parenthetical phrase, you would place commas directly before and after the phrase—making choice J the correct answer.

5. **To set off quoted text**

The last of the *Big Five* comma uses is setting off quotations in the passage. We're all used to seeing commas used this way, especially in novels and other works where characters are speaking. Here is the most common way we see commas used to set off spoken words:

"Wait," Alisha said.
"Please bring me a napkin," she said imperiously, "and a glass of
champagne."

In these instances, a comma is used inside the quotation marks at the end of the spoken phrase, or before the quotation mark that begins the spoken phrase. There are a few exceptions to this rule, however. When you introduce a quotation with "that," you don't use a comma:

The article I read last night reported that "the youth are rising up in
protest."

You also don't use a comma when the quoted word or phrase is embedded in another phrase or in a clause. Here's an example:

After saying "what?" a few times and still not understanding his answer,
I simply smiled and nodded as if I knew what he was talking about.

Finally, you use a colon, not a comma, when the quote is explanatory or the introduction is very long (more than one full sentence):

> Glancing down at the instructions, I found the following advice on how to assemble my new bookshelf: "First, gather the necessary tools. Next, take the . . ."

The dash

Dashes, like parentheses, are used to set apart words, phrases, or clauses that aren't essential to the meaning of a sentence. They can be used to indicate an abrupt change in thought, as well as to signal the inclusion of an explanation or an afterthought.

> The coyote's yipping—a harsh, guttural sound—could be heard throughout the valley that night.

Although dashes typically come in pairs (like commas that are used to set off phrases), they sometimes appear singly, when an idea is tacked onto the end of a sentence.

> After the terrible storm, a gorgeous rainbow lit up the sky—a sign, I hoped, of better things to come.

Keep in mind that dashes are used in pairs when the offset phrase or clause is in the middle of a sentence.

English 36 example

The last obstacle on the agility course

was the one that scared Anna the

most. But she didn't let that fear show.
_____
9

9. **A.** NO CHANGE
   B. most—but she didn't
   C. most—but—she didn't
   D. most—but she didn't—

It should be clear from the discussion above that the correct answer is choice B, which uses a dash to set off the "but" clause from the first part of the sentence, while maintaining a single sentence.

The colon

The colon introduces one or more details that pertain to the preceding statement. For example:

> Three parts of Charlie's car were broken: a window, a door, and the muffler.
> I bought all that I needed at the gas station: a stick of gum.

It's important to put the colon directly after the statement but before the list begins. A common trick in ACT English is the incorrect insertion of a colon in a sentence when the preceding statement is not a complete sentence. What does that mean? It means that the beginning part of the sentence—the part in front of the colon—needs to be able to stand alone and make sense if the sentence were to end right there. For example, in the above sentences, "Three parts of Charlie's car were broken" and "I bought all that I needed at the gas station" could both stand alone as complete sentences. Contrast these with the following example:

Martin got to see his two favorite people, who were: his mom and dad.

Since "Martin got to see his two favorite people, who were" could not stand alone as a complete sentence, the sentence would need to be written without a colon:

Martin got to see his two favorite people, who were his mom and dad.

You're ready to tackle an example involving colon use:

English 36 example

There were only a few items left on Tom's grocery list that he hadn't already bought. <u>Tomatoes</u>, spaghetti, and an onion.

10.
- **F.** NO CHANGE
- **G.** bought, tomatoes,
- **H.** bought tomatoes:
- **J.** bought: tomatoes,

Using the rules for colon use, you should recognize that a colon should be placed after the statement and before the list begins, as in answer choice J.

In the earlier discussion on commas, it was noted that a colon can be used before a long quotation.

The semicolon

Although a semicolon looks much like a colon, they are used in very different ways. A semicolon has two uses:

1. To separate items in a list where at least one item contains a comma

She had already lived in Hartford, Connecticut; Minneapolis, Minnesota; and New York City.

The items in the bakery window looked delicious: soft, buttery croissants; warm, flaky scones; decadent, gorgeous cakes; and delicate, artisanal chocolates.

Without semicolons to separate the items in these two examples, you wouldn't know where each item began and ended due to the commas already used within the items.

2. To join two complete and closely related sentences

Each sentence has to be able to stand on its own, and the two sentences should pertain to the same subject or be otherwise related.

> My mother has been knitting all her life; I don't think she'll ever stop.
> I was constantly reminded to stay strong by my sister; her encouragement and love helped keep me strong through some tough years.

Remember: a semicolon cannot be used to connect an incomplete phrase or clause to a complete sentence. It is a common error to place a semicolon between a sentence and a related phrase. If the second part of the sentence cannot stand by itself, the two elements need to be joined with a comma, not a semicolon, as in the example below:

> The ballerina twirled and twirled; beautiful and breathtaking. (INCORRECT)

Here's a question that tests your knowledge of semicolons:

English 36 example

My mother was a truly amazing

individual; selfless and devoted no

<small>11</small>

matter what.

11. A. NO CHANGE
  B. individual selfless
  C. individual. Selfless
  D. individual: selfless

The correct answer choice is D. As originally written, the sentence is incorrect, because the fragment "selfless and devoted no matter what" is not a complete sentence. Even though the fragment is related to the first sentence, a semicolon cannot be used to join them. A colon is used instead, because the fragment offers details that expand on why the mother was such an amazing individual.

The apostrophe

In the English language, apostrophes are used for two purposes: (1) to indicate possession and (2) to replace one or more letters in a contraction.

1. To indicate possession

Apostrophes are used to indicate possession in several ways. First, we'll discuss *singular possession*, in which a singular noun shows possession of something. Here are several examples:

> the boy's shoes
> the cat's meow
> Marla's paintings
> my father's glove

Notice that what is singular is the possessor, not the noun that follows. For singular possession, the apostrophe is placed after the possessive noun and is followed by "s."

For *plural possession,* the rule is different. First, you make the noun plural, then place the apostrophe after it. The same goes for family names: add an "s" to the name, then tack on the apostrophe. Take a look:

the four cats' toys
the brothers' room
my parents' bed
the Youngs' boat

With plural nouns that don't end in "s," you add the apostrophe + "s" after the noun:

the women's book club
the children's games

Don't make the common mistake of placing the apostrophe after the "s":

CORRECT	INCORRECT
the women's book club	the womens' book club
the children's games	the childrens' games

This is a rule that ACT exam writers love to test, and you will be sure to encounter at least one such question in the ACT English section. Try this example question:

English 36 example

The <u>furnitures</u> lovely craftsmanship
12

made Vicki fall in love with the set

immediately.

12. **F.** NO CHANGE
   G. furniture's
   H. furnitures'
   J. furnitures's

Because "furniture" is a collective noun that does not end in "s," the correct answer choice is G, which puts the apostrophe after the noun but before the "s." Even if you don't know the rules for possessives, the other choices may look or sound awkward to you—this is good! You are learning to recognize correct punctuation usage!

When a name ends in "s" (or with an "s" sound, like /z/), the second "s" is not required but is usually preferred. For example:

Ms. James's briefcase
Mr. Sanchez's breakfast

What if there are two possessors of a single item? You use an apostrophe + "s" only after the *second* possessor. For example:

the boys and girls' home
Alice and Peter's bedroom
Mr. and Mrs. Jones's car

If two people possess two different items, however, you use an apostrophe + "s" after *each* possessor. For example:

the boys' and girls' houses
Alice's and Peter's bedrooms
Mr. Jones's and Mrs. Jones's cars

Possibly the most common error made in the entire ACT English section is adding apostrophes where they don't belong. Unless the word is a contraction or you are showing possession, don't use an apostrophe! I can't tell you how often on Facebook and Twitter my friends post atrocities like these:

Just got back from the movie's! (INCORRECT)
Sister's are so annoying. (INCORRECT)
My brother's drive me crazy sometimes. (INCORRECT)

To avoid this costly and embarrassing mistake, ask yourself these questions every time you use an apostrophe: "Am I showing possession? Am I using a contraction?" If the answer to both questions is "no," don't use an apostrophe!

You should never use an apostrophe with possessive pronouns. The pronouns already show possession, so there's no need to add an apostrophe. Possessive pronouns include "yours," "his," "hers," "its," "ours," "theirs," and "whose." Compare these forms:

CORRECT	INCORRECT
his shoes	his' shoes
The book was hers.	The book was hers'.

If you can remember not to add apostrophes where possession is already implied, you can save yourself costly mistakes on apostrophe questions.

2. **To replace one or more letters in a contraction**

Apostrophes are also used to replace missing letters in contractions. Contractions are two words combined, with some letters taken out. Here are some examples:

can't	it's
couldn't	she's
doesn't	shouldn't
don't	wasn't
haven't	wouldn't
he's	you're
isn't	you've

An exhaustive list of contractions would not be particularly useful here, especially since most ACT English questions that deal with apostrophes focus on possessives, not contractions. However, it is important not to confuse contractions with possessive pronouns in some cases—we'll cover these in the DOUBLE TROUBLE section later in this chapter.

Other punctuation: ( ) ? ! *

Fortunately, the ACT seems uninterested in testing your knowledge of the correct use of any of these other punctuation marks. You'll likely never see an ACT English question that has to do with any of them—for whatever reason, the ACT only tests your understanding of commas, dashes, colons, semicolons, and apostrophes.

Try out your new ACT punctuation skills on the following practice problem set. Good luck!

Practice problem set Punctuation

The solutions follow the problem set.

Forget about <u>dogs: horses</u> have been
₁
man's true best friend since almost the dawn

of civilization. In ancient China, generals in

the Imperial Army used horses for a myriad

of critical <u>tasks, pulling</u> chariots, hauling
₂
supplies, and carrying soldiers into battle.

In medieval Europe, <u>knights' horses</u>
₃
were essential to their lifestyle as both

warriors and travelers. In the <u>United States</u>
₄
<u>where the Spanish settlers brought the first</u>
₄
<u>horses over from Spain the animals</u> quickly
₄
caught the interest and imagination of the

indigenous peoples.

1. **A.** NO CHANGE
   B. dogs horses
   C. dogs—horses
   D. dogs, horses—

2. **F.** NO CHANGE
   G. tasks: pulling
   H. tasks. Pulling
   J. tasks; pulling

3. **A.** NO CHANGE
   B. knight's horses
   C. knights horse's
   D. knights' horses'

4. **F.** NO CHANGE
   G. United States, where the Spanish settlers brought the first horses over from Spain, the animals
   H. United States, where the Spanish settlers brought the first horses over from Spain. The animals
   J. United States where the Spanish settlers brought the first horses over from Spain, the animals

Around the world, horses have captured the
hearts and minds of millions their beauty and
5
grace, combined with stunning athleticism,
generate admiration and awe. They frequently
appear in legends folktales and stories from a
6
myriad of cultures, usually as forces of good.

In the Koran, this is written, "When God
7
created the horse he said to the magnificent
creature: I have made thee as no other."

Although the advent of the motorized
vehicle means that horses are no longer
used for transportation—they still hold
8
an important place in people's—and

especially children's—hearts.
9
Popular media understands and takes
advantage of the popularity of horses. Every
year, one or two feature films are released
that center on the story of a horse and rider.
Some of these films enjoyed great commercial
success: *Hidalgo,* which stars a mustang,
10
Seabiscuit, which stars a racehorse, and *War*
10
Horse, which tells the story of a horse during
WWI.

Although it's not as common nowadays
for families to own horses many still enjoy
11

5. **A.** NO CHANGE
   B. millions their:
   C. millions; their
   D. DELETE the underlined portion.

6. **F.** NO CHANGE
   G. in: legends, folktales,
   H. in legends, folktales,
   J. in, legends, folktales,

7. **A.** NO CHANGE
   B. written
   C. written;
   D. written:

8. **F.** NO CHANGE
   G. transportation, they
   H. transportation: they
   J. transportation; they

9. **A.** NO CHANGE
   B. especially childrens
   C. especially childrens'
   D. especially child's

10. **F.** NO CHANGE
    G. success: *Hidalgo,* which stars a mustang; *Seabiscuit,* which stars a racehorse;
    H. success. *Hidalgo,* which stars a mustang; *Seabiscuit,* which stars a racehorse;
    J. success; *Hidalgo,* which stars a mustang, *Seabiscuit,* which stars a racehorse,

11. **A.** NO CHANGE
    B. horses. Many
    C. horses; many
    D. horses, many

the sport of riding. Avid <u>riders</u> love to develop
12
their relationship with their horses, regardless

of whether <u>theyre</u> competing at the highest
13

or lowest levels of the sport. <u>Its heartwarming</u>
14

to see how <u>horses and peoples lives</u> have
15
remained intertwined.

12. **F.** NO CHANGE
    G. rider's
    H. riders'
    J. riders,

13. **A.** NO CHANGE
    B. their
    C. there
    D. they're

14. **F.** NO CHANGE
    G. It's heartwarming
    H. It's heartwarming:
    J. Its heartwarming;

15. **A.** NO CHANGE
    B. horses and people's lives
    C. horse's and peoples' lives
    D. horses' and people's lives

Solutions for the practice problem set • *Punctuation*

1. **C.** The dash is the best choice here, because it indicates a shift in ideas. None of the other choices would be appropriate.
2. **G.** The colon introduces a list of tasks that horses of the Imperial Army performed. Neither a period nor a semicolon would work, because the list itself is not a complete sentence.
3. **A.** Multiple knights are being discussed, so the apostrophe is used to indicate plural possession, meaning that it comes after the "s" used to make "knight" plural. There is no reason for "horses" to be possessive.
4. **G.** The commas set off the parenthetical element "where the Spanish settlers brought the first horses over from Spain." If that element were removed, the sentence would still work, so we know it's a nonessential element that should be separated with commas.
5. **C.** The second sentence is closely related to the first, but each can operate as a complete, stand-alone sentence. None of the other choices makes sense.
6. **H.** You can't use a colon to set the list apart, because the fragment preceding the colon is not a complete sentence. You should use a comma after "legends," the first item in the list, as well as after "folktales."
7. **D.** The colon introduces a long, formal quotation.
8. **G.** A comma is appropriate, because it separates two clauses of a sentence. You can't use a dash, because the beginning of the sentence ("Although . . . transportation") is not a complete sentence.
9. **A.** "Children" is already plural, so you add the apostrophe after it and before the "s."
10. **G.** This list requires semicolons to separate the items, because each of the items contains a comma. A colon is used to introduce the list.

11. **D.** A comma is used, because the first part of the sentence ("Although . . . horses") is not a complete sentence. You can't use a period or semicolon, both of which can only be used to separate two complete sentences. The comma allows the sentence to read clearly and defines the separation in clauses.

12. **F.** "Riders" is not possessive (what would they possess?), and a comma after "riders" would separate the subject from the predicate.

13. **D.** "They're" is the contraction of "they are," so the apostrophe is necessary. Neither "their" nor "there" makes sense in the context of the sentence.

14. **G.** "It's" is the contraction of "it is," allowing the beginning of the sentence to read "It is heartwarming." "Its" is a possessive pronoun and makes no sense here. There is no reason to place any punctuation after "heartwarming."

15. **D.** The "lives," possessed by both the horses and the people, are different lives, so both "horses" and "people" need to be possessive. Since "horses" is plural, you put an apostrophe after the "s" ("horses'"); since "people" is already plural, you put an apostrophe plus "s" after it ("people's").

Grammar/usage

Grammar/usage questions on the ACT English section focus on the use of pronouns, subject-verb agreement, the use of verb tenses, parallel structure, the distinction between adjectives and adverbs, and idioms.

Pronouns

Pronouns, words used to replace nouns, are extremely common in everyday English. Pronouns include words like "I," "you," "he," "him," "she," "her," "it," and "them." Since they appear frequently on the ACT, you need to know how to use them correctly.

The correct use of pronouns is based on two keys: (1) agreement and (2) case.

Pronoun agreement means that the pronoun has to agree with the noun that it's replacing. Although this may sound obvious, a lot of people don't write with correct pronoun agreement, so incorrect answers may sound normal and correct because they occur so frequently in our everyday lives. Take a look at the following sentence and see if you can tell what's wrong:

> Any young girl who watched the Miss USA pageant that day probably left the show wishing that one day they too could be in the limelight.

To many of you, this sentence might sound perfectly all right. In standard written English, however, the subject, "any young girl," and the pronoun "they" don't match—one is singular, and one is plural! Instead of "they," we should write "she," so that the pronoun agrees with the noun it's replacing. Probably the most common pronoun error in ACT English is using a plural pronoun to replace a singular noun. Here is a list of pronouns that are, in fact, singular:

SINGULAR PRONOUN	EXAMPLE SENTENCE
either	*Either* the boy or the girl must sacrifice *his or her* candy.
neither	*Neither* of the boys standing near me could contain *his* excitement.
anybody	I don't know *anybody* who can lick *his or her* elbow.
anyone	I've never seen *anyone* treat *his or her* parents like that.
somebody	In every class, there is *somebody* who doesn't raise *his or her* hand.
someone	There's always *someone* who thinks *he or she* is the best.
everybody	*Everybody* at camp liked *his or her* counselor.
everyone	*Everyone* likes to see *his or her* name in print.
nobody	*Nobody* enjoys admitting that *he or she* is wrong.
each	*Each* of the artists used *her* brush masterfully.

In many of these examples, the italicized pronouns may look and sound awkward or wrong, and they might look and sound better if you replaced "his or her" with "their" and "he or she" with "they." Yet "their" or "they" in any of the sentences would be wrong. In the case of pronouns, you can't just listen to what sounds right—you have to make sure that you match up singular pronouns with singular nouns, and plural with plural. To determine whether a pronoun is singular or plural (for example, "everyone" seems fairly plural to me), you can check how it sounds with a plural verb. For example, you would say, "Everyone likes chocolate," not "Everyone like chocolate"; since "likes" is a singular verb ("he likes," "she likes"), you know that "everyone" is, in fact, singular. If you use this trick to determine whether a pronoun is singular or plural, you won't have to memorize the list above, or any list of singular and plural pronouns—saving you valuable time and energy.

English 36 example

Everyone at the concert wanted to see <u>their face</u> on the big screen!
₁₃

13. **A.** NO CHANGE
B. their faces
C. his or her faces
D. his or her face

The correct answer is choice D, which pairs the singular pronoun "everyone" with "his or her face."

The other key to the correct use of pronouns is case. *Case* means that a subject pronoun replaces the subject of a sentence and an object pronoun replaces the object of a sentence or the object of a preposition. Here's a list of subject and object pronouns:

SUBJECT PRONOUNS	OBJECT PRONOUNS
I	me
you	you
he	him
she	her
it	it
we	us
they	them
who	whom

In the following example, if you were to replace the nouns in brackets with pronouns, which would be "she" and which would be "her"?

[Caitlin] baked a batch of her famous chocolate chip cookies for [Priya].

Hopefully, you replaced "Caitlin" with "she" and "Priya" with "her." Since Caitlin is the person who is "doing," she's the subject of the sentence. Try this example question:

English 36 example

My father sent me out to the store to

buy a carton of eggs for he to bake with.
₁₄

14. **F.** NO CHANGE
G. him
H. his
J. he's

The correct answer is G, because "him" is the object of the preposition "for."

While most of the "he ~ him" / "she ~ her" / "they ~ them" questions will be easy for you, "who ~ whom" catches a lot of people off guard. We'll cover "who ~ whom" in the DOUBLE TROUBLE section later in this chapter.

Subject-verb agreement

If the subject of a sentence is singular, the verb should be too, and plural verbs should accompany plural nouns. In the present tense, singular nouns are typically accompanied by verbs that end in "s" ("he runs," "she plays," "the man cries"), while plural nouns accompany verbs without an added "s" ("we run," "they play," "the men cry"). Note that the "s" is only added if the subject is singular and in the third person (a noun or "he," "she," or "it"); "s" is not added if the subject is "I" or "you."

Because ACT exam writers know that most people are pretty good at subject-verb agreement, they like to shake things up by putting modifiers and extra words between the subject and the verb, hoping that you'll forget the subject by the time you get to the verb. Take a look:

The final minute of the race, the last of many grueling and punishing minutes, were a time when I felt my resolve was about to break.

Even though the plural noun "minutes" comes right before the verb, the subject is really the third word of the sentence ("minute"), and therefore the correct verb is "was." You can avoid mistakes like this by ignoring the "filler" and isolating the subject and verb from the rest of the sentence. See if you can do this in the following example:

English 36 example

The very last moments of the race—

except for the absolute last second—

<u>was the</u> hardest.
<small>15</small>

15. A. NO CHANGE
   B. was, the
   C. were the
   D. DELETE the underlined portion.

Choice C is the correct answer. The plural subject ("moments") requires a plural verb ("were").

Verb tense

ACT English often tests your understanding of verb tenses. First, a quick review:

PRESENT TENSE	She *sets* the timer.
PAST TENSE	She *set* the timer.
FUTURE TENSE	She *will set* the timer.
PERFECT TENSES	She *has set* the timer. (PRESENT)
	She *had set* the timer. (PAST)
	She *will have set* the timer. (FUTURE)
PROGRESSIVE TENSES	She *is setting* the timer. (PRESENT)
	She *was setting* the timer. (PAST)
	She *will be setting* the timer. (FUTURE)
PERFECT PROGRESSIVE TENSES	She *has been setting* the timer. (PRESENT)
	She *had been setting* the timer. (PAST)
	She *will have been setting* the timer. (FUTURE)

What does each verb tense mean, and when do you use it?

- The *present tense* is used to state facts and to describe habitual actions.
- The *past tense* is used to describe an action or event that happened in the past.
- The *future tense* is used to describe an action or event that is going to happen in the future.
- The *perfect tenses* are used to describe an action that started in the past but may continue into the present or future (present), a past action that was completed before another past action happened (past), and a future action that will have been completed before another future action is completed (future).
- The *progressive tenses* are used to describe actions that are ongoing; the verb ends in "-ing."

◄ The *perfect progressive tenses* are a combination of the perfect and progressive tenses; they convey the same idea as the perfect tenses but with an ongoing action.

You don't need to know the names of these tenses for the ACT. In fact, for many questions, you don't even need to know when certain tenses are used, so you can relax a little.

Verb-tense questions test *consistency* between verb tenses—that is, using the same or related verb tenses within a sentence. For example, take a look at these examples of inconsistent verb tenses:

John *was going* to get milk when he *will have gotten* eggs, too.
Sally *chews* gum as she *walked* to school.

To correct these sentences, change the verb tense of the second verb to match the first. On the real ACT, you could be asked to change the first verb to match the second, or the second verb to match the first, so be sure to check the sentence for clues as to what the verb tense should be. Here are the corrected sentences:

John *was going* to get milk when he *got* eggs, too.
Sally *chews* gum as she *walks* to school.

See the difference? In the first sentence, because "was" is a past tense, we need to change "will have gotten" (future tense) to "got" (past tense) in order to match the tense of "was." In the second sentence, "chews" is present tense, while "walked" is past tense, making it necessary to change "walked" to "walks" in order to match the tense of "chews."

Now, let's review verb-tense combinations that commonly occur, in addition to the present ~ present, past ~ past, and future ~ future combinations.

Any of the three perfect tenses can be used with its corresponding basic tense (for example, present perfect ~ present and past perfect ~ past). Here are some examples:

PRESENT Angelina *has curled up* in bed before she *begins* to read her book.
PAST Angelina *had curled up* in bed before she *began* to read her book.

English 36 example

After the rainstorm, a brilliant rainbow

lit up the sky as white, fluffy clouds
                                    16

reappear.
   16

16. **F.** NO CHANGE
   G. lit up the sky as white, fluffy clouds reappeared.
   H. lit up the sky as white, fluffy clouds reappears.
   J. lights up the sky as white, fluffy clouds reappeared.

The only answer choice in which the verb tenses agree is choice G, where "lit" (past tense) is matched with "reappeared" (past tense). Verb-tense inconsistencies make all the other choices incorrect.

Now wait just one second—in some sentences, verb tense is allowed to change! You'll be able to tell when this happens, though, because there will be an obvious clue. One of two things will occur:

1. **A transition**

    While I've enjoyed summer vacation, I'll be happy to go back to school.

2. **A phrase indicating a change in time period**

    Years after she left home, Carrie wishes she had spent more time with her mother.

You should be able to detect such clues when they appear. When no clue is present, be consistent with your verb tenses!

Keep in mind that the infinitive form of a verb, "to _____" (such as "to swim" and "to bike"), can be used with any verb tense.

Parallel structure

Here's another commonly tested principle: parallelism. *Parallelism* requires that two or more phrases or clauses in a sentence have the same structure. Even if this explanation sounds confusing, parallel structure is easy to spot and fix in sentences! Take a look at some examples of incorrect and correct parallel structure:

INCORRECT	The vase was filled with gorgeous roses, vibrant lilies, and carnations that were dazzling.
CORRECT	The vase was filled with gorgeous roses, vibrant lilies, and dazzling carnations.
INCORRECT	Sam loves boating and to tube on the lake.
CORRECT	Sam loves boating and tubing on the lake.

Parallelism is important in lists and with conjunctions. In lists (see the first example above), the items must mirror one another in structure. With conjunctions like "and" (see the second example above), the words or phrases being linked by the conjunction need to be parallel in structure. The same goes for other conjunctions, such as "or."

Adjectives and adverbs

Adjectives are words used to describe nouns:

    The roof was *blue*.
    Kenzie is a *talented* singer.

Adverbs, on the other hand, are words used to describe adjectives, verbs, and other adverbs. When you see an adverb on the ACT, chances are it will end with the telltale "-ly":

The girl *quickly* ran to the door.
The test was *really* difficult.

ACT exam writers often like to swap adjectives for adverbs and vice versa, then check to see if you notice the mistake. Be careful to spot and correct these errors!

INCORRECT   As the race went on, the runners became *increasing* tired.
CORRECT   As the race went on, the runners became *increasingly* tired.

Because "increasing" is being used to describe the word "tired," an adjective describing the word "runners," you should use the adverb "increasingly."

INCORRECT   Mr. Hess thought the singers were very *melodically*.
CORRECT   Mr. Hess thought the singers were very *melodic*.

The singers are being described as melodious; therefore, you should use "melodic," an adjective, because it is being used to describe a noun—not an adjective, verb, or adverb.

English 36 example

"You did that work very beautiful," said
           17
my mother about how I had arranged

the bouquets for the dinner party.

17. A. NO CHANGE
   B. well beautiful
   C. very beautifully
   D. very, beautiful

The correct answer is choice C, since a verb ("did") must be modified by an adverb ("beautifully").

Idioms

To score a 36 in ACT English, you'll need to be familiar with common idioms. An *idiom* is a common, everyday expression whose meaning can't be determined from its individual words. For most English speakers, correct idiom use comes naturally, because we encounter idioms in books, movies, and everywhere in our daily lives. However, if English isn't your first language, you may have trouble trying to answer the idiom questions. Either way, it's a good idea to review idioms before taking the exam. Take a look at the following example:

English 36 example

Much of the businessman's early

success was attributed from his
        18
connections to the Harvard Business

School.

18. F. NO CHANGE
   G. attributed by
   H. attributed to
   J. attributed of

Hopefully, you should be able to "say" each choice aloud in your head and pick the one that sounds right—in this case, choice H.

Sometimes, ACT exam writers try to trick you by inserting prepositional phrases or other "filler" to distract you from the correct answer. In this case, read the sentence without any of the filler, focusing only on the idiom that is being tested. An exhaustive list of English idioms is beyond the scope of this book, but here is a partial list of common idioms that you should know:

abide *by*	blame *for*	discriminate *against*
accuse *of*	care *about*	excuse *for*
agree *to*	compare *to*	hide *from*
apologize *for*	complain *about*	in charge *of*
apply *for*	consist *of*	insist *(up)on*
approve *of*	count *on*	stare *at*
argue *with*	depend *on*	subscribe *to*
believe *in*	differ *from*	succeed *in*

Double trouble

I call this topic "double trouble," because it's a list of common words that people use interchangeably when only one, in fact, is correct. Since there are quite a few of these questions in ACT English, it's a good idea to figure out which one is which.

◄ good ~ well

"Good" is an adjective, while "well" is an adverb. (If you're unsure about the difference between adjectives and adverbs, flip back to our discussion of them.) Use "good" to describe a noun, and "well" to describe an adjective or verb. For example:

The *pie* she baked was really *good*.
He can *play* baseball *well*.

◄ which ~ that

There's a lot of confusion over when to use "which" and "that" in writing. Simply put, you use "that" before so-called necessary clauses, and "which" before unnecessary clauses.

You use "that" when the meaning of the sentence would change if you took out the clause that follows "that." For example:

Dogs *that* have trust issues get very anxious.

Without "that have trust issues" in the above sentence, the whole meaning of the sentence would change. Instead of only some dogs getting nervous, the new sentence would suggest that all dogs get nervous, clearly changing the original meaning. We call these necessary clauses *restrictive clauses,* and they go with "that."

"Which," on the other hand, is used before so-called unnecessary clauses. While a "which" clause may offer more detail, the meaning of the sentence won't change if you remove it. Take a look:

The towers, *which* were made of steel, glinted in the setting sun.

Taking out "which were made of steel" wouldn't change the meaning of the sentence—the towers would still be glinting in the sun. These unnecessary clauses are called *nonrestrictive clauses,* and they go with "which."

◄ who ~ whom

Both "who" and "whom" are pronouns—so what's the difference? It all comes down to the distinction between a subject and an object. The *subject* of a sentence is the one doing the "doing," while the *object* is having something done to him, her, or it. "Who" is the subject of a sentence, and "whom" is the object. For example:

Who is riding the bike over there?
Whom are you taking to the concert?

In the first sentence, "who" is the subject and "bike" is the object. In the second sentence, "you" is the subject and "whom" is the object.

When I was little, my mom taught me an easy way to remember this—one I've never forgotten. If the question can be answered with "him," then the correct term is "whom." If the question can be answered with "he," the correct term is "who." For example:

_____ is riding the bike over there?
He is riding (→ *Who*). (NOT *Him* is riding.)

_____ are you taking to the concert?
I'm taking *him* (→ *Whom*). (NOT I'm taking *he*.)

Just remember that "him" and "whom" end with "m"—and take full advantage of the "he/him" trick. You will answer "who ~ whom" questions with ease and confidence.

◄ are ~ our

This one is fairly easy. "Are" is the plural form of the verb "is," while "our" is a possessive adjective.

The cats *are* cute.
That is *our* truck.

◄ less ~ fewer

This common mix-up happens even among accomplished writers. The bottom line is that you use "less" with things that can't be counted, and "fewer" with things that can. Like this:

I wish there were *less* pollution here.
There are *fewer* than 100 fish left in the lake.

See how "fish" can be counted, while "pollution" can't be? A quick and almost failproof test for whether a noun can be counted is to add an "s" to it; if it sounds wrong with an "s," it can't be counted. (Would you say "pollutions"?)

◄ among ~ between

ACT exam writers love to test this relatively subtle distinction. It comes down to the number of objects being discussed, and how distinct those objects are. If you are describing a set of (usually two) distinct objects, you use "between":

She needed to choose *between* physics and chemistry.
She needed to choose *between* physics, chemistry, and biology.

In the second example, even though you are discussing more than two objects, each of them is distinct, so you use "between." You use "among" when discussing multiple objects that are not distinct:

She was forced to choose *among* a myriad of science classes.
Fear spread *among* the students as the pop quiz was announced.

You use "between" when choosing from distinct, separately named objects, and you use "among" when choosing from multiple objects that are named together as a group ("a myriad of science classes") or as a plural noun ("students"). Sometimes, however, "between" can be used with a plural noun. Take a look at the following examples:

Simon walked *between* the pillars in the church.
Simon walked *among* the pillars in the church.

In these examples, both "between" and "among" could be correct. In the first sentence, Simon walked between two pillars or in an aisle flanked by rows of pillars. In the second sentence, "among" suggests that Simon wandered around the pillars, not between two individual pillars.

◄ -er ~ -est

This is an easy one. You use "-er" at the end of an adjective when comparing two things, and "-est" when comparing more than two things:

She was the *prettier* of the two girls.
She was the *prettiest* girl in the class.

◄ there ~ their ~ they're

The distinction between these three sound-alikes confuses about half the population of the country and at least 75 percent of my Facebook friends. Learn the difference between these words so that (1) you can ace the ACT and (2) you can stop embarrassing yourself online before friends and family.

"There" is used to state the existence of something:

There is a dog.
There's no place like home.

"There" also means "in/at/to that place."

There she goes!
We stopped *there* for a drink.

"Their" is a possessive adjective indicating that more than one person has possession of an object:

They played *their* music loud.
Their clothes were outlandish.
Their customs were very different.

"They're" is a contraction of "they" and "are" and means "they are":

They think *they're* pretty smart.
They're great dancers.
They're never going to make it to the movie.

◄ **lay ~ lie ~ laid**

"Lay" is a verb that requires an object; it often means "put," "build," or "produce."

Lay the book down now.
The workers *are laying* the foundation for a new house.
The hens *were laying* eggs in the barn.

"Lie" doesn't take an object; it usually means "be in a horizontal position" or "be located."

I *lie* down on the couch.
The corn fields *lie* to the west.

Both "lay" and "lie" have past tense forms—the past tense form of "lay" is "laid" (not so bad), while the past tense form of "lie" is "lay" (ouch!).

PRESENT TENSE	PAST TENSE
Lay down the book now.	She *laid* down the book.
I *lie* down on the couch.	I *lay* down on the couch after dinner.

To avoid this trap, ask yourself: should I be using the present or past tense here? If your answer is the present tense, you have a choice between "lay" (which requires an object) and "lie" (which doesn't take an object). If your answer is the past tense, you have a choice between "laid" (which requires an object) and "lay" (which doesn't take an object).

◄ it's ~ its

Even though the difference between these two words should be clear from our discussion of punctuation and contractions, you will almost certainly encounter a question on the ACT that tests your understanding of the difference.

Because an apostrophe is used to indicate possession, many people think that if an object belongs to "it," they should write "it's." Erase this thinking from your mind. "It's" can only be used as a contraction of "it" and "is," so even if an object belongs to "it," you never write "it's object"— you write "its object."

Every time you see "it's," read it as "it is." If "it is" doesn't make sense (as in "it is object"), you need to use "its" instead.

Done with double trouble! Now try this practice set:

Practice problem set Grammar/usage

The solutions follow the problem set.

Nobody likes to find out that theyre wrong.
                                    1
Yet realizing and addressing our weaknesses

1. **A.** NO CHANGE
   B. that they're wrong.
   C. that he or she is wrong.
   D. that they are wrong.

is an important part of the learning process.
2
One of the best ways to identify our personal

weaknesses is to seek help from our peers.

2. **F.** NO CHANGE
   G. are an
   H. is, an
   J. are: an

Last year, I was struggling a bit with one

of my essays when I have asked one of my
                         3
friends for some advice.

3. **A.** NO CHANGE
   B. had asked
   C. will ask
   D. asked

    After reading through my essay twice, she

let out a lengthy sigh. I braced myself, ready

for biting criticism or laughter that was jeering.
                         4

4. **F.** NO CHANGE
   G. laughter that is jeering.
   H. laughter, jeering.
   J. jeering laughter.

Yet when she spoke, she spoke gentle. "The
                         5
core idea of this essay is strong," she told me,

5. **A.** NO CHANGE
   B. she spoke gently.
   C. she spoke with gentle.
   D. she spoke with gently.

"something I can believe in as a reader." She
6
pointed me to one or two unclear sentences,

insisting that if I changed them, I could

score good when I turned it in.
7

Relieved that she had given me

advice which was helpful and clear, rather
8
than accusatory, I smiled. I felt grateful to

have a friend whom could give me honest,
9
clear advice.

Even though I was afraid to ask for help

at first, that experience taught me how

reaching out to those around us can help us

strengthen are weakest areas. So don't be
10
afraid to reach out—the risk in doing so is far

fewer than the potential benefit.
11

Still, choose advisers with care—between
12
your friends, make sure to pick those whom

you can count on to give you genuine and

clear advice. Ask people who are good

communicators, as the clearer advice comes
13
from those who can articulate what you

should change. Their comments will be the
14
easiest to understand and use effectively when

editing.

6. **F.** NO CHANGE
   G. believe on
   H. believe for
   J. believe at

7. **A.** NO CHANGE
   B. score—good
   C. score—well
   D. score well

8. **F.** NO CHANGE
   G. advice; that
   H. advice that
   J. advice, which

9. **A.** NO CHANGE
   B. friend, whom
   C. friend, who
   D. friend who

10. **F.** NO CHANGE
    G. strengthen. Are
    H. strengthen. Our
    J. strengthen our

11. **A.** NO CHANGE
    B. fewer then
    C. less then
    D. less than

12. **F.** NO CHANGE
    G. between,
    H. among
    J. among,

13. **A.** NO CHANGE
    B. as the clearest
    C. as the most clearest
    D. as the most clearer

14. **F.** NO CHANGE
    G. They're
    H. There
    J. There's

In short, remember this: while it's easy

to <u>lie back</u> passively and not go out of your
₁₅

way to find your own weaknesses, identifying

them is the only way to help your writing

<u>reach it's full potential.</u>
₁₆

15. **A.** NO CHANGE
    B. to lay back
    C. to laid back
    D. to lie back,

16. **F.** NO CHANGE
    G. reach its
    H. reach it is
    J. reach its'

Solutions for the practice problem set • *Grammar/usage*

1. **C.** Since "nobody" is singular, only this choice includes singular pronouns: "he or she." The other choices would result in inconsistency.

2. **G.** "Realizing and addressing" make the subject plural, thus requiring a plural verb: "are." Choice J uses the colon incorrectly.

3. **D.** This question is about verb-tense agreement. The author is talking about "last year," so that should be an indication that the verb must be past tense. "Have asked" is present perfect tense, and "will ask" is future tense, so "had asked" and "asked" are the only choices left. "Had asked" is incorrect, because the past perfect tense is used for an action in the past that preceded another action in the past, which doesn't apply here.

4. **J.** "Jeering laughter" fulfills the principle of parallelism by mirroring the phrase "biting criticism."

5. **B.** An adverb is required, because it is a verb, not a noun, that is being modified; thus, "gently" is correct. "With gentle" and "with gently" don't make sense.

6. **F.** This question tests your knowledge of idioms. "Believe" goes with "in," not with "on," "for," or "at."

7. **D.** "Well" is correct, because an adverb, not an adjective, is required to modify the verb. The dash in choice C interrupts the flow of the sentence and is clearly incorrect.

8. **H.** If the clause "which . . . accusatory" were removed, the meaning of the sentence would change. Therefore, "that" is required here, without a preceding comma. The semicolon in choice G is incorrect, since it would create two incomplete sentences.

9. **D.** "Who" is correct; applying the "he/him" rule eliminates "him could give me," so "who" is the subject, not the object. The comma after "friend" would make the "who" clause a nonrestrictive clause, meaning that the clause doesn't change the basic meaning of the sentence, when in fact it does.

10. **J.** "Our," not "are," is correct, because a possessive adjective is required to modify "weakest areas." Introducing a period, as in choices G and H, would create two incomplete sentences.

11. **D.** Since this is a comparison, "than" is used, not "then." That leaves only a choice between "fewer" and "less." Since "risk" is not a plural, countable noun, "less" is correct.

12. **H.** "Among" is correct, because there are more than two "friends," and they are not distinctly named. The comma after "among" in choice J is incorrect, because it separates "among" from its object.

13. **B.** Since the choice is between more than two "people," "clearest" is correct. Using "most" is redundant and incorrect.

14. **F.** The comments belong to "those who can articulate what you should change" in the preceding sentence, so the possessive adjective "their" is correct.

15. **A.** "Lie" is correct, because the verb has no object and because the present tense is required.

16. **G.** "It is," as in choice H, makes no sense. Since the word is a possessive adjective, not a contraction, an apostrophe is incorrect.

Sentence structure

Sentence structure is a critical part of ACT English; in fact, it's the largest subsection. Sentence structure is the focus of 18 questions—almost a quarter of the entire section. Luckily, sentence structure comes naturally to many students and is far more intuitive than some of the punctuation and grammar rules. To make the topic manageable, we'll address it point by point:

- ◄ Connectors and coordinating/subordinating conjunctions
- ◄ Comma splices
- ◄ Run-on sentences
- ◄ Sentence fragments
- ◄ Misplaced modifiers

Connectors and coordinating/subordinating conjunctions

One of the most important categories of connecting words is *coordinating conjunctions*. These are used to connect words or phrases that are of equal importance in a sentence and that are grammatically equivalent. Examples are "and," "but," "or," "nor," and "yet."

> I wasn't sure if I wanted both this *and* that.
> He was heavy-set *but* athletic.
> You can saddle the horse *or* sweep out the stable.

Notice how the conjunction connects words, phrases, or clauses without a comma. You need a comma only if you're connecting more than two objects. In such a list, a comma is placed after all but the last item, including before the conjunction:

She liked to eat doughnuts, drink coffee, *and* sleep.

Another category of connecting words is *subordinating conjunctions.* Unlike coordinating conjunctions, subordinating conjunctions make one clause dependent on the other. Examples are "after," "although," "because," "before," "until," and "when."

To use a subordinating conjunction, first determine which clause of the two is dependent on the other. Take a look at the following two sentences and see if you can tell which clause is dependent and which is independent:

I overslept.
I was late for school.

To join these sentences with a subordinating conjunction, establish the correct relationship between them:

Because I overslept, I was late for school.

Since being late for school is the result of oversleeping, being late for school becomes the independent clause and oversleeping becomes the dependent clause. If you accidentally invert the relationship, the sentence doesn't make sense:

Because I was late for school, I overslept.

A common error tested on the ACT is the use of a coordinating conjunction where a subordinating conjunction should be used, and vice versa. Treating two clauses as equivalent when one is actually dependent on the other can make a sentence hard to understand, as can subordinating one clause to another when the two are actually equally important. Take a look at the examples below:

Sarah trained every day and ran thousands of miles, *and* she succeeded in her goal of running a marathon.
Since Sarah trained every day and ran thousands of miles, she succeeded in her goal of running a marathon.

Even though the first sentence is not technically incorrect, it does not make the relationship between Sarah's training and her results as clear as the second, which demonstrates that her success in the race was dependent on her training. ACT English tests your proficiency in identifying and correcting these coordinating/subordinating conjunction mix-ups.

Let's look at another example, one where a subordinating conjunction is used when the relationship between clauses is equal:

Because Rafael loves to run, he also loves to paint and ski.

The fact that Rafael loves to paint and ski has absolutely nothing to do with his love of running—it is highly unlikely that his love of running somehow contributes to his love for the other two activities. Instead of a subordinating conjunction, a coordinating conjunction is used to put the clauses on equal footing:

Rafael loves to run, paint, and ski.

This sentence makes a lot more sense and is more concise than the one above. This is why it's important to be able to understand when each of the types of conjunctions needs to be used; the ACT is sure to test you on this at least a few times in the English section. Let's see how you do on the following example problem:

English 36 example

Rebecca studied hard, read over all of

her notes, and went to all the lectures,

and scored very well on the final exam.
    19

19. **A.** NO CHANGE
    B. so she scored
    C. scored
    D. but scored

The correct answer is choice B. The word "so" makes the dependent relationship clear: Rebecca's scoring well on the final exam was the result of her performing the previous actions.

Comma splices

ACT exam writers love to challenge your ability to spot and fix comma splices. A *comma splice* occurs when two independent clauses are joined by a comma but with no conjunction—leading to an awkward, choppy sentence:

I took my dog for a walk, my brother mowed the lawn.

Awkward, right? It seems like it should be two sentences, yet it isn't. This incorrect use of the comma should be detected and repaired.

To fix a comma splice, you have a couple of options:

1. Make it two sentences.

    I took my dog for a walk. My brother mowed the lawn.

    If the sentences are closely related, you can use a semicolon instead of a period. Sometimes, though, the clauses are so short that the period or semicolon makes them sound choppy. In that case, you might want to consider option 2.

2. Add a coordinating or subordinating conjunction.

    I took my dog for a walk, *and* my brother mowed the lawn.
    I took my dog for a walk, *while* my brother mowed the lawn.

The method you use often depends on the length of the clauses. For long, complex clauses, separating them into two sentences is usually cleaner. For short clauses, joining them with a conjunction usually makes them read more smoothly.

English 36 example

Wesley is from <u>Cleveland, he</u> loves
₂₀
drinking chocolate milk.

20. **F.** NO CHANGE
    G. Cleveland, and he
    H. Cleveland; and he
    J. Cleveland. And, he

As you read the sentence, your comma-splice detection alarm should be ringing: there it is, two independent clauses, separated by a comma. Of all the available answer choices, only G makes a smooth transition from one clause to the other. The sentences are not related enough to merit the use of a semicolon; and if you used a semicolon, you would need to omit "and." A period, as in choice J, would be acceptable, were it not for the word "and" at the beginning of the next sentence.

Run-on sentences

These are similar to comma-spliced sentences, except run-on sentences don't even have a comma to separate the clauses. It's usually easier to detect run-on sentences than comma splices, because run-ons look and sound so awkward:

> Emma loves to eat cake Olivia hates cake.
> Writing a book is difficult it can be stressful.

Detecting the run-ons in these examples isn't hard. Fixing them isn't hard, either: to remedy a run-on sentence, use the same strategies you would use to fix a comma splice. Either use a coordinating or subordinating conjunction to join the clauses, connect them with a semicolon, or separate them into two sentences.

Sentence fragments

Unlike comma splices and run-on sentences, sentence fragments don't have enough material to make a complete sentence. To be considered a sentence, a group of words must have a subject and a verb and must make sense by itself. A sentence fragment is incomplete, unable to stand alone as a complete sentence. When you read a sentence fragment, you should have a sense of incompleteness, as if the sentence was getting ready to go somewhere and then didn't:

> Not daring to peek above the covers. The little girl shook with fear.

"The little girl shook with fear" is a fine, complete sentence. However, "Not daring to peek above the covers" is not—there is only a description with no subject to latch onto. This is clearly a sentence fragment.

So how do you fix such a fragment? One easy way is to join it to a neighboring, related clause or sentence. In the example above, you could simply replace the period with a comma:

Not daring to peek above the covers, the little girl shook with fear.

Because the ideas naturally flow together, this is a great way to correct the sentence fragment.

English 36 example

Conrad, nicknamed "Conradical" by <u>his peers. Loved</u> to study all things
₂₁
mathematical.
	21. A. NO CHANGE
	  B. his peers; loved
	  C. his peers: loved
	  D. his peers, loved

Answer choice D joins both fragments into a complete sentence. We know the sentence had fragments as originally written, so choice A is out. A semicolon, as in choice B, requires two complete sentences, and a colon, as in choice C, is inappropriate—there is no explanation or list to introduce.

You can also fix sentence fragments by converting them into complete sentences, using colons or dashes where appropriate (see the PUNCTUATION section above). In ACT English, a lot of sentence fragments are dependent clauses masquerading as complete sentences. These can often be linked to a neighboring independent clause. Remember, let no fragment stand alone!

Misplaced modifiers

Knowing how to use modifiers is a key skill in ACT English, since misplaced modifiers are a favorite of exam writers year after year. They can be a lot trickier than comma splices, run-on sentences, and sentence fragments, because they can be much harder to spot. In addition, misplaced modifiers are common in everyday speech, so they may not set off alarms like other grammar violations do.

A modifier is a word, phrase, or clause that describes or modifies a noun in a sentence. An example is the italicized phrase in the example below:

Able to speak Spanish fluently, Gabe was praised by the professor.

This modifier is meant to describe Gabe, so it is correctly placed. Would the altered arrangement below also work?

Able to speak Spanish fluently, the professor praised Gabe.

The new sentence doesn't mean the same thing at all. If we hadn't read the first sentence, we would think that the professor, not Gabe, was the one who could speak Spanish. To be in the correct position, a modifier needs to be either directly in front of or behind the noun it modifies. Take a look at these examples:

Amy put her water bottle on her bike, *which she planned to drink from as she rode.*
Amy put her water bottle, *which she planned to drink from as she rode,* on her bike.

In the first sentence, the modifier describes Amy's bike—which she almost certainly is not planning to drink from. In the second sentence, the modifier has been moved to the correct position so that it describes the water bottle. Here's another example:

Having eaten a bag of chocolates, sickness debilitated the dog.
Having eaten a bag of chocolates, the dog was overwhelmed by sickness.

In the first sentence, the modifier seems to describe "sickness." I highly doubt that "sickness" ate a bag of chocolates. The second sentence shows the correct modifier placement, making plain that it was the dog that ate the bag of chocolates.

Misplaced modifiers can also cause confusion when modifying words, rather than phrases or clauses, are involved. In these cases, the placement of the word may not make a sentence "incorrect," but it may alter its meaning. Compare these three sentences:

Just Megan worked for two hours on her homework.
    (Only Megan worked on it—no one else.)
Megan *just* worked for two hours on the homework.
    (She didn't do anything else during those two hours.)
Megan worked for *just* two hours on the homework.
    (I can't believe she finished so quickly!)

Each of the sentences is grammatically correct, but the placement of the modifier "just" changes the meaning from one sentence to the next. In these instances, be sure to place the modifier so that the sentence expresses the meaning you intend.

English 36 example

Some of the girls in track are extremely fast runners: <u>Only Claudia and four</u>
₂₂
<u>other girls could run a mile in</u> five
₂₂
minutes.

22. F. NO CHANGE
 G. Claudia and only four other girls could run a mile in
 H. Claudia and four other girls could only run a mile in
 J. Claudia and four other girls could run a mile in only

Without the hint provided by the first clause, you wouldn't know which of the choices is correct. The first clause makes it clear, however, that the rest of the sentence must be consistent with the idea that the track team has some very fast members.

Answer choice F expresses surprise that only five girls could run a five-minute mile—that's not right. Choice G implies a similar idea, that only four girls besides Claudia could run a five-minute mile—that's not right. Choice H expresses the notion that running a mile in only five minutes isn't much of an achievement—also not the idea we're looking for. Choice J is correct, because the modifier "only" emphasizes how quickly the girls could run the mile, which coincides nicely with the idea expressed in the first clause.

When you encounter a potentially misplaced modifier, ask yourself, "What noun is being modified? Is this the noun that should be modified?" If the answer to the second question is yes, great! If not, figure out which noun should be modified and select the choice that pairs the modifier with that noun.

Practice problem set **Sentence structure**

The solutions follow the problem set.

Staying fit and healthy is an important

part of everyone's lifestyle, regardless of

age, gender or race. In America, there is a
₁

staggeringly high number of overweight and

obese individuals, because of many studies
₂

only see this number rising in the next 20

years. However, there are many small changes

we can make in our lives for to be healthier.
₃

One of the best things you can do to stay

healthy is easy, drink water. Having water
₄

running through your body throughout the day

helps to remove toxins it keeps your digestive
₅

system running smoothly. Repeatedly, studies

performed on participants who exercised

daily and were given varying amounts

1. **A.** NO CHANGE
    B. age gender or race.
    C. age, gender, or race.
    D. age, gender, yet race.

2. **F.** NO CHANGE
    G. and many studies
    H. and because of many studies
    J. after many studies

3. **A.** NO CHANGE
    B. for
    C. and be
    D. in order to be

4. **F.** NO CHANGE
    G. easy. Drink water.
    H. easy: drink water.
    J. easy drink water.

5. **A.** NO CHANGE
    B. helps to remove toxins, and it
    C. helps to remove toxins. It
    D. helps to remove toxins, keeps

of water. <u>Found that</u> those who drank at least
₆
8 cups of water a day lost, on average, more

weight than those who drank only 4 cups per

day.

    In addition to keeping yourself hydrated,

it's important to make a plan for regular

exercise. <u>Offering a lot of nice equipment and</u>
₇
<u>fellow fitness enthusiasts, you might find</u>
₇
<u>joining the local gym very motivating!</u>
₇

    Another great way to get your body

moving while having a <u>great time is to join</u>
₈
a local recreational sports team.

<u>Playing sports with friends is so much fun, and</u>
₉
you'll be surprised when hours have gone by

in healthful activity.

    The last piece to transitioning to a healthy

<u>lifestyle, is watching</u> what—and how—you
₁₀
eat. Rather than counting calories or obsessing

over <u>food. Try</u> to eat foods that are minimally
₁₁

6. F. NO CHANGE
  G. water: found that
  H. water, found that
  J. water found that

7. A. NO CHANGE
  B. You might find joining the local gym, which offers a lot of nice equipment and fellow fitness enthusiasts, very motivating!
  C. Offering a lot of nice equipment and fellow fitness enthusiasts, the local gym might find you joining it very motivating!
  D. You might find, offering a lot of nice equipment and fellow fitness enthusiasts, joining the local gym very motivating.

8. F. NO CHANGE
  G. great time, is to join
  H. great time. Join
  J. great time is to join,

9. A. NO CHANGE
  B. Because playing sports with friends is so much fun,
  C. Playing sports with friends is so much fun,
  D. After playing sports with friends is so much fun,

10. F. NO CHANGE
  G. lifestyle. Watching
  H. lifestyle, watching
  J. lifestyle is watching

11. A. NO CHANGE
  B. food try
  C. food, try
  D. food; try

processed. <u>Fresh and raw, you'll find sliced</u>

<u>vegetables</u> to be a great snack in between
₁₂
meals.

With those three tips in mind (drink water, move your body, eat nutritious food), you can change your lifestyle for the better.

12. **F.** NO CHANGE
    G. You'll find sliced vegetables, fresh and raw,
    H. Fresh and raw—you'll find sliced vegetables—
    J. You'll find sliced vegetables fresh and raw

Solutions for the practice problem set • *Sentence structure*

1. **C.** A coordinating conjunction is used to link three items: "age," "gender," and "race." The first two items are followed by a comma, then the coordinating conjunction "or" is placed before the last item.

2. **G.** The phrase, as originally written, uses the preposition "because of" to imply that the first clause is dependent on the second—that is, that people are obese because studies say that more people will be obese in the future. This relationship doesn't make sense. The correct choice is G, which uses the coordinating conjunction "and" to link the two independent clauses in a way that does not erroneously state that one is the cause of the other.

3. **D.** As originally written, the end of this sentence looks and sounds incorrect; "for to" is substandard English. The conjunction should imply a dependent relationship between the two clauses, indicating that being healthier is dependent on making small changes. Answer choice D suggests that relationship.

4. **H.** This is a comma splice, where a comma has been used to connect two parts of a sentence incorrectly. A colon should be used to indicate that an explanation follows; "drink water" is an example of "one of the best things you can do to stay healthy."

5. **B.** As originally written, this sentence is a run-on, where two complete ideas are joined without any separation. The two clauses should be connected with a coordinating conjunction.

6. **J.** Despite its length, the "sentence" that begins with "Repeatedly" and ends with "of water" is not really a sentence at all; it is a sentence fragment. In fact, "studies . . . of water" is a noun phrase and "found . . . per day" is a verb phrase. Combining the two phrases without separating punctuation creates a very long but well-formed sentence.

7. **B.** The sentence, as originally written, contains a misplaced modifier: "Offering . . . enthusiasts" should describe the gym, not "you"! The modifier should be placed next to what it describes, as in answer choice B.

8. **F.** The sentence is correct as written. It would be incorrect to separate "great time" from the linking verb "is." Adding a period, as in choice H, would create sentence fragments. Adding a comma, as in choice J, would create a comma splice.

9. **B.** A subordinating conjunction ("because") is required to show causation. The fact that "you'll be surprised" by how much time went by is directly dependent on how much fun you had "playing sports with friends."

10. **J.** The original wording contains a comma splice. Choice G would create two sentence fragments, and choice H would create an incomplete sentence.

11. **C.** As originally punctuated, "Rather . . . over food" is a sentence fragment. You need to link the sentence "Try . . . processed" to the fragment, separating them with a comma due to the shift in ideas.

12. **G.** Another misplaced modifier! The original wording incorrectly indicates that "you" are "fresh and raw"—a description that should be assigned to the sliced vegetables. Choice G places the modifier directly next to the noun it modifies.

Rhetorical skills (47%)

Rhetorical skills are far less concrete and cut-and-dried than the skills tested on the earlier part of ACT English. Rhetorical skills involve your ability to write effectively and clearly, to recognize good writing, and to correct and improve writing. The ACT breaks down rhetorical skills into three categories:

- ◄ Strategy (16%)
- ◄ Organization (15%)
- ◄ Style (16%)

By learning to evaluate strategies and answer example questions, you will strengthen your grasp of each of these topics and prepare yourself for these questions on the ACT.

Strategy

Although "strategy" means lots of things in the real world, on the ACT, "strategy" simply means making the point of a passage clearer through effective editing. You will be tested in three areas:

- ◄ The big picture
- ◄ Topic sentences and transitions
- ◄ The details

The big picture

Big-picture questions on the ACT test how well you can recognize the main idea of a passage; these questions usually appear at or near the end of a passage. They focus not only on recognizing the main point of a passage, but also on articulating the purpose of the passage and predicting the passage's intended audience. Helpful strategies are covered thoroughly in the ACT Reading chapter, so wait a hundred pages and you won't have to study it twice!

Topic sentences and transitions

Topic-sentence and transition questions test your understanding of how best to introduce, connect, and conclude an argument. Transitions can appear almost anywhere in a passage, even several times in a single paragraph. The key to nailing transition questions is to ask yourself what kind of transition the author is trying to make:

◄ **Continuation**

Is the author trying to continue with the same idea by adding additional examples or exploring a related idea?

> Franco loved to help out at his local food pantry. *In addition,* he worked hard during all the food drives to make sure he could keep the shelves full.

Common continuation words and phrases follow:

along the same lines	in other words
also	in the same way
and	likewise
by the same token	moreover
further	similarly
furthermore	that is
in addition	then

◄ **Contradiction**

Is the author trying to indicate that there's been a contradiction or a change in idea? Is the author highlighting a contrast?

> In general, Megan was a very hard-working and smart girl. *However,* she was unable to keep her grades up when she entered high school.

Common contradiction words follow:

although	nevertheless
as opposed to	not
but	on the contrary
conversely	on the other hand
despite	rather
however	unlike
in contrast	while
instead	yet

◄ **Cause and effect**

Is the author trying to communicate a causal relationship? Is the author asserting that one event led to another?

> Only the boys' bathroom had graffiti in it. *Therefore,* the girls were allowed to keep their recess privileges while the boys were punished.

Common cause-and-effect words follow:

as a result	in response to
because of	thanks to
consequently	therefore
due to	thus
hence	

These are the three types of transitions most often encountered in ACT English, so it's important to know when to use each one and which transition words fall in which categories.

You're probably already pretty good at figuring out which types of transitions to use within sentences. However, this section tests your ability to position and use transitions correctly not only within sentences, but also within a passage. Let's take a crack at an example problem:

English 36 example

Everyone in my family loves puppies. Over the course of my childhood, we've never had fewer than three dogs in the family, and once we had six at the same time! They eat with us, sleep with us, and play with us every day, and I'm sure my family will continue to keep dogs long after I head off to college.

In addition, my family has a keen
                22
dislike for the neighbor's dog. He's a mean, grungy old thing who uses any excuse he can to bark and growl at our dogs.

22. **F.** NO CHANGE
   G. Therefore, my family
   H. Consequently, my family
   J. However, my family

Ask yourself: What relationship between the first and second paragraphs should the author be making clear? The first paragraph reveals that the author's family really likes dogs. The second paragraph indicates that the family dislikes the neighbor's dog. Is this a continuation? A contradiction? Cause and effect? You should be able to rule out cause and effect (does the family dislike the neighbor's dog because they love dogs in general?) and continuation (does the family dislike the neighbor's dog in the same way they like their own dogs?). You should settle on contradiction: the family's love for their own dogs clashes with their dislike of the neighbor's dog. By comparing the transition words offered by the four answer choices—"in addition," "therefore," "consequently," and "however"—it is obvious that the contradiction word, "however," is the correct answer.

Transitions involve determining the relationship between two ideas:

CONTINUATION	A, and B
CONTRADICTION	A, but B
CAUSE AND EFFECT	A, so B

The appropriate transition word provides a clue to the reader about what's coming next.

Other types of transitions appear less frequently in ACT English. Here are some helpful word lists:

◄ **Words that indicate explanation**

> for example
> for instance
> that is

◄ **Words that suggest an order**

> before
> after
> first
> then
> last
> finally

◄ **Words that hint at a conclusion**

> in conclusion
> in summary
> in the end

Now, one more example:

English 36 example

Energy drinks can have negative effects

on teens in a variety of different ways.

<u>In conclusion,</u> some energy drinks
    23
contain levels of caffeine that in some

rare cases have caused heart attack

and death. Another negative impact

23. A. NO CHANGE
    B. In the end,
    C. Similarly,
    D. For instance,

of energy drinks is that they often

are linked to sleep deprivation and

depression.

The transition should indicate that the author is moving from the general ("negative effects . . . in a variety of ways") to the specific (a particular example of detrimental effects). Because the author is introducing an example, the correct answer is choice D.

The details

Some ACT English questions ask you to add substance to a paragraph by choosing the most appropriate detail to include. Other questions ask you to add a sentence that agrees with the evidence already presented; you'll have to identify the theme or pattern in the rest of the paragraph and continue in that vein.

Process of elimination becomes especially important in answering these questions, since you can easily rule out details that are irrelevant or unrelated to the current topic. If a question asks you to add a point in support of details that have already been given, look in the answer choices for sentences that begin with continuation transition words, like "in addition" and "furthermore." You can probably eliminate any choice that begins with a contradiction transition word, like "however" or "nevertheless"; by their nature, these words imply that the following point will *not* be in agreement with the points already made. Be careful, however: you also need to make sure that the point itself agrees with the preceding point. Both the transition word *and* the point that follows must agree with the earlier point.

A question may ask you to select a detail or additional sentence that contradicts the points already made. Such a question is rare, but it is very clearly worded. Never choose a contradicting detail unless the question specifically asks you to. To answer such a question, look for contradiction transition words and rule out any choices that contain a continuation word. Again, make sure that the actual detail also contradicts the previous point. Both the transition word *and* the point that follows must contradict the earlier point.

A question may ask you to identify or select a logical concluding sentence for a paragraph; you'll select a choice that sums up the information already presented. A helpful clue in such a case is a cause-and-effect transition word like "therefore" or "consequently." As noted before, the point presented after the transition word must make sense as the concluding idea for the paragraph.

Try the following example:

English 36 example

Global warming describes the phenomenon by which the accumulation of greenhouse gases in the atmosphere reflects more of the sun's light back to the earth's surface, warming global temperatures. Scientists are very concerned with the possible effects of global warming, which include the melting of polar ice caps and the raising of the sea level around the world. The rising of the oceans will put many cities and millions of people under water. 24

24. The author wants to add a sentence here to further support his points about global warming. Which of the following sentences will do that most effectively?

F. However, this melting will also mean extreme habitat loss for the polar bears, who will be forced into a smaller and smaller area as the polar ice caps continue to melt.

G. Furthermore, some scientists argue that the so-called global warming is no more than a continuation of the natural cycles of the earth's warming and cooling.

H. In addition, this melting will also mean extreme habitat loss for the polar bears, who will be forced into a smaller and smaller area as the polar ice caps continue to melt.

J. As a result, some scientists argue that the so-called global warming is no more than a continuation of the natural cycles of the earth's warming and cooling.

First, decide which of the transition words in the answer choices you would use. Since the question asks you to select a point that *further supports* the argument about global warming, you know immediately that you should use a continuation transition word. You can therefore rule out choices F and J without wasting the time to read the entire choices. Both choices G and H begin with a continuation transition word, so you need to decide which of the two points better supports the points already made. Clearly, choice H is correct, since the point made in choice G contradicts the argument of the author.

Practice problem set **Strategy**

The solutions follow the problem set.

College admissions can be a tricky process. Most high school students spend hours slaving over applications, trying to leverage their advantages in order to secure a spot at the universities of their choice. <u>However,</u>
[1]
pressure from friends and family only adds to the burden.

<u>That being said, there</u> are several great
[2]
resources you can consult when trying to put your application together. Your high school counselor is an excellent resource for reading and commenting on your application. <u>Moreover, it's important</u> that you are the one
[3]
who makes the ultimate decisions about what you write and how you write it.

Keep in mind when applying that thousands (or tens of thousands, depending on the university) of students are applying to the same institution. <u>Yet, it's</u> important to set
[4]
yourself apart from the other applicants in the pool.

A great place to start is the Common App, which you can find online. The Common App

1. **A.** NO CHANGE
   B. As a result,
   C. In addition,
   D. Yet,

2. **F.** NO CHANGE
   G. Along the same lines, there
   H. Therefore, there
   J. Similarly, there

3. **A.** NO CHANGE
   B. However, it's important
   C. And, it's important
   D. In the same way, it's important

4. **F.** NO CHANGE
   G. Thus, it's
   H. Nonetheless, it's
   J. Even so, it's

is accepted by almost all the schools you'll end up applying to. [5]

Try to let your spirit shine through in your essay. Show, rather than tell, the admissions officers why they should accept you. Show your friends and family your essay—they should know right away that it's your essay. [6]

The letters you get from your teachers are incredibly important. Make sure you ask your teachers well in advance for your letters so that they can devote adequate time to writing a thoughtful letter that highlights your best qualities.

5. Here, the author wants to add another sentence to continue his point about the benefits of the Common App. Which is the best choice to add here?

A. The Common App can save you a lot of time, as you only have to fill out one application rather than one for each individual school you're applying to.
B. Unfortunately, the Common App does take a great deal of time to complete—between 10 and 12 hours for a quality application.
C. Some applications require extra, additional essays that can take many hours as well.
D. A lot of my friends use the Common App too.

6. You want to insert a sentence here that signals the topic of the new paragraph. Choose a transition/conclusion sentence that effectively moves from this paragraph to the next.

F. The essay is a critical part of your application package.
G. In conclusion, your essay should tell the person who reads it why you deserve to get in.
H. Besides the essay, your letters of recommendation play an important role in the admissions process.
J. Your letters of recommendation are very important as well.

Solutions for the practice problem set ▪ *Strategy*

1. **C.** Pressure from friends and family is a continuation of the ideas already expressed in the passage. Therefore, you should select a continuation transition word, in this case, "in addition."

2. **F.** To mark the contrast between the negative ideas of the first paragraph and the positive, "here's what you can do about it" ideas in the second paragraph, you should select an answer choice with a contradiction transition word paired with a contrasting idea. Choice F is the only answer that fits.

3. **B.** While your high school counselor is a good resource, the point here is that you shouldn't rely too much on his or her help in writing your essay. Since this is a contrasting idea, you should select the answer choice with a contradiction transition word.

4. **G.** A causal relationship is implied between the fact that there are many applicants and the importance of setting yourself apart. The transition word should indicate a cause-and-effect relationship; "thus" is the only appropriate choice.

5. **A.** To support the idea about how useful the Common App is, you need to select the choice that relates to the Common App in a positive, relevant way.

6. **H.** Choice H is the only answer that both wraps up the current paragraph ("besides the essay") and introduces the idea of the next paragraph ("your letters of recommendation").

Organization

The ACT's organization questions assess how well you're able to reposition parts of sentences, paragraphs, and the passage as a whole to increase the clarity and effectiveness of the writing. We'll discuss the three types of organization questions that you'll encounter:

- ◄ Organization of sentences
- ◄ Organization of paragraphs
- ◄ Organization of passages

Organization of sentences

In reorganizing sentences, you decide which parts of a sentence go where. You'll be asked to move the parts around so that the finished sentence reads clearly and expresses the desired idea. About half of the reorganizing questions are about sentences, and they often involve misplaced modifiers, discussed earlier in the chapter. Fortunately, you've already learned almost everything you need to know about sentence reorganization—specifically, modifiers, conjunctions, and sentence structure.

Your goal is to make sure that the sentence reads clearly and that it's easy to understand which adjectives and adverbs go with which nouns and verbs. Modifiers should be next to the words they modify, and the sentence should flow logically.

Organization of paragraphs

The basic logic used to reorganize a paragraph is the same as that used to reorganize a sentence. Ideas should flow logically from beginning to end, usually with an introductory sentence at the beginning, details in the middle, and a concluding sentence at the end. There should be no extraneous or unrelated material in the paragraph; in fact, for many questions, "DELETE the underlined sentence" is the correct choice. Paragraph reorganization questions occur at the ends of paragraphs.

Most paragraphs have the following organization:

◄ **An introduction/topic sentence (general)**

This sentence, which often relates to the previous paragraph, prepares the reader for what follows. After reading the first sentence, the reader should know exactly what he or she is about to read in the rest of the paragraph. If you read the first sentence and have no clue as to the topic of the paragraph, chances are that the sentence doesn't belong at the beginning of the paragraph. Extremely detailed or specific sentences typically aren't found at the beginnings of paragraphs.

◄ **Two to five detailed sentences (specific)**

This is the "meat" of the paragraph. These sentences provide details and supporting points that elaborate on the idea expressed in the topic sentence. Be aware that there is no place in a paragraph for random, extraneous, or irrelevant information. If a sentence doesn't relate directly to the topic, it doesn't belong in the paragraph and should be deleted.

◄ **A conclusion/summary sentence (general)**

At the end of the paragraph is a sentence that often begins with "in summary," "in conclusion," "therefore," or "thus." These words are a clue that the sentence is summarizing the main idea presented in the paragraph. The last sentence of a paragraph is not the place to introduce new ideas or include specific evidence.

Here's what a sample question looks like:

English 36 example

[1] The summer after my freshman year, I spent hours flipping burgers at the local McDonald's. [2] The next summer, I got a slightly better gig painting fences in the neighborhood—out of the heat of the kitchen and into the heat of the

25. Which of the following provides the most logical ordering of the sentences above?

A. 1, 2, 3, 4, 5
B. 5, 1, 2, 3, 4
C. 4, 1, 2, 3, 5
D. 4, 1, 3, 2, 5

Georgia, summertime sunshine.

[3] The pay wasn't great, but it was my first real job and the chocolate shakes that they served with the burgers were really something. [4] I've worked ever since I entered high school. [5] Thus, although none of my jobs has been easy, each has given me valuable experience and—more importantly— cash in my pocket. [25]

The correct answer is choice D. Sentence 4 introduces the topic; sentences 1, 3, and 2 (in that order) provide the details; and sentence 5 neatly wraps up the paragraph. The content of sentence 3, relating to shakes and burgers, indicates that it should immediately follow sentence 1, which describes the author's first job at McDonald's.

The best approach to a paragraph reorganization question is to identify the introduction and concluding sentences first. Any answer choices that don't have these in the correct position (first and last) can be immediately eliminated, often leaving only one or two choices and saving you valuable time.

A question may provide a new sentence and ask you to place it correctly in the paragraph.

Organization of passages

Passage reorganization questions are almost always at the end of the passage and are typically the last question in the section. These questions ask you to confirm the order of the paragraphs within the passage, to suggest a new order, or to determine where to place a specific paragraph in the passage.

The key to solving a passage reorganization question is to focus on the topic sentence of each paragraph. By reading only the first sentence of each paragraph, you should see a natural and logical sequence of information. The topic sentences should indicate which paragraph belongs at the beginning of the passage and which belongs at the end. Much like sentences in a paragraph, paragraphs in a passage tend to begin with a general introduction, go to specific details, and end with a general conclusion. Detailed topics tend to be sandwiched in the middle, with broad, general statements or arguments being made at the beginning or end.

The first paragraph should introduce the passage, the middle paragraphs should support or elaborate on the ideas presented in the introduction, and the last paragraph should recap the passage's most important points and draw a conclusion. In some passages, the introductory and conclusion paragraphs mirror one another, with the concluding paragraph revisiting an idea that appeared in the introductory paragraph.

Frequently, a transition word introducing a new paragraph relates to the previous paragraph, and this can help you figure out where a paragraph belongs. If, for example, a paragraph begins "In addition to X, Y is important," you have a clue that this paragraph directly follows the paragraph that discusses X.

One last tip: points in the middle paragraphs should be in the same order as they are mentioned in the introductory paragraph. Use this tip if you know which paragraphs make up the body of the passage, but you don't know their order and you don't have enough information from transition words and topic sentences to guess confidently.

Style

Style questions test your ability to assess and analyze the writing style of the author, as well as to make changes that add to the flow and consistency of the passage. Solving style questions involves several tactics:

- ◄ Eliminating redundancy
- ◄ Avoiding ambiguity
- ◄ Recognizing tone
- ◄ Choosing appropriate language

All of these areas relate to making the passage flow smoothly from one paragraph to another, remaining consistent in tone and writing style throughout. Errors are signaled by choppy, awkward-sounding sentences, changes in tone from one part of the passage to another, and style variation between parts of the passage.

Eliminating redundancy

This topic was addressed earlier in the chapter—see English 36 Strategy 4: *Shorter is sweeter*. The key is to cut any words or phrases that repeat ideas, based on the principle that any time you say the same thing twice, you're wasting the reader's time. Because the ACT in general hates filler material, you should seek out and remove repeated ideas wherever you find them. Take a look at the repetition in the following sentences:

INCORRECT	My brother led me down the road as I followed him up to the green house.
CORRECT	My brother led me down the road to the green house.

The fact that you followed your brother is already expressed by the fact that he is leading you—repeating the fact is a waste of words and ACT exam writers expect you to remove them.

INCORRECT	Dinner was at 6 PM in the evening.
CORRECT	Dinner was at 6 PM.

The abbreviation "PM" implies evening, so "in the evening" isn't necessary.

In general, if you can remove part of the sentence without losing any important information, you should remove it. Redundancy, on the ACT as well as in the real world, is a sign of bad writing style and should be eliminated.

Avoiding ambiguity

Your writing—and the writing you see in ACT English—should be as clear and specific as possible. Avoid general, vague terms like the plague. Especially avoid using "this" and "that," as in "This shows . . ." and "That shows . . .". *What* shows? Sentences like "this shows that he's very upset" fail to demonstrate what exactly "shows that he's very upset." Instead of using these general terms, specify the subject. For example:

INCORRECT	This shows that Bill is upset.
CORRECT	Bill's caustic tone and accusatory glare show that he's upset.

After reading the second sentence, you have a much better idea of what's actually going on. Be as clear and specific in your writing as possible; using general terms makes your writing less accurate and harder to understand. Here's a short list of words to avoid:

good
bad
happy
sad
this
that
important
special

Wherever possible, replace these words with accurate, specific counterparts. Why paint a story with a sloppy magic marker when you could be sketching with an ultrafine-point pen?

Recognizing tone

These questions ask you to assess the tone of a passage, that is, to decide whether certain phrases and ways of writing are consistent with the author's tone. You'll explore this concept more extensively in the chapter on ACT Reading.

My high school teachers constantly proclaimed that tone isn't what you say, it's how you say it. Since tone is often considered the "mood" or manner in which content is delivered, the choices for tone are nearly endless. Light-hearted, somber, jovial, triumphant, playful, gloomy—all these are tones you may encounter in ACT English. The content of a passage should help narrow down the choices. For example, a presentation of historical or literary material is usually done in an academic tone: long, complex sentences; big words; and little or no humor. On the other hand, personal accounts are often conversational and peppered with shorter, simpler sentences; familiar vocabulary; and, often, humor.

Once you ascertain the mood of the author's writing by reading the passage, you need to choose phrases or sentences consistent with that mood. If the essay is formal, don't opt for a choice that includes slang or familiar language. If the essay is informal, avoid long, complex sentences and archaic words. It should be relatively easy to tell which answer choices are appropriate and which aren't.

Choosing appropriate language

While recognizing tone focuses on phrases and sentences, this tactic concentrates on words. The same approach is used, however: assess the tone of the passage and select words that reflect the same degree of formality. In a history of the life and achievements of John Hancock, you wouldn't write "John was a cool guy." Similarly, in a casual note to a friend, you wouldn't write "John consistently displays deep affection for his classmates and genuine interest in the subject material."

There are no black-and-white rules for assessing tone and choosing the right word. Instead, rely on your intuition to help you know whether a word can and should be used in a certain context. For clues, look at the length and type of neighboring words. Let's say you need to describe the facial expression of a disappointed friend. If the surrounding sentences contain words like "somber," "morose," and "disheartened," you should choose a complex word—"dejected," for example. On the other hand, if the surrounding sentences contain words like "sad," "hurt," and "frowning," your word choice should reflect that level of simplicity, so "gloomy" would be better than "dejected."

Reading widely and working through practice questions will help you develop the skill to recognize tone and choose appropriate language.

The solutions follow the problem set.

[1]

[1] Finding a balance between academics, extracurriculars, and social activities is a challenge that faces almost every high school student. [2] <u>Wanting to succeed not only in class but also on the field and in the social scene, it is the school's responsibility to help the student find resources and assistance</u> when they need it. [3] With careful planning and good time management, you'll be able to achieve your goals and then some! [4] While it may all seem rather overwhelming, your

school is there to help. [2]

[2]

The transition to high school can be a <u>trying time, or a difficult period in their lives,</u> for many students. A new environment, new people, and increasing demands on time and energy are all factors that make the jump from middle to high school a tough one. <u>This means</u> that some students will struggle through it.

1. A. NO CHANGE
B. It is the school's responsibility to help the student, wanting to succeed not only in class but also on the field and in the social scene, find resources and assistance
C. It is the school's responsibility to help the student find resources, wanting to succeed not only in class but also on the field and in the social scene, and assistance
D. It is the school's responsibility to help the student find resources and assistance, wanting to succeed not only in class but also on the field and in the social scene,

2. Which of the following provides the most logical ordering of the sentences in Paragraph 1?
F. 1, 2, 3, 4
G. 1, 3, 2, 4
H. 1, 4, 3, 2
J. 1, 4, 2, 3

3. A. NO CHANGE
B. trying time
C. trying time—or a difficult period in their lives—
D. trying time,

4. F. NO CHANGE
G. The shock of the transition means
H. This jump means
J. DELETE the underlined portion.

However, most students happily adjust within the first months, which is cool.
5

[3]

The sheer newness of the physical environment can also make students uncomfortable. High schools, which are usually bigger than middle schools, are easier for new students to get lost in. However, with the help of a map and a few friends, students will learn their way around fairly quickly.

Yay!
7

[4]

[1] In addition to a new physical environment, a new social environment also confronts incoming freshmen. [2] Meeting all new friends can be difficult at first, and some shy students have more trouble reaching out to their peers. [3] Within a few weeks, though, most students will be comfortable and happy with many new friends. [4] Many high schools combine multiple middle schools, and some new students may even come in from other school districts. 8

5. **A.** NO CHANGE
   B. which is greatly beneficial to the environment and community of students and staff.
   C. that is cool.
   D. DELETE the underlined portion.

6. **F.** NO CHANGE
   G. can also sometimes, in some cases, make students uncomfortable.
   H. can also make students uncomfortable, or not 100% confident.
   J. can also make students uncomfortable in the new school.

7. **A.** NO CHANGE
   B. Wahoo!
   C. How great!
   D. DELETE the underlined portion.

8. The most logical place for Sentence 4 in Paragraph 4 is:
   F. NO CHANGE
   G. before Sentence 1.
   H. after Sentence 1.
   J. before Sentence 3.

[5]

In summary, starting high school can be a difficult transition—but with the right tools and a can-do attitude, students will find themselves at home in no time. ⑨

9. For the passage to make the most sense and flow smoothly from idea to idea, the 5 paragraphs should be ordered as follows:
   A. 1, 2, 3, 4, 5
   B. 2, 3, 4, 1, 5
   C. 2, 1, 3, 4, 5
   D. 2, 4, 1, 3, 5

Solutions for the practice problem set • *Organization and style*

1. **B.** This is an example of a misplaced modifier. The phrase "wanting . . . social scene" needs to be placed directly next to "the student," which it modifies.
2. **J.** Sentence 1 should remain at the beginning—it introduces the topic. Sentence 3 seems to contain a concluding idea, so it should be last. Sentence 4 introduces the idea of school assistance, on which Sentence 2 elaborates. Therefore, the correct order should be 1, 4, 2, 3.
3. **B.** This is an example of redundancy. "A trying time" and "a difficult period in their lives" are essentially the same thing, and stating this idea twice does not give the reader any new information. Thus, the best choice is to remove the redundant phrase.
4. **G.** The vague "this" in the original sentence leaves the reader wondering what exactly it is that means some students will struggle. Choice G provides an explicit answer, and it is the only response that successfully eliminates ambiguity from the sentence.
5. **D.** This question concerns recognizing tone. Thus far, the passage has been fairly formal—written in the style of a school newspaper article. "Which is cool" is too casual for the passage and adds no new information, so it should be removed. Choice B, at the other extreme, is too wordy to match the style of the passage.
6. **F.** There is no need to add redundant information. None of the other choices would provide any valuable or new information.
7. **D.** As pointed out earlier, the tone of the passage isn't extremely formal, but it certainly isn't the casual, perky style that would work with an exclamation like "Yay!" In the context of the paragraph and passage, this exclamation is unexpected and unprofessional, and should be eliminated.

8. **H.** Sentence 4 provides the reason for the "new social environment" in Sentence 1 and sets the stage for "meeting all new friends" in Sentence 2. Therefore, Sentence 4 belongs after Sentence 1.

9. **B.** Since Paragraph 2 introduces the topic of the transition to high school, it should be placed first. Paragraph 5 clearly belongs where it is, because it sums up the ideas in the passage. The three middle paragraphs should mirror the order in which they appear in the new first paragraph: "a new environment" (Paragraph 3), "new people" (Paragraph 4), and "increasing demands on time and energy" (Paragraph 1).

Prepare for ACT Math

Depending on your background in math, you'll be approaching the Mathematics section of the ACT with fear or excitement. Either way, the strategies in this chapter will improve your score.

ACT Math is probably quite similar to the math you've seen on other standardized tests. The keys to success are (1) knowing the techniques and properties necessary to solve all the problems and (2) applying them quickly enough to answer all 60 questions in the section. The first time I took the ACT, I didn't finish before time was called. I had to become familiar with the types of questions and the strategies to solve them before I was able to answer all 60 questions in 60 minutes, with a few moments to check my answers. Fortunately, you won't have to waste one of your ACT exams getting used to the Math section—I've laid it all out here! Once you've worked through this chapter, you'll know exactly what's on the longest section of the ACT.

Stats

Time allowed	60 minutes
Number of questions	60 questions
Time allowed per question	60 seconds

⬕ Breaking down ACT Math

"The ACT Mathematics Test is designed to measure the mathematical skills students have typically acquired in courses taken by the end of 11th grade. The test presents multiple-choice questions that require you to use reasoning skills to solve practical problems in mathematics. You need knowledge of basic formulas and computational skills to answer the problems, but you aren't required to know complex formulas and perform extensive computation."

—ACT.org

Since I don't know your background in math, I've organized this chapter differently. First, I'll "teach" all of the mathematical concepts covered on the ACT, so it doesn't matter what math classes you've already taken. Using the checklist in the MATHEMATICAL CONCEPTS section on the following pages, you will identify which concepts you understand and which you need to review. The checklist is based on the content listed on ACT.org. Next, I'll present the *Math 36 Strategies* that will help you ace this section of the ACT. Unlike the SAT, the ACT provides no list of formulas; in the EQUATIONS TO MEMORIZE section at the end of this chapter, I provide a list of formulas that you'll need to memorize before exam day.

Logistics

Two important issues involve how you should pace yourself in ACT Math and how you should use a calculator.

Timing

Unlike other sections of the ACT, the Math section organizes its questions from easiest to most difficult. The first 20 questions are relatively easy, the next 20 are of medium difficulty, and the last 20 are fairly challenging. As a test taker, you shouldn't stick to the 60-seconds-per-question guide if you expect to be able to finish the entire section in 60 minutes. If you spend 40 minutes on the easy and medium-difficulty questions, you simply won't be able to finish the last 20 (difficult) questions in the remaining 20 minutes.

When I took the ACT the first time, I wasn't aware that the difficulty of the questions increased as I went along. Halfway through the section, I checked my watch and was relieved that I had only used half an hour—with plenty of time to finish the section before time was called. Wrong! When the five-minute warning was issued, I had 10 questions left and flew through six of them; I had to guess on the remaining four. Needless to say, I didn't get a 36 on the Math section.

You should be able to finish some of the easy questions in 20 to 30 seconds, which will allow extra time for the most difficult problems, some of which may take several minutes to solve. Here's a useful guideline for time allocation on the ACT Math section:

First 20 questions	10–15 minutes
Second 20 questions	15–20 minutes
Last 20 questions	25–35 minutes

Should you double-check your calculations as you go or after you've answered all 60 questions? I advise waiting until you've completed the section before you double-check your calculations. If you don't double-check as you work problems and have extra time at the end to review and check, great! If you don't have extra time at the end, it means that you needed all the time to solve the 60 questions. Furthermore, studies have shown that in most cases, your first answer is the correct one.

There is one exception to this rule: if your solution doesn't match any of the answer choices, immediately redo your calculations. You know that you made a mistake, either in the way you set up your calculations or in a computation. Redoing the problem while it's fresh in your mind is more efficient than skipping the question and returning to it later.

Using a calculator

A calculator will save lots of time on complex multiplication, division, and multistep problems in ACT Math; it will also help you avoid mistakes frequently made when calculations are done by hand.

Not all calculators are permitted during the ACT Math section. The second time I took the ACT, one of my close friends brought her TI-89 calculator; she was informed by the test proctor that she wasn't allowed to use it. She didn't have a replacement calculator, and there were no extra calculators available. She told me afterwards that there were at least four problems that were impossible to solve without a calculator and performing calculations by hand had taken so much time that she wasn't close to finishing the test when time was called. Make sure you have a legal calculator.

A graphing calculator is fine, but not one that has a computer algebra system (for example, a TI-89, TI-92, or TI-Nspire CAS) or any calculator with a QWERTY keyboard. The ACT website states that the most common reason for students being dismissed from testing is using the TI-89. TI-84s are allowed; consider buying one, since it will be useful in many of your high school math classes, as well as in college math and physics classes. If you can't afford to buy one—they cost about $100 new—ask your math teacher if you can borrow one to prepare for the ACT. Many schools have a calculator-checkout program.

Be sure to practice with your calculator before the test. Know how to use your calculator for basic addition, subtraction, multiplication, division, some simple trigonometric functions, and graphing. Use your calculator on practice exams and on all of the math problem sets in this book. In this way, you'll become quick and efficient.

Finally, don't forget to bring extra batteries on exam day. Dead calculators are useless.

Mathematical concepts

As we review basic math concepts, I will present actual math problems and their solutions.

Topics covered

Here is a complete list of topics that the ACT Math section covers:

◄ Pre-algebra (23%)
- ☐ Number problems
- ☐ Square roots
- ☐ Exponents
- ☐ Scientific notation
- ☐ Factors and multiples
- ☐ Ratio, proportion, and percentage
- ☐ Linear equations
- ☐ Absolute value and ordering
- ☐ Mean, median, and mode
- ☐ Probability
- ☐ Data representation

◄ Elementary algebra (17%)
- ☐ Substitution
- ☐ Using variables to express relationships
- ☐ Algebraic operations and inequalities
- ☐ Factoring

◄ Intermediate algebra (15%)
- ☐ Roots of polynomials
- ☐ The quadratic formula
- ☐ Radicals and radical expressions
- ☐ Absolute values in equations
- ☐ Sequences and patterns
- ☐ Functions
- ☐ Matrices
- ☐ Complex numbers
- ☐ Logarithms

◄ Coordinate geometry (15%)
- ☐ Points and lines
- ☐ Polynomials
- ☐ Circles
- ☐ Graphing inequalities
- ☐ Slope
- ☐ Parallel and perpendicular lines
- ☐ Distance and midpoints
- ☐ Conics

- ◄ Plane geometry (23%)
  - ☐ Angles
  - ☐ Circles
  - ☐ Triangles and the Pythagorean theorem
  - ☐ Polygons
  - ☐ Transformations
  - ☐ Volume and 3-D geometry

- ◄ Trigonometry (7%)
  - ☐ SOHCAHTOA
  - ☐ Values and properties of trigonometric functions
  - ☐ Graphing trigonometric functions
  - ☐ Trigonometric identities
  - ☐ Solving trigonometric equations

Scoring

The ACT Math score is a composite of three subscores based on the six content areas listed above:

Pre-algebra and elementary algebra	40%
Intermediate algebra and coordinate geometry	30%
Plane geometry and trigonometry	30%

The subscores (each with a maximum of 36 points) are averaged and rounded to the nearest integer.

Basic math

I assume that you know how to add, subtract, multiply, and divide. Other essential math concepts are explained below. If you are already proficient in some of these areas, you may skip them.

Order of operations

Mathematical calculations are performed in a specific order. The acronym *PEMDAS* is used to remember this order:

Parentheses
Exponents
Multiplication
Division
Addition
Subtraction

Here's an example:

$$\frac{(5-3)^2 - (4 \times 3 - 2)}{3}$$

$$\frac{(2)^2 - (12 - 2)}{3}$$

$$\frac{4 - (10)}{3}$$

$$\frac{-6}{3}$$

$$-2$$

Distribution

Distribution involves multiplication when there are two or more terms inside parentheses. For example, you can distribute $x(y + z)$ as $(xy + xz)$. Here's another example:

$$3(2 + x)$$
$$3(2) + 3(x)$$
$$6 + 3x$$

Even and odd numbers

Even numbers are those that are evenly divisible by 2; examples are 2, 6, 10, and 14. Odd numbers are those that are not evenly divisible by 2; examples are 1, 5, 9, and 13.

When two even numbers or two odd numbers are added, the sum is an even number. When an even number and an odd number are added, the sum is an odd number. When two even numbers are multiplied, the product is an even number. When two odd numbers are multiplied, the product is an odd number. When an even number and an odd number are multiplied, the product is an even number. You don't need to memorize this; simply test it in your head by using 2 as your even number and 1 as your odd number.

Positive and negative numbers

A positive number is any number greater than zero; no sign is written in front of the number. A negative number is any number less than zero; a negative sign is written in front of the number.

Adding a positive number and a negative number is the same as subtracting the second number from the first:

$$3 + (-2) = 3 - 2 = 1$$

Subtracting a negative number is the same as adding its positive value:

$$3 - (-2) = 3 + 2 = 5$$

When two positive numbers are multiplied, the product is a positive number. When two negative numbers are multiplied, the product is a positive number. When a positive number and a negative number are multiplied, the product is a negative number.

$$2 \times 2 = 4$$
$$-2 \times -2 = 4$$
$$2 \times -2 = -4$$

Integers

ACT Math questions often ask you to "round your answer to the nearest integer" or "find all the integers between 1 and 20 that . . .". An *integer* is a number that can be expressed without a decimal point or fraction (for example, 1, 3, and 849, but not 2.4, ½, and 7⅝). Negative numbers can also be integers (for example, -2, -6, and -87).

Real and rational numbers

A *real number* is any number that can be placed on an infinite number line stretching from negative infinity to positive infinity. Integers, fractions, and decimals, including infinite decimals (for example, .333333 . . .), are real numbers. ACT Math uses only real numbers, so you don't have to worry about imaginary numbers, such as i (the square root of -1).

Both rational and irrational numbers are used in ACT Math. A *rational number* can be expressed as a fraction consisting of an integer divided by another integer. Expressed as a decimal, a rational number can be recognized as a finite or repeating decimal (for example, 3, .5, .3333, and .3232323). Most numbers on the ACT are rational, but some are irrational (for example, π (3.1415 . . .), $\sqrt{2}$, and e). You probably won't be asked to distinguish between rational and irrational numbers on the test; just remember that rational numbers can be represented by a single fraction of two integers or as a finite or repeating decimal, and that irrational numbers cannot.

Pre-algebra

The pre-algebra section accounts for 23% of ACT Math questions.

Number problems

These are word problems that require you to make calculations (addition, subtraction, multiplication, and division) with integers, decimals, and fractions. Here is an example of adding fractions with different denominators:

$$\frac{1}{2} + \frac{1}{4} = \frac{2}{4} + \frac{1}{4} = \frac{3}{4}$$

To multiply fractions, multiply the numerators and multiply the denominators:

$$\frac{2}{7} \times \frac{3}{4} = \frac{(2 \times 3)}{(7 \times 4)} = \frac{6}{28} = \frac{3}{14}$$

To divide fractions, "cross multiply" the numerators and denominators, that is, multiply the first fraction by the reciprocal of the second. (The *reciprocal* of a fraction is the result of flipping the numerator and denominator. For example, the reciprocal of $\frac{1}{2}$ is $\frac{2}{1}$, which is 2.)

$$\frac{2}{3} \div \frac{4}{5} = \frac{2}{3} \times \frac{5}{4} = \frac{10}{12} = \frac{5}{6}$$

Instead of dividing $\frac{2}{3}$ by $\frac{4}{5}$, $\frac{2}{3}$ is multiplied by the reciprocal of $\frac{4}{5}$, which is $\frac{5}{4}$. Then, the result, $\frac{10}{12}$, is simplified by dividing both the numerator and denominator by 2 to get $\frac{5}{6}$. Here's an example of an ACT number problem:

Math 36 example

1. Liz rode her horse, Hannah, $1\frac{3}{7}$ miles on Monday and $2\frac{7}{8}$ miles on Tuesday. What was the total distance, in miles, that Liz rode Hannah during those 2 days?

   A. $4\frac{17}{56}$

   B. $5\frac{6}{17}$

   C. $4\frac{4}{7}$

   D. $4\frac{19}{56}$

   E. $3\frac{17}{56}$

First, you add the whole numbers: $1 + 2 = 3$. Then, you convert the fractions so that they share a common denominator:

$$3 + \frac{3}{7} + \frac{7}{8} = 3 + \frac{3(8)}{7(8)} + \frac{7(7)}{8(7)} = 3 + \frac{24}{56} + \frac{49}{56} = 3 + \frac{73}{56}$$

$$= 3 + 1\frac{17}{56} = 4\frac{17}{56}$$

The correct answer is A.

Square roots

The *square root* of a number is the number that, multiplied by itself, yields the first number. The square root of x is y such that:

$$y \times y = x \quad \text{OR} \quad y^2 = x$$

This can also be written as $\sqrt{x} = y$ or as $x^{1/2} = y$.

You probably already know several common square roots (for example, $\sqrt{1} = 1$, $\sqrt{4} = 2$, and $\sqrt{9} = 3$). It is important to know how to find a square root on your calculator.

Cube roots are rarely encountered on the ACT. The cube root of x is y such that:

$$y \times y \times y = x \quad \text{OR} \quad y^3 = x$$

This can also be written as $\sqrt[3]{x} = y$. To find a cube root on your calculator, use the exponent (^) key and raise the number to the $\frac{1}{3}$ power. Higher roots (for example, fourth and fifth roots) can be calculated in the same way (for example, ^¼ and ^⅕ on your calculator); they are written as $\sqrt[4]{}$ and $\sqrt[5]{}$.

Math 36 example

2. A mathematical box takes a number x and returns a number y by performing the calculation $x^2 = y$. Tomás uses the box and it returns the number 100. What was the value of x, the input to the box?

F. 100
G. 10,000
H. 10
J. 1
K. 0

You are asked to calculate the square root of 100, which is 10. To verify your answer, calculate $10 \times 10 = 100$. The correct answer is H.

Exponents

The *exponent* of a number indicates how many times the number is to be multiplied by itself.

$$x^2 = x \times x$$
$$x^3 = x \times x \times x$$

These expressions can be read, respectively, as "x squared" or "x to the second power" and "x cubed" or "x to the third power."

To multiply two terms with exponents, combine the terms by adding the exponents:

$$x^2 \times x^3 = x^{(2+3)} = x^5$$

If the terms are different, the exponents can't be combined.

$$x^2 \times y^4 \neq xy^{(2+4)}$$

If one of the terms is in parentheses, the exponents are multiplied.

$$(x^2)^3 = x^{(2 \times 3)} = x^6$$

For a negative exponent, raise the number to the power indicated, then use the reciprocal of the result.

$$x^{-1} = \frac{1}{x}$$

$$(x + y)^{-4} = \frac{1}{(x + y)^{-4}}$$

To calculate numbers with exponents on your calculator, use the exponent (^) key. For example, to calculate 2^3, key 2^3, which yields 8.

Remember: exponents are not distributive.

$$(x + y)^2 \neq (x^2 + y^2)$$

Instead:

$$(x + y)^2 = (x + y)(x + y) = x^2 + 2xy + y^2$$

Math 36 example

3. For all positive integers a, b, and c, which of the following expressions is equivalent to $\dfrac{(a + b)}{c}$?

  A. $ac^{-1} + bc^{-1}$
  B. $a^{-1} + b^{-1} + c^{-1}$
  C. $(ac)^{-1} + (bc)^{-1}$
  D. $a^{-1} - b^{-1} - c^{-1}$
  E. $ab^{-1} + c$

Since c is in the denominator, the answer must contain a c^{-1} term, which eliminates answer choice E. Since a and b are in the numerator, they aren't being raised to a negative power, which eliminates choices B, C, and D. Choice A remains and can be verified by the following simplification:

$$ac^{-1} + bc^{-1} = a\left(\frac{1}{c}\right) + b\left(\frac{1}{c}\right) = \frac{a}{c} + \frac{b}{c} = \frac{(a + b)}{c}$$

Scientific notation

Scientific notation appears rarely in ACT Math, but occurs regularly in ACT Science. It is used to express very large and very small numbers efficiently. For example, instead of writing 6,785,000,000,000, you could use scientific notation: 6.785×10^{12}. To convert a number to scientific notation, place a decimal point after the first nonzero number, then count the number of places you moved the decimal point. The number of places is the power of 10 to which the number is to be raised. If the number is greater than 1, the power is positive; if the number is less than 1, the power is negative. Finally, delete all leading and trailing zeros. Here are two examples:

$$1,354,000 = 1.354000 \times 10^6 = 1.354 \times 10^6$$
$$.00000073 = 0000007.3 \times 10^{-7} = 7.3 \times 10^{-7}$$

Factors and multiples

The *factors* of a number are all the integers that can evenly divide into the number. Put another way, the factors of a number is the set of all integers that can be multiplied by a single integer to obtain the number. Here are the factors of the number 24:

1, 2, 3, 4, 6, 8, 12, 24 (because $1 \times 24 = 24$, $2 \times 12 = 24$, and so on)

Factors can also be listed in pairs whose products are the number. Here are the factor pairs for the number 70:

1×70
2×35
5×14
7×10

The greatest common factor (GCF) is often used in ACT Math. The *greatest common factor* of two numbers is the largest integer that is a factor of both numbers. For example, the GCF of 12 and 8 is 4, because $3 \times 4 = 12$, $2 \times 4 = 8$, and there is no larger factor that both numbers share.

GCFs can be used to reduce fractions: divide both the numerator and the denominator by the GCF of the two numbers to obtain the simplest form of the fraction. Here's an example:

$$\frac{36}{54} = \frac{2}{3} \quad \text{(because the GCF of 36 and 54 is 18)}$$

Multiples are even easier than factors. The *multiples* of a number are all the products of the number multiplied by any integer. While there is a finite number of factors for a given number, there is an infinite number of multiples for a number. For example, the multiples of 4 are 4, 8, 12, 16, 20, and so on.

The least common multiple (LCM) is often used in ACT Math. The *least common multiple* of two numbers is the smallest integer that is a multiple of both numbers. For example, the LCM of 12 and 20 is 60, the LCM of 54 and 9 is 54, and the LCM of 2 and 3 is 6. The LCM is used when adding and subtracting fractions: to calculate a common denominator, the smallest common denominator is the LCM of the original denominators. In the following example, the LCM of 8 and 12 is 24:

$$\frac{1}{8} + \frac{1}{12} = \frac{3}{24} + \frac{2}{24} = \frac{5}{24}$$

Ratio, proportion, and percentage

The concepts of ratio, proportion, and percentage are closely linked. Ratio and proportion relate one part of a whole to another part of the whole, while percentage relates one part to the whole itself. For example, if $a + b = c$, ratio and proportion relate a and b to one another, while percentage relates a or b to c.

Ratio

A ratio can be written in several ways. Most frequently, it has the form $a:b$; for example, if there are three red bricks and two green bricks, the ratio of red bricks to green bricks is $3:2$. This relationship can also be expressed as $\frac{3}{2}$. When working on ratio problems, remember to relate one part to another part, even if the question provides only one part and the whole. For example, a question may state that Sally flipped a coin 30 times and got 18 heads, then ask for the ratio of heads to tails. The number of tails is $30 - 18 = 12$, so the ratio of heads to tails is $18:12$. In ratios, the order of the numbers is important. Be sure that your ratio reflects the order expressed in the question. In the coin example, $12:18$—the ratio of tails to heads—is incorrect.

In summary, ratios are used to compare parts and may require some calculation. The ACT exam writers know that many students are prone to blindly use the two numbers in the question, so they offer one or two answer choices that use only those numbers.

Proportion

A *proportion* applies a ratio to more than one whole. For example, a question may state that the ratio of blue to green sprinkles on your cupcake is $5:3$ and ask you to calculate the number of green sprinkles if there are 800 sprinkles on the cupcake. If there were eight sprinkles, five of them would be blue and three would be green, so you can write the proportion as follows:

$$\frac{3}{8} = \frac{?}{800}$$

The proportion can be solved by using cross-multiplication ($3 \times 800 = 8x$; solve for x) or inspection (just by looking at the proportion, you can see that $x = 300$).

Percentage

At least one ACT Math problem will test your ability to calculate and use percentages. A percentage is expressed as a fraction of 100; for example, $50\% = \dfrac{50}{100}$. A percentage can be expressed in the following way:

$$\frac{\text{Part}}{\text{Whole}} = \text{Percentage}$$

A question will provide two of the quantities and ask you to calculate the third.

To calculate the percentage from the part and the whole, divide the part by the whole, then multiply the resulting decimal by 100. For example, a question may state that Gabriel hugged his sister on 5 of the 7 days of the week and ask what percentage of the days he hugged his sister.

$$\frac{5}{7} = .714 = 71.4\%$$

To calculate the part from the whole and the percentage, multiply the whole by the percentage (expressed as a decimal). For example, a question may state that Professor Interrante read 89% of 27 term papers and ask the number of papers she read.

$$27 \times .89 = {\sim}24$$

To calculate the whole from the part and the percentage, divide the part by the percentage (expressed as a decimal). For example, a question may state that Birch used 52 photos on a project, which represented 6% of all the photos she took last year, and ask how many photos she took last year.

$$\frac{52}{.06} = {\sim}867$$

When a problem involves a percentage increase, be aware that the total percentage is the percentage increase plus 100%; thus, a 50% increase means 150% of the original value. When a problem involves a percentage decrease, subtract the percentage decrease from 100%; thus a 20% decrease means 80% of the original value.

Math 36 example

4. If 125% of a certain number is 100, what is 60% of that same number?

   F. 24

   G. 65

   H. 36

   J. 48

   K. 64

Since you know the part and the percentage, you first calculate the whole: $100/1.25 = 80$. You then calculate 60% of the whole: $80 \times .6 = 48$. The correct answer is J.

Linear equations

Graphing

Linear equations are usually written in the form $y = mx + b$, where m is the slope and b is the y-intercept. For example, in the equation $y = 3x + 2$, the slope is 3 and the y-intercept is 2. If you are questioned about the graph of a linear equation, first verify that the y-intercept is in the correct place; it is the y-value of the point where $x = 0$. For example, if the y-intercept is 2, look for the point (0,2).

Next, make sure that the slope of the graph matches the slope in the equation: count the number of units up or down that a point moves for every unit that it moves to the right. For a slope of 3, the point should be 1 unit to the right and 3 units higher than the last point.

To solve a set of two linear equations graphically, find the point on the graph where the two lines cross. For example, if a question asks you to find the solution to $y = 4x + 2$, $y = -x + 7$ graphically, look at a graph of both equations and find the point at which the two lines cross: (1,6); therefore, $x = 1$ and $y = 6$.

If a fractional slope is involved (for example, $\frac{4}{5}$), remember the phrase "rise over run": the number in the numerator is the number that you move up (the rise), while the number in the denominator is the number that you move to the right (the run). With a slope of $\frac{4}{5}$, the next point would be 4 units above and 5 units to the right of the last point.

Solving linear equations in one variable

This is the first step in learning to solve more complex systems of equations. In general, the number of variables that you're asked to solve for is equal to the number of equations that you're given that describe the variables. For example, if you need to find both x and y, you'll be given two equations; if you're asked to solve for only one variable, you'll be given only one equation. Consider the following equation:

$$3x + 17 = 32$$

The key to solving this equation is to get the variable "by itself," which means that you should eventually have x on one side of the equation and everything else on the other side. First, eliminate all the terms on the x side that don't have x in them; you do this by adding or subtracting from both sides of the equation. In algebra, you do this to ensure that the equation remains true. Here, you need to subtract 17 from the left-hand side to leave $3x$ by itself, and you need to subtract 17 from the right-hand side:

$$3x + 17 \, (- \, 17) = 32 \, (- \, 17)$$
$$3x = 32 - 17$$
$$3x = 15$$

Next, you need to divide both sides by the coefficient of x. (The *coefficient* is the number that is multiplied by x—in this case, 3.)

$$\frac{3x}{3} = \frac{15}{3}$$
$$x = 5$$

If the coefficient of x were a fraction ($\frac{x}{3} = 15$, for instance), dividing by the coefficient of x ($\frac{1}{3}$) would be equivalent to multiplying by the reciprocal of the fraction, that is, 3:

$$\frac{x}{3}(3) = 15(3)$$
$$x = 45$$

If there are terms on both sides of the equation that contain x, they must be moved to the same side and combined; then, you proceed as if you had only one x term.

$$4x + 10 = 7x - 20$$
$$4x + 10 \, (- \, 4x) = 7x - 20 \, (- \, 4x)$$
$$10 = 3x - 20$$
$$10 \, (+ \, 20) = 3x - 20 \, (+ \, 20)$$
$$30 = 3x$$
$$30 \, (\div \, 3) = 3x \, (\div \, 3)$$
$$10 = x$$

Math 36 example

5. If $5x + 4 = 10x - 16$, then $x = ?$

A. $\dfrac{1}{4}$

B. $\dfrac{4}{3}$

C. $1\dfrac{1}{4}$

D. -4

E. 4

The following calculations are performed:

$$5x + 4 = 10x - 16$$
$$5x + 4\,(-\,5x) = 10x - 16\,(-\,5x)$$
$$4 = 5x - 16$$
$$4\,(+\,16) = 5x - 16\,(+\,16)$$
$$20 = 5x$$
$$20\,(\div\,5) = 5x\,(\div\,5)$$
$$4 = x$$

The correct answer is E.

Solving linear equations in two variables

When working with two variables and two equations, the same approach is used, except that one equation is used to solve for one variable in terms of the other variable; you find the solution by entering the result from the first equation into the second equation. Here are two equations with two variables:

$$6x - 10 = 2y$$
$$40 - 10x = y - 7$$

First, select one of the equations to solve for a variable. Select the equation with the fewest steps to solve—in this case, the first equation, because it can be solved by dividing both sides of the equation by 2:

$$6x - 10 = 2y$$
$$\frac{6x}{2} - \frac{10}{2} = \frac{2y}{2}$$
$$3x - 5 = y$$

Next, replace y in the second equation with the expression in terms of x $(3x - 5)$. In this way, you will have an equation with only one variable:

$$40 - 10x = y - 7$$
$$40 - 10x = (3x - 5) - 7$$
$$40 - 10x = 3x - 12$$
$$40 - 10x \, (+ \, 10x) = 3x - 12 \, (+ \, 10x)$$
$$40 = 13x - 12$$
$$40 \, (+ \, 12) = 13x - 12 \, (+ \, 12)$$
$$52 = 13x$$
$$\frac{52}{13} = \frac{13x}{13}$$
$$4 = x$$

Finally, enter the value for x into the equation for y:

$$3x - 5 = y$$
$$3(4) - 5 = y$$
$$12 - 5 = y$$
$$7 = y$$

The solution to this set of equations is $x = 4$, $y = 7$.

If there are three equations with three variables, use the same approach: solve for and replace one variable, repeat the process to solve for a second variable, and solve for the remaining variable. The ACT typically doesn't include problems with three variables.

Absolute value and ordering

Absolute value, denoted by the straight bracket symbol $|x|$, is the value of a number without regard to sign. For example, the absolute value of 4 is 4, and the absolute value of -4 is also 4. When working with absolute values, leave positive numbers unchanged and make negative numbers positive.

Math 36 example

6. If $5 + |4 - 6| = x + 6$, what is x?

  F. 9
  G. -3
  H. 3
  J. 1
  K. 11

The absolute value of $4 - 6$ is 2. Therefore, if $5 + 2 = x + 6$, then $x = 1$ and the correct answer is J. Absolute-value problems are fairly straightforward; just remember to make negative numbers positive.

The ACT exam writers love to ask you to place a set of numbers in increasing or decreasing order. The set of numbers is usually a combination of fractions, decimals, square roots, operations, and absolute values. A question may ask you to place the following terms in ascending order:

$$\frac{5}{4}, \ \sqrt{2}, \ .77, \ |-1.3|, \ 2.4, \ \sqrt[3]{8}$$

First, use your calculator to reduce each number to its decimal form:

1.25, 1.41, .77, 1.3, 2.4, 2

Then put each number in ascending order:

.77, 1.25, 1.3, 1.41, 2, 2.4

Mean, median, and mode

These concepts will certainly be tested on your ACT exam.

Mean

Mean is another way of saying "average." To calculate the mean of a set of values, add the values and divide by the number of values. As an example, to calculate the mean of test scores 81, 74, 92, 96, and 83, perform the following calculation:

$$\frac{81 + 74 + 92 + 96 + 83}{5} = \frac{426}{5} = 85.2$$

Sometimes, you are given the mean and part of a set of numbers and asked to find the remaining number, as in the following example:

Math 36 example

7. Rebecca needs a test average of 90 to ensure that she will get an A in her multivariable calculus class. So far, she's earned a 92, a 97, and a 96. What's the lowest score she can receive on her last test and still get an A?

   A. 75
   B. 72
   C. 81
   D. 100
   E. 68

The problem can be set up as follows:

$$\frac{92 + 97 + 96 + x}{4} = 90$$

Multiply both sides of the equation by 4:

$$92 + 97 + 96 + x = 360$$
$$285 + x = 360$$
$$x = 75$$

The correct answer is A.

Median

The *median* of a set of numbers is the number whose value is in the middle of the set. To find the median, write the elements of the set in numerical order, then cross off the largest and smallest elements pair by pair until you reach the middle number. If there's an odd number of elements in the set, one number will remain, and it is the median. If there's an even number of elements in the set, two numbers will remain; average these numbers to find the median.

Math 36 example

8. Kelly is in the same multivariable calculus class as Rebecca, but she wants to determine her median score. So far, she's earned a 78, an 82, a 94, and an 89. What is Kelly's median score?

   F. 82
   G. 89
   H. 85.5
   J. 85
   K. 86.5

In ascending order, Kelly's scores are as follows:

$$78, 82, 89, 92$$

Crossing off the largest and smallest scores, two scores remain: 82 and 89. Finding the mean of these scores ($(82 + 89) \div 2$) yields a median of 85.5. The correct answer is H.

Mode

The *mode* is the element in a set that occurs the greatest number of times. For example, in the following set, the mode is 46, which occurs four times:

$$23, \mathbf{46}, 7, 94, \mathbf{46}, 32, 54, 32, \mathbf{46}, 78, \mathbf{46}, 12, 99$$

If no element occurs more than once, or if every element occurs the same number of times, there is no mode.

Probability

Probability is the likelihood that a particular outcome will happen as a fraction of all possible outcomes. For example, what's the probability of drawing an ace from a deck of 52 playing cards? Since there are four aces and 52 total cards, the probability is as follows:

$$\frac{4}{52} = \frac{1}{13}$$

As with percentages, remember to divide by the *total* number of options, not the number of other options. The following problem tests your skill at computing probability:

Math 36 example

9. Jen is helping Sam choose a saddle pad for his new pony. The bin contains 3 navy blue pads, 2 black pads, and 5 maroon pads. What is the chance that Jen will randomly select a maroon pad?

   A. $\dfrac{1}{2}$

   B. $\dfrac{5}{2}$

   C. $\dfrac{1}{5}$

   D. $\dfrac{5}{3}$

   E. 1

The number of maroon pads is 5, and the total number of pads is $3 + 2 + 5 = 10$. Thus, the probability is as follows:

$$\frac{5}{10} = \frac{1}{2}$$

The correct answer is A. Note that two of the incorrect answer choices offer probabilities that result from mistakenly comparing the number of maroon saddle pads to the number of saddle pads of other colors.

Sometimes, you are asked to express probability as a percentage chance that a particular outcome will happen. In this case, divide the fraction probability to obtain the percentage. In the example above, $1 \div 2 = 50\%$. In the playing card example, the chance of drawing an ace is $1 \div 13 = 7.7\%$.

Data representation

ACT Math tests your ability to read and interpret charts, graphs, and other methods of data representation. These include pie charts (where relative percentages are displayed as portions of a circle), bar graphs, and graphic representations that use miniature pictures to model data. I assume that you're proficient in reading and interpreting pie charts and bar graphs, so I present here an example of a miniature-picture problem:

Math 36 example

10. The following graph shows how many packages were delivered in the last year to 3 different planets, to the nearest 1,000 packages. According to the graph, what fraction of all packages delivered last year was sent to Tweenis 12?

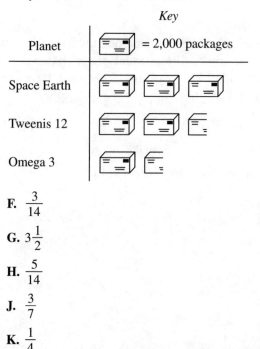

F. $\dfrac{3}{14}$

G. $3\dfrac{1}{2}$

H. $\dfrac{5}{14}$

J. $\dfrac{3}{7}$

K. $\dfrac{1}{4}$

This problem tests your knowledge of fractions as well as data representation. First, count the number of boxes in the graph, including halves: 3 + 2.5 + 1.5 = 7. Since each box represents 2,000 packages, there is a total of 14,000 packages (the denominator). Of these packages, 5,000 (2.5 boxes × 2,000) were sent to Tweenis 12 (the numerator).

$$\frac{5,000}{14,000} = \frac{5}{14}$$

The correct answer is H.

Data representation questions are not difficult; the key is to multiply the number of graphic objects by the number of real-world items they represent.

Elementary algebra

The elementary algebra section accounts for 17% of ACT Math questions.

Algebra is a powerful tool for solving problems. In order to work quickly enough to finish all 60 problems in ACT Math, you will use algebra to solve problems rapidly. If you avoid using algebraic solutions or if you use trial-and-error by plugging in answer choices and checking whether they work, you will move through the test slowly and probably not score well. To become proficient in algebra, you can use online resources and math textbooks to review basic concepts, then practice solving equations until solutions come easily and—most importantly—quickly.

Substitution

Substitution replaces variables with equivalent functions. You used substitution when you replaced y in solving linear equations with two variables (see the SOLVING LINEAR EQUATIONS IN TWO VARIABLES section). Here's an example of substitution as used in ACT Math:

Math 36 example

11. If $x = 3t + 4$ and $y = \dfrac{4}{3} + t$, which of the following answers accurately expresses y in terms of x?

A. $y = \dfrac{x}{3}$

B. $y = 3x$

C. $y = x$

D. $y = \dfrac{3x}{3}$

E. $y = \dfrac{3x}{t}$

Solve the first equation for t:

$$x = 3t + 4$$
$$x\,(-\,4) = 3t + 4\,(-\,4)$$
$$x - 4 = 3t$$
$$\frac{x - 4}{3} = \frac{3t}{3}$$
$$\frac{x - 4}{3} = t$$

Substitute the expression for t in the second equation:

$$y = \frac{4}{3} + \left(\frac{x - 4}{3}\right)$$

$$y = \frac{4 + x - 4}{3}$$

$$y = \frac{x}{3}$$

The correct answer is A.

Using variables to express relationships

You can use variables to write equations that model the facts stated in a question, then solve the equations. An ACT Math question may present a word problem and ask you to select the equation or set of equations that best models the situation. Here's an example:

Math 36 example

12. The larger of two numbers exceeds three times the smaller number by 2. The sum of twice the larger number and four times the smaller number is 115. If a is the smaller number, which equation represents the correct value of a?

    F. $2(3a) + 2 + 4a = 115$
    G. $2(3a + 2) + 4a = 115$
    H. $3(2a + 2) + 4a = 115$
    J. $2(3a - 2) + 4a = 115$
    K. $3(2a + 2) - 4a = 115$

Use a to represent the smaller number and b to represent the larger number. One by one, convert the statements in the question to equations:

(1) The larger of two numbers exceeds three times the smaller number by 2:

$$b = 3a + 2$$

(2) The sum of twice the larger number and four times the smaller number is 115:

$$2b + 4a = 115$$

Using substitution, enter the expression for b from the first equation into the second equation:

$$2(3a + 2) + 4a = 115$$

The correct answer is G.

When using variables to express relationships, it is important to work slowly (sentence by sentence or phrase by phrase) and express the relationships in mathematical form.

Algebraic operations and inequalities

Following are a few more tips on modifying algebraic expressions.

Combining like terms

You can only combine terms of the same degree and variable. The *degree* of a term is the exponent to which the variable in the term is raised; for example, the degree of x^4 is 4, the degree of x^{-2} is -2, and the degree of 6 is 0 (because there is no x term). If two terms have the same degree but different variables (for example, x^2 and y^2), you cannot combine them. The following equation shows which terms can be combined:

$$y = 3x^3 - 4x^{-1} + 6x^5 - 5x^3 - 7 + 2x^{-1} + 8 + 2x$$

The result is as follows:

$$y = 6x^5 - 2x^3 + 2x + 1 - 2x^{-1}$$

Multiplying binomials

ACT Math tests your ability to multiply binomials, which are of the form $x + c$, where x is a variable and c is a constant. A question may ask you to multiply the following expression:

$$(x + 4)(x - 3)$$

To perform this operation, use a technique called FOIL, which stands for *First, Outside, Inside, Last*. FOIL is applied as follows:

(1) Multiply the two **F**irst numbers:

$$(x)(x) = x^2$$

(2) Multiply the two **O**utside numbers:

$$(x)(-3) = -3x$$

(3) Multiply the two **I**nside numbers:

$$(4)(x) = 4x$$

(4) Multiply the two **L**ast numbers:

$$(4)(-3) = -12$$

The result of combining these products follows:

$$x^2 - 3x + 4x - 12$$
$$x^2 + x - 12$$

It helps to realize that the coefficient of the second term is the sum of the two constants ($-3x + 4x = x$) and that the final term is the product of the two constants ($(4)(-3) = -12$). Applying this shortcut can save time.

Algebraic inequalities

The symbols $>$, $<$, $\geq$, and $\leq$ indicate the presence of an inequality. When solving an equation with an inequality, you use the same methods that you use when solving an equation with an equals sign ($=$). The only difference is that when an inequality is involved, you reverse the direction of the inequality when you multiply both sides of the equation by a negative number:

$$-x > 5$$
$$-x(-1) > 5(-1)$$
$$x < -5$$

In a square root involving an inequality, the square root of x^2 is $|x|$, not x. Here is a common error of this sort:

$$x^2 > 9$$
$$\sqrt{x^2} > \sqrt{9}$$
$$x > 3$$

This error causes you to miss half of the possible solutions. This is how to avoid the error:

$$x^2 > 9$$
$$\sqrt{x^2} > \sqrt{9}$$
$$|x| > 3$$
$$x > 3 \text{ OR } x < -3$$

The ACT exam writers are aware of this error and include answer choices that assume that the square root of x^2 is only positive x, not negative x.

Factoring

You can simplify an algebraic expression by factoring. In order to factor, find a number that is a factor of all the terms in the expression, then divide the terms by the factor. Here's an expression that can be factored:

$$4x^6 + 8x^3 + 12x - 4$$

Since each of the terms is divisible by 4, you can factor the 4 out and place it as a multiplier of the factored expression:

$$4(x^6 + 2x^3 + 3x - 1)$$

Factoring often helps solve problems by simplifying complex equations.

Fractions can also be factored; each term is multiplied by a common fraction:

$$\frac{1}{4}x^4 - \frac{1}{2}x^2 + \frac{1}{8}x - 1$$

$$\frac{1}{8}(2x^4 - 4x^2 + x - 8)$$

Intermediate algebra

The intermediate algebra section accounts for 15% of ACT Math questions.

Roots of polynomials

Earlier, you used FOIL to multiply two binomials, yielding an expression of the type $ax^2 + bx + c$, where a, b, and c are constants (see the MULTIPLYING BINO-MIALS section). This expression is a second-degree quadratic polynomial; it is second degree because the highest exponent of x is 2.

You can reverse the process and turn $ax^2 + bx + c$ into two binomials. This is necessary to solve a quadratic equation, which has the form $ax^2 + bx + c = 0$. In order to solve the equation and find its "roots," the polynomial expression must be factored into two binomials. Here is a sample quadratic equation:

$$x^2 + 5x - 14 = 0$$

To factor this equation, you need to find two integers m and n such that $m + n = 5$ and $m \times n = -14$. The easiest way to do this is to consider which factors of -14 would add up to equal 5. Do -1 and 14 add up to 5? No. Do -2 and 7 add up to 5? Yes! The equation can now be written as follows:

$$(x - 2)(x + 7) = 0$$

The two solutions are $x = -2$ and $x = 7$.

The more you practice factoring quadratic equations, the easier it becomes. For some equations, however, it seems impossible to find factors that work. This rarely happens, but when it does, you can use the quadratic formula to solve such equations.

The quadratic formula

The quadratic formula uses the a, b, and c of $ax^2 + bx + c$ to solve a quadratic equation. The formula is complicated, and you must memorize it for ACT Math:

$$x = \frac{-b \pm \sqrt{b^2 - 4ac}}{2a}$$

This formula is used to solve the following problem:

Math 36 example

13. Find the two solutions to the quadratic equation
$x^2 - 7x + 9 = 4$.

A. $x = \dfrac{7 + \sqrt{49}}{2} \approx$ and $x = \dfrac{7 - \sqrt{49}}{2}$

B. $x = \dfrac{7 + \sqrt{29}}{2} \approx$ and $x = \dfrac{7 - \sqrt{29}}{2}$

C. $x = \dfrac{2 + \sqrt{49}}{7} \approx$ and $x = \dfrac{2 - \sqrt{49}}{7}$

D. $x = \dfrac{-7 + \sqrt{29}}{2} \approx$ and $x = \dfrac{-7 - \sqrt{29}}{2}$

E. $x = \dfrac{7 + 3}{2} \approx$ and $x = \dfrac{7 - 3}{2}$

First, the terms are placed on the left side of the equation and set to 0.

$$x^2 - 7x + 5 = 0$$

The values of the constants are entered: $a = 1$, $b = -7$, and $c = 5$.

$$x = \frac{-(-7) \pm \sqrt{(-7)^2 - 4(1)(5)}}{2(1)}$$

$$x = \frac{7 \pm \sqrt{49 - 20}}{2}$$

$$x = \frac{7 \pm \sqrt{29}}{2}$$

The correct answer is B. Obviously, you would not have been able to solve this equation by factoring alone.

Radicals and radical expressions

The ACT Math section may ask you to solve problems involving the manipulation of radicals.

Multiplying radicals

You may be required to multiply two square roots. Multiplying radicals, as long as they have the same degree, is quite easy:

$$\sqrt{x} \times \sqrt{y} = \sqrt{xy}$$

For example, $\sqrt{2} \times \sqrt{8} = \sqrt{16} = 4$.

The process is the same when multiplying radicals with coefficients:

$$a\sqrt{x} \times b\sqrt{y} = ab\sqrt{xy}$$

For example, $3\sqrt{2} \times 6\sqrt{8} = 18\sqrt{16} = 72$.

Dividing radicals

The same principle applies to the division of radicals:

$$\frac{\sqrt{x}}{\sqrt{y}} = \sqrt{\frac{x}{y}}$$

For example, $\frac{\sqrt{2}}{\sqrt{8}} = \sqrt{\frac{2}{8}} = \sqrt{\frac{1}{4}} = \frac{1}{2}$. The process is the same when dividing radicals with coefficients:

$$\frac{a\sqrt{x}}{b\sqrt{y}} = \frac{a}{b}\sqrt{\frac{x}{y}}$$

Simplifying radicals

Sometimes, a radical can be simplified by factoring out squares in the radical. A *square factor* is a factor of a radicand (the number inside a radical sign) that is itself a square. Consider the radical $\sqrt{54}$, which contains the square factor 9; the radical can be simplified to $\sqrt{9} \times \sqrt{6}$, or $3\sqrt{6}$. Here's another example:

$$\sqrt{75} = \sqrt{25 \times 3} = \sqrt{25} \times \sqrt{3} = 5\sqrt{3}$$

Adding and subtracting radicals

Adding and subtracting radicals is similar to adding and subtracting fractions; instead of a common denominator, however, you need a common radicand. You can only add or subtract radicals that contain the same value:

$$a\sqrt{x} + b\sqrt{x} = (a + b)\sqrt{x}$$
$$a\sqrt{x} - b\sqrt{x} = (a - b)\sqrt{x}$$

Here's an example:

$$5\sqrt{3} + 3\sqrt{3} = 8\sqrt{3}$$

Never add or subtract radicals like this:

$$\sqrt{x} + \sqrt{y} = \sqrt{x + y} \quad \text{(INCORRECT)}$$
$$\sqrt{x} - \sqrt{y} = \sqrt{x - y} \quad \text{(INCORRECT)}$$

Absolute values in equations

It is important to know how to use absolute values in equations. Here's an example:

$$|x + 4| = 3x - 17$$

To solve absolute-value problems, write and solve two separate equations—one with a positive absolute value and the other with a negative absolute value. For example, the equation above would be written as follows:

$$x + 4 = 3x - 17 \qquad -(x + 4) = 3x - 17$$
$$4 = 2x - 17 \qquad\qquad -x - 4 = 3x - 17$$
$$21 = 2x \qquad\qquad\qquad 13 = 4x$$
$$10.5 = x \qquad\qquad\qquad 3.25 = x$$

If an equation contains an absolute value, there are always two solutions.

Sequences and patterns

Arithmetic sequences

Occasionally, the ACT exam writers ask a question about recognizing patterns in a list of numbers. An arithmetic sequence, in which each new term is obtained by adding a fixed number, d, to the previous term, is the most likely sequence to appear on the test. Here's an example of an arithmetic sequence:

$$3, 7, 11, 15, 19, 23, \ldots$$

In this example, $d = 4$, so the next number in the sequence would be 27.

A question about arithmetic sequences may ask for one of two values: (1) the value of a specified term (for example, What is the 100th term of the series?) or (2) the sum of the first n terms (for example, What is the sum of the first 50 terms?). Here is the formula to determine the value of a specified term in an arithmetic sequence:

$$a_n = a_1 + (n - 1)d$$

This formula gives the value of the nth term a_n for a sequence with a first term a_1 and a difference d.

Here is the formula to determine the sum of the first n terms in an arithmetic sequence:

$$\Sigma_n = \frac{n(a_1 + a_n)}{2}$$

This formula gives the partial sum Σ_n of the first n terms of a sequence with a first term a_1 and an nth term a_n.

You should memorize both of these formulas before exam day and know how to use them.

Geometric sequences

In a geometric sequence, each new term is equivalent to the previous term multiplied by a common ratio r. Here's an example of a geometric sequence:

$$2, 8, 32, 128, 512, \ldots$$

In this example, $r = 4$, so the next number in the sequence would be 2,048.

As with arithmetic sequences, you need to memorize two formulas. Here is the formula to determine the value of a specified term in a geometric sequence:

$$a_n = a_1(r^{n-1})$$

This formula gives the value of the nth term a_n for a sequence with a first term a_1 and a common ratio r.

Here is the formula to determine the sum of the first n terms in a geometric sequence:

$$\Sigma_n = \frac{a_1(1 - r^n)}{1 - r}$$

This formula gives the partial sum Σ_n of the first n terms of a sequence with a first term a_1 and a common ratio r.

Math 36 example

14. What 3 numbers should be placed in the following sequence so that the distances between consecutive numbers are equal?

13, …, …, …, 37

F. 17, 24, 31
G. 18, 23, 28
H. 19, 25, 32
J. 19, 25, 31
K. 19, 27, 32

Some problems involving sequences don't require an equation for their solution, merely an understanding of how sequences work. In this problem, three terms are missing, so there will be four "jumps" of equal value between 13 and 37. Subtract 13 from 37, then divide the result (24) by 4 to determine the size of each "jump" ($24 \div 4 = 6$). Since each new term represents an increase of 6 over the previous term, the complete sequence is 13, 19, 25, 31, 37. The correct answer is J.

Functions

Equations not only represent the relationship between two variables, but are *functions* that modify an input to produce an output. To encourage you to think about equations in this way, some math textbooks (and some problems on the ACT) use "$f(x) =$" instead of "$y =$." These two types of notation are equivalent; however, questions that use "$f(x)$" are more likely to ask you to find inverses ($f^{-1}(x)$) or composite functions ($f(g(x))$, or $f \circ g$).

Inverses

ACT Math questions refer to the inverse of a function as $f^{-1}(x)$ or simply as the "inverse." To find the inverse, you supply a new function that does the exact opposite of the original function: given the output of the first function, the inverse returns the input of that function. For example, a question may ask you to find $f^{-1}(x)$, given $f(x) = 3x - 4$. Using the original equation, replace x with $f^{-1}(x)$ and $f(x)$ with x, then rearrange the equation so that you have $f^{-1}(x)$ alone on one side of the equation.

$$f(x) = 3x - 4$$
$$x = 3f^{-1}(x) - 4$$
$$x + 4 = 3f^{-1}(x)$$
$$\frac{x + 4}{3} = f^{-1}(x)$$

Not all functions have an inverse. For example, a function that sends two inputs to the same output (for example, a quadratic function) doesn't have an inverse because you wouldn't be able to determine which of the two inputs to return. The ACT, however, won't ask you to calculate the inverse of a function that doesn't have an inverse.

Domain and range

The *domain* of a function is the set of all possible inputs; for most functions on the ACT, the domain will be the set of all real numbers. Earlier, I made the point that a denominator of zero makes a function undefined. For example, the function $f(x) = \dfrac{1}{x - 2} + 7$ can't have an input of $x = 2$, because the function would be undefined. The domain of this function is the set of all real numbers *except* 2.

Logarithmic functions also have domain restrictions. You can't calculate the logarithm of a nonpositive number, so the domain of basic logarithmic functions is all *positive* real numbers. On a graph, you can determine the domain of a function by finding the values of x for which the function exists. With logarithmic functions, for example, the line exists only for positive x, but there won't be a point on the graph for a negative value of x or 0.

The *range* of a function is the set of all possible outputs; for most functions on the ACT, the range is also the set of all real numbers. However, some very important functions (quadratic functions, for example, and trigonometric functions, which will be discussed later in the chapter) have ranges that are restricted to certain values of y.

To find the range of a function on a graph, simply determine how far up and down the graph the function extends. If it seems to extend to positive infinity and to negative infinity, chances are that the function's range is the set of all real numbers. However, if there are certain y-regions into which the function doesn't extend (for example, on a graph of x^2, which extends from 0 to positive infinity in the y direction), you can conclude that those y-values are not in the range of the function.

Composite functions

The ACT exam writers may ask you to combine two functions into a composite function. Instead of simply using x as your input, you'll use $h(x)$, where $g(x)$ itself is a function. Consider the following two functions:

$$f(x) = 5x - 1$$

$$g(x) = \frac{x}{3} + 24$$

To find $f(g(x))$ (sometimes written $f \circ g$), enter the function $g(x)$ everywhere that x appears in the $f(x)$ equation:

$$f(g(x)) = 5\left(\frac{x}{3} + 24\right) - 1 = \frac{5x}{3} + 120 - 1 = \frac{5x}{3} + 119$$

To find $g(f(x))$, enter the function $f(x)$ everywhere that x appears in the $g(x)$ equation:

$$g(f(x)) = \frac{5x - 1}{3} + 24 = \frac{5x}{3} - \frac{1}{3} + 24 = \frac{5x}{3} + \frac{71}{3}$$

Notice that $f(g(x))$ and $g(f(x))$ are *not* equal. Unless f and g are the same function, they will probably be different.

Math 36 example

15. If $f(x) = x^3 - 4$, then $f(x + h) = ?$
    A. $x^3 + 3x^2h + 3xh^2 + h^3 - 4$
    B. $x^3 - 4 + h$
    C. $x^3 + 3xh + h^3 + 4$
    D. $x^3 + x^3h^3 + h^3 + 4$
    E. $3xh - 4$

To find $f(x + h)$, enter $(x + h)$ everywhere that x appears in the $f(x)$ equation:

$$f(x + h) = (x + h)^3 - 4 = (x^3 + 3x^2h + 3xh^2 + h^3) - 4$$

The correct answer is A.

Matrices

There will be, at most, one ACT Math question involving matrices. Although many complex operations can be performed with matrices, the ACT won't ask you to do anything more complex than add or subtract two matrices. Fortunately, matrix addition and subtraction are quite easy. Here are two matrices:

$$A = \begin{bmatrix} 1 & 4 \\ 3 & -2 \end{bmatrix} \text{ and } B = \begin{bmatrix} 8 & 6 \\ -1 & 3 \end{bmatrix}$$

To find $A + B$, simply add the corresponding entries of the two matrices:

$$A + B = \begin{bmatrix} 1 + 8 & 4 + 6 \\ 3 + (-1) & -2 + 3 \end{bmatrix} = \begin{bmatrix} 9 & 10 \\ 2 & 1 \end{bmatrix}$$

To find $A - B$, subtract the entries of B from the corresponding entries of A.

To perform scalar multiplication (for example, $3A$), multiply every entry in matrix A by the scalar (in this case, 3).

Complex numbers

Questions involving complex numbers appear rarely on the ACT. As stated earlier, the imaginary number i is equivalent to $\sqrt{-1}$; thus, $i^2 = -1$, $i^3 = -i$, $i^4 = 1$, $i^5 = i$, and so on. For ACT Math, you need to know what i is equal to when raised to any of these powers, as well as to be able to multiply i by an assortment of elements, including other positive and negative is and positive and negative constants. Here's a problem involving complex numbers:

Math 36 example

16. In complex numbers, where $i^2 = -1$, choose the answer that best fits the following equation:

$$\frac{1}{(1 + i)}(-i) = \,?$$

　　F. $\dfrac{i}{1 + i}$

　　G. $-\dfrac{1}{i + 1}$

　　H. $-\dfrac{2}{i + 1}$

　　J. $\dfrac{1}{i - 1}$

　　K. $-\dfrac{2}{i - 2}$

First, multiply $-i$ by the fraction:

$$-\frac{i}{(1 + i)}$$

Since this doesn't match any of the answer choices, and since all of the choices have a constant for the numerator, multiply the numerator and denominator by i:

$$-\frac{(-1)}{(i - 1)} = \frac{1}{i - 1}$$

The correct answer is J.

Logarithms

Problems involving logarithms rarely appear on the ACT. Nevertheless, it is important to know that $\log_m(x) = n$ means $m^n = x$; for example, $\log_{10}(100) = 2$.

Be familiar with the LOG key on your calculator. Keep in mind that $\ln(x)$ is equivalent to $\log_e(x)$. If no base is listed (for example, $\log(x)$), the default base of 10 is assumed; the LOG key on your calculator will return log base 10 for the given input.

Coordinate geometry

The coordinate geometry section accounts for 15% of ACT Math questions.

Points and lines

You should already know how to find points in a 2-D coordinate plane. For example, point $(2,3)$ is two units to the right of the origin and three units above it, while point $(-4,-1)$ is four units to the left of the origin and one unit below it. The first number of the pair is the x-coordinate; it indicates the point's location along the (horizontal) x-axis. The second number is the y-coordinate; it indicates the point's location along the (vertical) y-axis. You can review graphing linear equations like $y = 3x + 4$ in the LINEAR EQUATIONS section.

An ACT question may ask you to find the location of the vertex of a figure; simply sketch the figure and record the location of the vertex. The following problem tests your general knowledge of the coordinate plane:

Math 36 example

17. Point A is to be placed in a specific quadrant, not along an axis, of the coordinate plane shown on the following graph. If point A's x-coordinate and y-coordinate are both positive, then what quadrant must point A be found in?

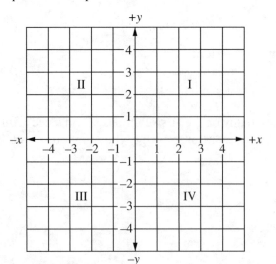

A. Quadrant I only
B. Quadrant II only
C. Quadrant I or II only
D. Quadrant II or IV only
E. Point *A* could be in any quadrant.

If point *A* has both a positive *x*-coordinate and a positive *y*-coordinate, it must be in quadrant I. The correct answer is A.

Polynomials

The ACT exam writers are likely to ask you to graph polynomials, like quadratic equations and third-degree equations. First, you should know the general shape of the graphs $y = x^2$ (the dashed line in the graph below) and $y = x^3$ (the solid line).

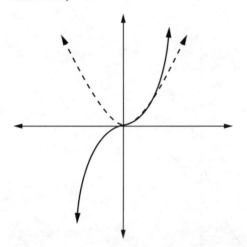

For $y = -x^2$ and $y = -x^3$, flip the graphs over the *x*-axis. In matching an equation to a graph, make sure that the *y*-intercept is the same. In the equation, the *y*-intercept is the value of *y* when *x* is 0; for example, in $y = x^2 + 4x + 4$, the *y*-intercept is 4. On the graph above, the *y*-intercept should be at point (0,*y*-intercept), that is, (0,4).

A quadratic equation can have zero, one, or two *x*-intercepts; these are the roots of the equation. For example, if you found the solutions for $y = x^2 - 3x - 10$ to be $x = 5$, $x = -2$, the two *x*-intercepts would be at points (5,0) and (−2,0).

Sometimes, it is possible to enter points on a likely-looking graph to verify that it correctly represents the equations. It is best, however, to use the other strategies first to narrow the choices, since checking points can be time-consuming.

The next problem tests your ability to apply these general strategies:

Math 36 example

18. From the following graphs, choose the one that most accurately depicts $f(x) = x^2 + 3x - 3$ on the standard (x, y) coordinate plane.

F.

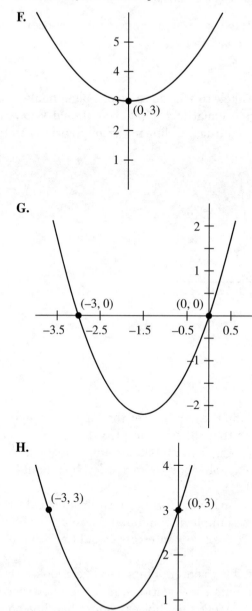

G.

H.

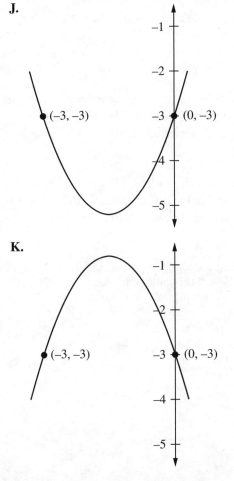

J.

K.

First, verify the y-intercept (since it's the quickest and easiest to verify); it is $(0, -3)$. Only answer choices J and K have a y-intercept of -3, so choices F, G, and H can be eliminated. Choice J opens upward, indicating a positive x^2 value, while choice K opens downward, indicating a negative x^2 value. Since the equation shows that x^2 is positive, the correct answer is J.

Modifying quadratic functions

When working with quadratic functions, it is important to know how changes in the equation relate to changes in the graph of the function. Here are changes in the basic quadratic, x^2, that cause changes in the graph:

- $x^2 + c$ moves the graph c units in the y direction (up if c is positive, down if c is negative).
- $(x - c)^2$ moves the graph c units to the right. $(x + c)^2$ moves the graph c units to the left.
- ax^2 stretches the graph vertically by a factor of a. If $a < 1$, the graph shrinks vertically.

◂ $\left(\dfrac{x}{a}\right)^2$ stretches the graph horizontally by a factor of a. If $a < 1$, the graph shrinks horizontally.

Circles

ACT Math may test your knowledge of the properties of equations that result in circles. A circle is the set of points that are all equidistant from a point at the center. In equation form, a circle looks like this:

$$(x - h)^2 + (y - k)^2 = r^2$$

where (h,k) is the center and r is the radius. This equation, which you should memorize before exam day, will help you solve most circle-related questions on the ACT. The following problem tests your ability to use the equation:

Math 36 example

19. A circle in the standard coordinate plane is tangent to the x-axis at 10 and tangent to the y-axis at 10. Which of the following answers is the equation of this circle?

   A. $(x - 10)^2 + (y - 10)^2 = 100$
   B. $(x - 10)^2 + (y - 10)^2 = 10$
   C. $(x + 10)^2 + (y + 10)^2 = 100$
   D. $x^2 + y^2 = 100$
   E. $x + y = 10$

First, sketch the circle:

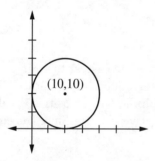

From the sketch, it is clear that the radius of the circle is 10, so answer choices B and E can be eliminated. Next, since the center of the circle is at (10,10), entering these values into the equation yields $(x - 10)^2 + (y - 10)^2 = 100$. The correct answer is A.

Graphing inequalities

The ACT exam writers are likely to ask you to represent inequalities in a graphical way, either by plotting equations in the standard 2-D coordinate plane or by plotting them on a number line.

Plotting inequalities in the 2-D coordinate plane

Graphing inequalities is only slightly different from graphing linear equations. First, sketch in the line as if the inequality had an equals sign instead of the inequality. If the inequality is $>$ or $<$, the line should be dotted (to indicate that values along the line itself are *not* included); if the inequality is $\geq$ or $\leq$, the line should be solid (to indicate that values along the line *are* included). Next, decide which side of the line you will shade. If your inequality has a $>$ or $\geq$ sign (so that y is greater than, or greater than or equal to, x), then shade above the line. If your inequality has a $<$ or $\leq$ sign (so that y is less than, or less than or equal to, x), then shade below the line.

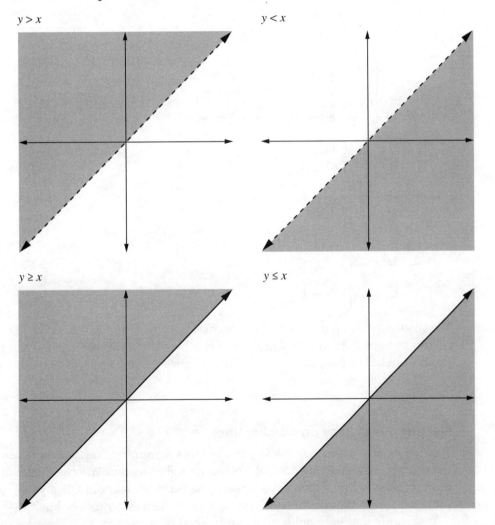

Test your graphing skills on the following problem:

Math 36 example

20. From the systems of inequalities that follow, select the system that best defines the shaded area in the graph below.

(4,11)

(4,0)

F. $y \leq \dfrac{4x}{11}, x \leq 4$

G. $y \geq \dfrac{4x}{11}, x > 4$

H. $y \geq \dfrac{4x}{11}, x \geq 4$

J. $y \leq \dfrac{4x}{11}, x = 4$

K. $y \geq \dfrac{4x}{11}, x = 4$

The shaded area is to the right of the vertical line $x = 4$, so $x \geq 4$ must be in the correct system. Fortunately, only one of the answer choices has $x \geq 4$—choice H. This can be verified, since the shading is above the line and the inequality is $y \geq \dfrac{4x}{11}$.

Plotting inequalities on number lines

The ACT exam writers may ask you to identify the number line that represents the solution to a given inequality. You may need to manipulate the inequality to find the solution; this was covered in the previous section. Once you have those solutions, though, how do you represent them on a number line?

Assume that your solution to an inequality is $-3 < x < 3$. Because the signs are "less than" and not "less than or equal to," the points on the number line aren't filled in; this indicates that the point at which the solution begins is itself not included in the solution set. Here is how the number line would look:

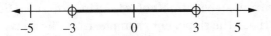

As you can see, the points at -3 and 3 are not filled. If the equation had been $-3 \le x \le 3$ instead, the points would have been filled. The distinction between filled and open points is the most important detail that you'll need to remember when matching solution sets to number lines. Once this is understood, you simply place the ends of the set at the right points. For an equation like $-2 < x$, where there is only one edge to the set, the line will begin at a point and continue, with an arrow at the end in the increasing x direction.

Inequality questions are typically straightforward; you should be able to solve each one in less than a minute, saving time for more challenging problems.

Slope

The ACT Math section may have several questions involving the slope of a line. Questions range from simply determining whether the slope of a line is positive or negative (it's positive if y is increasing as you move to the right, it's negative if y is decreasing as you move to the right), to calculating the slope of a line from an equation.

You need to be able to recognize certain characteristic slopes. For instance, in problem No. 20 above, $x = 4$ is a vertical line passing through the point $(4,0)$. In fact, any equation $x = c$, where c is a constant (for example, 1, 4, or 78), is a vertical line at that value of x. Similarly, any equation $y = c$ is a horizontal line spanning all the points where the value of y is c. The slope of such a horizontal line would actually be zero, because as x is increasing, y is neither increasing nor decreasing.

The slope of a line is calculated by dividing its "rise" by its "run"—that is, how many units the line moves up for each unit it moves to the right. With a vertical line $x = c$, the slope is undefined, because vertical lines don't have a "run": the fraction $\dfrac{\text{Rise}}{\text{Run}}$ used to determine the slope has a denominator of 0, which makes it undefined.

To find the slope of a line from a graph, count the number of units (or fractions of a unit) that the y value changes when you move one unit in the positive x direction. If the y value increases as you move to the right, the slope is positive; if the y value decreases, the slope is negative. You can also use the following equation to find the slope of a line passing through two points (x_1, y_1) and (x_2, y_2):

$$\text{Slope} = \frac{(y_2 - y_1)}{(x_2 - x_1)}$$

To find the slope of a line from an equation, solve for y in terms of x, then examine the coefficient of x—that's the slope. For example, from the equation $y = -2x + 17$, you can conclude that the slope is -2.

An ACT Math question may ask you to rewrite equations in slope-intercept form. This is not complicated: slope-intercept form is the way that most equations appear:

$$y = mx + b$$

where m is the slope of the line and b is the y-intercept. If an equation isn't written in slope-intercept form, you can convert the equation by rearranging it to solve for y. Here's an example:

$$3x + 4 = 6y - 20$$
$$3x + 4\ (+\ 20) = 6y - 20\ (+\ 20)$$
$$3x + 24 = 6y$$
$$\frac{3x + 24}{6} = \frac{6y}{6}$$
$$\frac{1}{2}x + 4 = y$$

The final equation is in slope-intercept form, where m (the slope) is $\frac{1}{2}$ and b (the y-intercept) is 4.

Parallel and perpendicular lines

Parallel lines have the same slope, while the slopes of perpendicular lines are the negative reciprocal of one another. For example, from the equation $y = -7x + 3$, you can conclude that the slope of a parallel line is -7, while the slope of a perpendicular line is $\frac{1}{7}$.

On a graph, parallel lines never cross, and perpendicular lines cross at a 90° angle. On the ACT Math section, never assume that two lines in a graph are parallel or perpendicular based simply on how they appear. If they are parallel or perpendicular, this will be stated in the question or shown on the graph (parallel lines by two arrows at the center of each line, perpendicular lines by a small square where the lines intersect).

If you are asked to identify the equation of a parallel or perpendicular line from a set of choices, remember that slope is all that matters. In a $y = mx + b$ equation, the value of b has no effect on whether the two lines are parallel or perpendicular. For example, $y = 2x + 4$ and $y = 2x + 456$ are parallel even though their b values are drastically different, and $y = -\frac{1}{3}x + 76$ and $y = 3x + 2,456$ are perpendicular.

Distance and midpoints

The ACT exam writers love to test your ability to calculate midpoints and distances on the 2-D coordinate plane. These calculations are straightforward—they are essentially "plug and chug" operations that require you to memorize intuitive formulas.

Distance

To calculate the distance between two points (x_1, y_1) and (x_2, y_2) in the coordinate plane, enter the values in the following equation:

$$\text{Distance} = \sqrt{(x_2 - x_1)^2 + (y_2 - y_1)^2}$$

This equation derives from the Pythagorean theorem, which will be discussed later in this chapter. You need to memorize this formula and know how to use it.

Math 36 example

21. What is the distance between the points (4,4) and (2,6) on the standard x, y coordinate plane?

   A. $\sqrt{8}$
   B. 8
   C. 4
   D. 2
   E. $\sqrt{20}$

First, enter the values into the distance equation:

$$\begin{aligned}
\text{Distance} &= \sqrt{(2 - 4)^2 + (6 - 4)^2} \\
&= \sqrt{(-2)^2 + (2)^2} \\
&= \sqrt{4 + 4} \\
&= \sqrt{8}
\end{aligned}$$

The correct answer is A.

Midpoints

The midpoint of two points (x_1, y_1) and (x_2, y_2) can be determined with the following formula:

$$\text{Midpoint} = \left(\frac{x_1 + x_2}{2}, \frac{y_1 + y_2}{2} \right)$$

Conics

Conics questions appear only rarely in the ACT Math section. One type of conic section—circles—has already been discussed. Two other types are parabolas and ellipses.

Parabolas

On a graph, a parabola looks like the mouth of a smiley face or frowny face, depending on whether it opens upward or downward. A familiar example of a parabola is x^2. Since all parabolas are graphs of quadratic functions, they can be represented by the equation $y = ax^2 + bx + c$, where a, b, and c are constants. You can answer any question about parabolas by knowing this equation and the values of a, b, and c. A parabola question may take one of five forms:

◄ **What is the vertex of the parabola?**

The *vertex* is the point where a parabola has a maximum (if it opens downward) or a minimum (if it opens upward). Use the following equation to find the vertex of a parabola:

Vertex located at $\left(-\dfrac{b}{2a}, \dfrac{4ac - b^2}{4a}\right)$

◄ **Where is the axis of symmetry of the parabola?**

This question asks along what line can you fold the parabola in half and have the sides match up. Use the following equation to find the axis of symmetry of a parabola:

Axis of symmetry is the vertical line $x^2 = -\dfrac{b}{2a}$

◄ **What is the y-intercept of the parabola?**

The *y*-intercept is the point $(0,c)$.

◄ **What is/are the x-intercept(s) of the parabola?**

The *x*-intercept(s) is/are the solution(s) to the equation $ax^2 + bx + c = 0$, which was discussed earlier in the chapter.

◄ **Does the parabola open upward or downward?**

If $a > 0$, the parabola opens upward; if $a < 0$, it opens downward.

Ellipses

An ellipse in the 2-D coordinate plane looks like an oval. Here's the basic equation for an ellipse:

$$1 = \frac{(x - h)^2}{a^2} + \frac{(y - k)^2}{b^2}$$

Notice the similarity to the equation for a circle, discussed earlier.

Center of the ellipse	(h,k)
Length of the horizontal axis (width of the ellipse)	$2a$
Length of the vertical axis (height of the ellipse)	$2b$

If $a > b$, the ellipse is wider than it is tall; if $b > a$, the ellipse is taller than it is wide.

It is important to memorize these equations and know how to use them before exam day.

Plane geometry

The plane geometry section accounts for 23% of ACT Math questions. If you've taken geometry in high school, most of the discussion here will be a review of familiar concepts.

Angles

ACT Math tests your knowledge of several types of angles, as well as how to measure certain angles given the measurement of other angles.

Right angles

Right angles measure exactly 90 degrees and look like a corner. Triangles with right angles (called right triangles) have useful properties that will be explored later.

Two lines that meet at a right angle are always perpendicular.

Acute angles

Acute angles measure less than 90 degrees.

Obtuse angles

Obtuse angles measure more than 90 degrees.

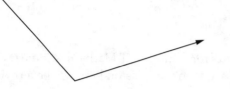

Complementary angles

Two complementary angles add up to 90°.

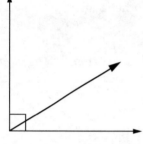

Supplementary angles

Two supplementary angles add up to 180°.

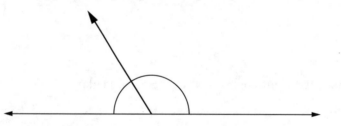

Vertical angles

Vertical angles are opposite each other when two lines cross. This very important property will definitely be tested in ACT Math.

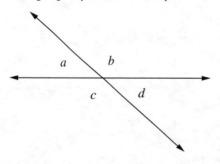

In this diagram, angle $a = d$, angle $b = c$, angles $b + d = a + b = a + c = c + d$ $= 180°$, and angles $a + b + c + d = 360°$.

Angles in parallel lines

ACT Math will likely test your knowledge of the relationships among angles of parallel lines intersected by a transversal:

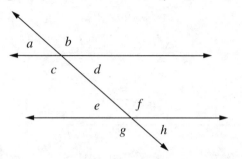

In this diagram, the pairs of corresponding angles are equal: $a = e = d = h$ and $b = f = c = g$.

Circles

There are two circle equations that you need to know and be able to apply:

$$C = 2\pi r$$
$$A = \pi r^2$$

where C is the circumference of the circle, r is its radius, and A is its area. The diameter of a circle is twice the radius ($d = 2r$).

Triangles and the Pythagorean theorem

Triangles are frequent topics in the ACT Math section. The basic properties and types of triangles, as well as the Pythagorean theorem, are discussed below.

All triangles

For all triangles, the sum of the internal angles is $180°$. In a right triangle, the sum of the two nonright angles is $90°$.

Math 36 example

22. The trapezoid *DEFG* is depicted with angles as marked. Using the information available in the diagram, what is the angle measure of *GDF*?

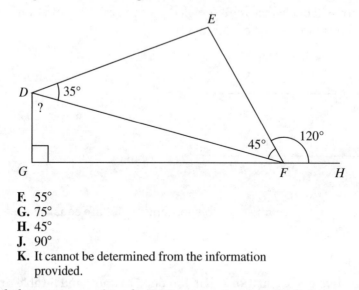

F. 55°
G. 75°
H. 45°
J. 90°
K. It cannot be determined from the information provided.

To find the measure of angle *GDF*, you must first find the measure of the other unknown angles in triangle *DGF*. The sum of angles *GFD*, *DFE*, and *EFH* is 180°, because they span the entire upper side of line *GH*. Since angle *GFD* + 45° + 120° = 180°, angle *GFD* = 15°. Angle *DGF* is a right angle (denoted by the square box at the angle), so it measures 90°. Since the sum of the internal angles of a triangle is 180°, angle *GDF* = 180° − 15° − 90° = 75°. The correct answer is G.

Helpful facts about triangles

- ◄ The longest side of a triangle is opposite the largest angle, and the smallest side is opposite the smallest angle.

- ◄ The area of a triangle can be calculated using the following equation:

$$A = \frac{1}{2}bh$$

where *b* is the length of the triangle's base and *h* is the triangle's height.

- ◄ The perimeter of a triangle is the sum of the lengths of its three sides.

- ◄ The hypotenuse of a triangle is the longest of its three sides, but it can't be longer than the sum of the other two sides.

Equilateral triangles

The three sides of an equilateral triangle are equal in length. The measure of each of the three angles is also the same: 60°.

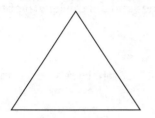

Isosceles triangles

An isosceles triangle has two sides that are equal in length and two angles of the same measure; these angles are called the base angles.

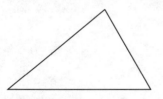

Scalene triangles

In a scalene triangle, all sides are unequal in length and all angles are unequal in measure.

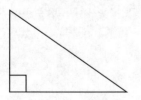

Right triangles

A right triangle has one angle that measures 90°. The longest side of the triangle—the one opposite the 90° angle—is called the hypotenuse.

The Pythagorean theorem

The Pythagorean theorem is used to calculate the length of any side of a right triangle if you know the lengths of the other two sides. In the following equation, a and b are the lengths of the two shorter sides and c is the length of the hypotenuse:

$$a^2 + b^2 = c^2$$

The Pythagorean theorem is extremely useful in ACT Math. Here's how it may be used on exam day:

Math 36 example

23. The right triangle below has side lengths of 3 and 4 for the two shorter sides. What is the length of the hypotenuse?

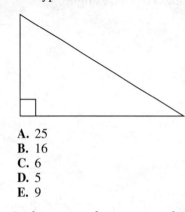

   A. 25
   B. 16
   C. 6
   D. 5
   E. 9

Use the Pythagorean theorem to solve this problem:

$$a^2 + b^2 = c^2$$
$$3^2 + 4^2 = c^2$$
$$9 + 16 = c^2$$
$$25 = c^2$$
$$5 = c$$

The correct answer is D.

Special right triangles

There are two types of right triangles whose angles have special ratios. Usually referred to by their angle measures, they are the 45-45-90 triangle and the 30-60-90 triangle.

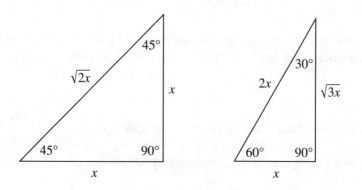

Make sure that you understand the ratios between the side lengths, since these relationships are critical in solving problems with triangles, as well as trigonometry problems. Recognizing these ratios saves time and mental energy on calculations.

Similar and congruent triangles

Two triangles are similar if they have the same three angle measures, but don't necessarily have the same side lengths. Note, however, that their side lengths have the same ratios. For example, one 30-60-90 triangle has side lengths of 2, 4, and $2\sqrt{3}$, while a second triangle has side lengths of 10, 20, and $10\sqrt{3}$; even though the side lengths of the triangles are different, the triangles are similar.

An ACT Math question may provide the side lengths of one of two similar triangles, plus one side length of the second triangle, and ask you to find the other side lengths. The keys to solution are (1) knowing that similar triangles have the same ratios among their side lengths and (2) using these ratios properly to solve for the unknown side lengths. Here are two similar triangles:

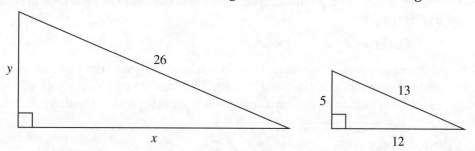

You are asked to find the measure of x and y. You recognize that the triangles are similar and that the larger triangle's hypotenuse is twice as long as that of the smaller triangle. Since the ratios among the side lengths are the same, x is twice as long as 12 and y is twice as long as 5. Thus, x is 24 and y is 10.

Congruent triangles have identical angle measures *and* identical side lengths.

Polygons

A polygon is a closed, two-dimensional shape with at least three straight sides. Triangles are polygons, and so are squares, rectangles, diamonds, and octagons.

Squares

The sides of a square are equal in length, and its angles all measure 90°. The diagonals of a square are perpendicular to one another, and each diagonal crosses the other at its midpoint. In the following equations, s is the side length of a square:

$$\text{Area} = s^2$$
$$\text{Perimeter} = 4s$$

Rectangles

A rectangle has two pairs of equal sides; a square is a rectangle, but a rectangle is not necessarily a square. A rectangle has four 90° angles. As with squares, the diagonals of a rectangle are equal in length. In the following equations, w is the width of a rectangle and h is its height:

$$\text{Area} = w \times h$$
$$\text{Perimeter} = 2w + 2h$$

Parallelograms

Parallelograms are an even broader category of polygon. A parallelogram has four sides, and opposite sides are parallel to each other and have the same length. Both rectangles and squares are parallelograms. The opposite angles of a parallelogram are equal, and two adjacent angles are supplementary (they add up to 180°). In the following equation, w is the width of a parallelogram and h is its height:

$$\text{Perimeter} = 2w + 2h$$

The area of a parallelogram can't be found by multiplying the two side lengths. Instead, the width of the base is multiplied by the vertical distance (the altitude) from the top to the bottom, shown as a dotted line in the diagram below:

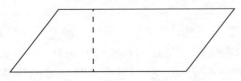

$$\text{Area} = \text{base} \times \text{altitude}$$

Math 36 example

24. Parallelogram *QRST,* shown below, has its dimensions shown in meters. What is the area of the parallelogram, in square meters?

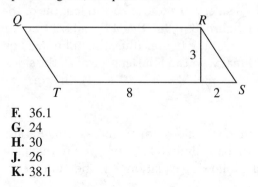

F. 36.1
G. 24
H. 30
J. 26
K. 38.1

The altitude is provided, so you calculate the length of the base (8 + 2 = 10 meters) and multiply it by the altitude (3 meters). The result is 30 square meters, and the correct answer is H.

Perimeters

A perimeter question often involves an oddly shaped figure with many sides and corners. From incomplete information about the lengths of sides, you are asked to calculate the perimeter of the figure by adding the lengths of all the sides. This can be time-consuming. Here's an example of a perimeter problem:

Math 36 example

25. Assuming each pair of intersecting lines meets at a right angle and all lengths are shown in feet, what is the perimeter, in feet, of the figure below?

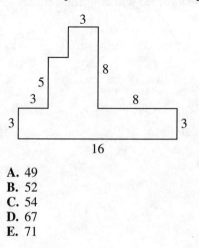

A. 49
B. 52
C. 54
D. 67
E. 71

All of the side lengths are known except for the two at the top left of the polygon. The length of the unknown vertical side plus 5 must equal 8, since the two sides combined are the same vertical length as the vertical side labeled 8. Thus, the unknown vertical side length is calculated as 3 feet. To calculate the length of the unknown horizontal side, you add the known lengths of the horizontal sides along the top of the figure (3 + 3 + 8 = 14) and subtract the sum from 16, the length of the bottom of the figure. Thus, the unknown horizontal side length is calculated as 2. Finally, you add the lengths of all the sides of the polygon (3 + 3 + 5 + 2 + 3 + 3 + 8 + 8 + 3 + 16 = 54). The correct answer is C.

Other polygons

For polygons with more than four sides (for example, octagons and decagons), an ACT Math question is usually limited to asking you to calculate the sum of the interior angles. In the following equation, n is the number of sides of the polygon:

$$\text{Sum of interior angles} = 180°(n - 2)$$

Transformations

Of the several types of transformations you may be asked about on the ACT, reflections and translations are the most common.

Reflections

You may be asked to reflect a point, line, or shape about a given line, frequently the x or y axis. Unfortunately, there's no cut-and-dried formula for determining the position of the new vertices after reflection; it depends on which line you are reflecting across. If you are reflecting across the x-axis (the horizontal axis), the y values will be flipped (for example, 1 to –1 or –3 to 3) while the x values are unchanged. If you are reflecting across the y-axis (the vertical axis), the x values will be flipped and the y values will stay the same.

Math 36 example

26. The triangle *DEF* has been reflected to the other side of the *x*-axis on the standard coordinate plane to appear as *D′E′F′*. Assuming that *D* reflects to *D′* and the coordinates of *D* are (*c,d*), what are the coordinates of *D′* ?

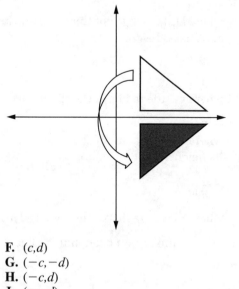

    F. (*c,d*)
    G. (−*c,*−*d*)
    H. (−*c,d*)
    J. (*c,*−*d*)
    K. Cannot be determined from the information given

It may help to draw a sketch of the reflection if one is not provided. Even if you only picture the transformation in your head, you will see that the *x* values of the new vertices are the same and that the *y* values have been flipped. Thus, the *y* values will be negative. Answer choice J is correct.

Translations

A translation is, essentially, a "slide." For example, a translation up 3 units and right 2 units means that the original point, line, or shape was slid 3 units up and 2 units to the right.

    The key to a translation question is to accurately visualize the new location of the object. For the coordinates of the vertices, remember that moving side to side changes the *x*-coordinate (it increases moving to the right and decreases moving to the left) and moving up and down changes the *y*-coordinate (it increases moving up and decreases moving down).

Volume and 3-D geometry

ACT Math also tests your knowledge of three-dimensional shapes.

Volume

Here are the formulas for calculating the volume of common shapes:

Rectangular solid $V = l \times w \times h$
where l is the length of the solid, w is its width,
and h is its height

Sphere $V = \dfrac{4}{3}\pi r^3$
where r is the radius of the sphere

Cylinder $V = \pi r^2 h$
where r is the radius of the cylinder and h is
its height

Cone $V = \dfrac{1}{3}\pi r^2 h$
where r is the radius of the cone and h is its height

The ACT sometimes provides the formulas you need, but it's best to have these formulas memorized.

Surface area

Here are the formulas for calculating the surface area of common shapes:

Rectangular solid $SA = 2lw + 2wh + 2lh$
where l is the length of the solid, w is its width,
and h is its height

Sphere $SA = 4\pi r^2$
where r is the radius of the sphere

Cylinder $SA = 2\pi rh + 2\pi r^2$
where r is the radius of the cylinder and h is
its height

Cone $SA = \pi rs + \pi r^2$
where r is the radius of the cone and s is the
hypotenuse of the triangle created by r and h
$(s = \sqrt{r^2 + h^2})$

3-D diagonals

The ACT exam writers may ask you to calculate the length of three-dimensional diagonals. A 3-D diagonal has x, y, and z components (respectively, horizontal, vertical, and out of the page/into the page).

For a 2-D diagonal, the Pythagorean theorem is used to determine the hypotenuse of the triangle spanned by the length and the width of the rectangle, using the following equation:

$$d = \sqrt{w^2 + h^2}$$

The formula for calculating the length of a 3-D diagonal is similar; it includes the variable l to account for the third dimension of the diagonal:

$$d = \sqrt{w^2 + h^2 + l^2}$$

A 3-D diagonal looks like this:

Trigonometry

The trigonometry section accounts for 7% of ACT Math questions. There are four or so questions of this type on the test. Only the basic concepts of trigonometry are tested.

SOHCAHTOA

An introduction to trigonometry is most likely in the form of triangles. A typical problem gives the length of a ladder and the angle at which it's leaning against the top of a building, then asks you for the building's height. Or the length of two sides of a right triangle are given, and you are asked to calculate the angle between them. This is the kind of trigonometry question that usually appears in ACT Math, and it's also the most straightforward.

To work these problems, it is important to know and be able to apply the acronym SOHCAHTOA:

SOH $\quad \sin \theta = \dfrac{\text{opposite}}{\text{hypotenuse}}$

CAH $\quad \cos \theta = \dfrac{\text{adjacent}}{\text{hypotenuse}}$

TOA $\quad \tan \theta = \dfrac{\text{opposite}}{\text{adjacent}}$

where θ is the angle of the triangle (not the right angle) and opposite, hypotenuse, and adjacent are as follows:

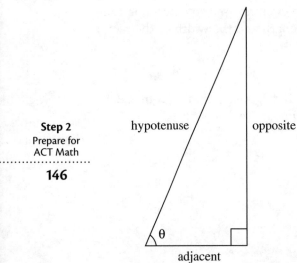

These ratios specify how to calculate the sine, cosine, and tangent of an angle by using the side lengths of the right triangle shown below:

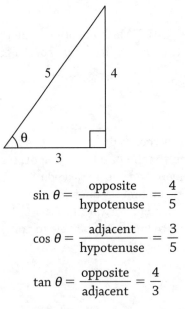

$$\sin \theta = \frac{\text{opposite}}{\text{hypotenuse}} = \frac{4}{5}$$

$$\cos \theta = \frac{\text{adjacent}}{\text{hypotenuse}} = \frac{3}{5}$$

$$\tan \theta = \frac{\text{opposite}}{\text{adjacent}} = \frac{4}{3}$$

Note that the sine and cosine can never be greater than 1 or less than -1, while the tangent can be any real number.

These ratios allow you to solve three types of right-triangle problems in the trigonometry section of ACT Math:

◄ **The sine, cosine, or tangent of an angle**
These problems are the easiest to solve. Simply enter the side lengths in the ratios.

◂ The measure of an angle

These problems involve an additional step. First, you use the ratios to produce an equation of the following type:

$$\sin \theta = c$$

where c is a constant (the result of your calculation using the ratio). Next, you solve for θ to find the measure of the angle. To do this, take the inverse sine of both sides:

$$\sin^{-1}(\sin \theta) = \sin^{-1} c$$
$$\theta = \sin^{-1} c$$

Using your calculator's SIN^{-1}, COS^{-1}, and TAN^{-1} keys, enter the value of c to find the angle θ. You can work through this process in the following problem:

Math 36 example

27. Ian and Dan want to climb into a window, so they lean a 10-foot ladder up against a building, with the base of the ladder on the ground 5 feet away from the building. What angle does the ladder make with the ground?

    A. 90°
    B. 60°
    C. 180°
    D. 30°
    E. 50°

Some problems provide a diagram, but others—like this one—don't. First, sketch the problem and label what you know:

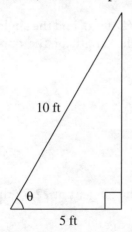

As you can see, the side lengths of the hypotenuse and the adjacent side are known; you need to find the measure of angle θ. Select the trigonometric function that uses hypotenuse and adjacent: cosine. Use the formulas above to calculate the cosine of θ:

$$\cos\theta = \frac{\text{adjacent}}{\text{hypotenuse}} = \frac{5\text{ ft}}{10\text{ ft}} = \frac{1}{2}$$

$$\cos^{-1}(\cos\theta) = \cos^{-1}\left(\frac{1}{2}\right)$$

Using your calculator, solve for the inverse cosine of $\frac{1}{2}$, which is 60°.

The correct answer is B.

NOTE: If you had recognized the triangle as a 30-60-90 triangle by noting the relationship between the shortest side and the hypotenuse, you would have known, without any calculations, that the answer was B. This would have saved you valuable seconds.

◂ The length of a side

A trigonometry question may ask you to calculate the length of one side of a triangle, given the length of another side and the angle between them. Consider the following diagram:

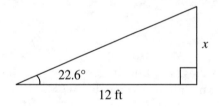

The length of the adjacent side is given (12 feet), and the angle is known (22.6°). Since you are asked to find the length of the opposite side (called x), the tangent ratio is used.

$$\tan\theta = \frac{\text{opposite}}{\text{adjacent}}$$

$$\tan 22.6° = \frac{x}{12}$$

$$12(\tan 22.6°) = x$$

Using your calculator, multiply 12 by the tangent of 22.6°; the result is $x \cong 5$.

There are two keys to solving problems about triangles using trigonometric functions: (1) knowing which ratio to use (determined by the side lengths given) and (2) being able to rearrange and manipulate the ratio to solve for the unknown quantity. Be sure to sketch the problem if no diagram is provided; the sketch will show which angles and side lengths are which. Also, make sure that your calculator is in degree mode, not radian mode (MODE > DEGREE).

Values and properties of trigonometric functions

Several facts about trigonometric functions are useful on this section of ACT Math.

Sine and cosine

The domain (the set of all possible inputs) of the sine and cosine functions is the set of all real numbers, while the range of each is -1 to 1, inclusive:

$$-1 \leq \sin x \leq 1$$
$$-1 \leq \cos x \leq 1$$

Tangent

The domain of the tangent function is the set of all real numbers that aren't odd multiples of 90 (for instance, 45, 112, and 180 are in the domain, and 90, 270, and -90 aren't), while the range of the tangent function is all real numbers:

$$\tan \theta = \frac{\text{opposite}}{\text{adjacent}} \text{ for all } \theta \text{ that aren't odd multiples of } 90°$$

Knowing the domain and range of trigonometric functions helps identify their graphs.

Graphing trigonometric functions

You should be familiar with the general shape of the graph of each trigonometric function and know how it can be stretched or shrunk.

It is important to understand radians when discussing the graphs of trigonometric functions. Like degrees, a *radian* is a unit for measuring angles; when trigonometric functions are graphed, the x-axis is almost always measured in radians instead of degrees. Converting between the two types of measurement is easy.

A full circle, or 360°, is an angle of 2π radians; 180° is π radians. Here's the formula for converting degrees and radians:

$$\text{degrees} \times \frac{\pi}{180} = \text{radians}$$

Following are graphs of sines, cosines, and tangents:

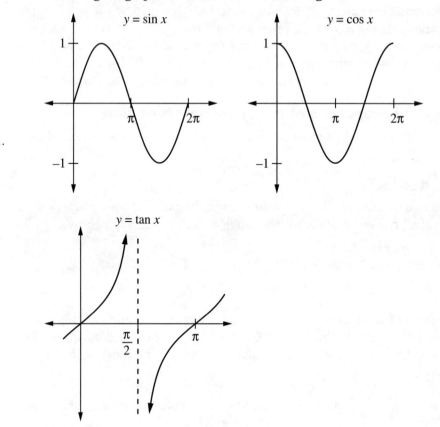

It is important that you be able to recognize the general shapes of the graphs of these three trigonometric functions.

Trigonometric functions can be altered by changing their equations. For example, the following equation stretches the graph of sine vertically by a factor of a:

$$y = a \sin x$$

The following equation stretches the graph of sine horizontally by a factor of a:

$$y = \sin \frac{x}{a}$$

The same alterations apply to equations for cosine and tangent functions.

Trigonometric identities

For the ACT Math section, you need to know only two (of a dozen or so) trigonometric identities:

$$\tan x = \frac{\sin x}{\cos x}$$

$$\sin^2 x + \cos^2 x = 1$$

These identities can be used to simplify long trigonometric expressions into shorter ones.

Solving trigonometric equations

The ACT tests your ability to use trigonometric functions and their identities to solve trigonometry problems. Following are two example problems and their solutions:

Math 36 example

28. Which of the following is equivalent to the expression below?

$$\cos x - \cos x \sin x \tan x - \cos x \,(1 + \cos x)$$

F. 1
G. −1
H. 0
J. $\cos x$
K. There is no solution.

First, enter trigonometric identities where possible:

$$\cos x - \cos x \sin x \frac{(\sin x)}{(\cos x)} - \cos x - \cos^2 x$$

$$\cos x - \cos x \frac{\sin^2 x}{\cos x} - \cos x - \cos^2 x$$

$$\cos x - \sin^2 x - \cos x - \cos^2 x$$

$$-\sin^2 x - \cos^2 x$$

$$-(\sin^2 x + \cos^2 x)$$

Using the identity $\sin^2 x + \cos^2 x = 1$, you can conclude that the expression is equivalent to −1. The correct answer is G.

Don't be intimidated by a long, seemingly complex trigonometric expression on the ACT; it usually simplifies to a very short expression, sometimes even 0 or 1.

Math 36 example

29. Which of the following is a solution to the equation below?

$$\sin^2 x + 2\sin x + 1 = 0$$

A. $x = 0$

B. $x = \dfrac{\pi}{2}$

C. $x = \pi$

D. $x = 2\pi$

E. $x = \dfrac{3\pi}{2}$

Here, a quadratic equation has been inserted into a trigonometry problem. While this may seem unusually complex, treat it as you would any quadratic: factor to find the roots.

$$0 = \sin^2 x + 2\sin x + 1 = (\sin x + 1)(\sin x + 1)$$

Thus, $(\sin x + 1) = 0$, so $\sin x = -1$. Use your calculator to solve for x:

$$\sin^{-1}(\sin x) = \sin^{-1}(-1)$$

$$x = 270°, \text{ or } \dfrac{3\pi}{2} \text{ radians}$$

The correct answer is E.

Although this problem may have intimidated you at first, this chapter has given you all the concepts and tools you need to solve it. The difference between a 34 and a 36 on ACT Math is the ability to apply these concepts and tools to problem types you have never encountered.

Math 36 Strategies

ACT Math, more than any other section of the ACT, is content-driven. If you don't know important equations or the correct approach to a certain problem type, you won't be able to solve it. Therefore, it's critical that you have mastered *all* the material covered in the chapter so far. You can use the checklist in the MATHEMATICAL CONCEPTS section to mark off concepts as you master them.

The strategies in this section will transform you from a good test taker to a great one. To achieve success on ACT Math, you must work through the questions efficiently and accurately. These strategies will save you time and enable you to answer as many math questions as possible.

1 · Write it down
2 · Draw a picture
3 · Perform a sanity check
4 · Don't trust your eyes
5 · Target the unknown
6 · Use your calculator—last
7 · Don't be afraid to take the first step
8 · When in doubt, test it out

Math 36 Strategy 1 ⟋ *Write it down*

If you were allowed to write down your thoughts and work during only one section of the ACT, the math section would be it. Not only does writing your work down help you solve a problem, it allows you to review your work for errors in case none of the answer choices matches your solution.

This is when the "show your work" mantra of high school math teachers really pays off—write down your work, step by step, as you move through a problem. If you get stuck, reviewing your work may jog your memory.

Even if you have no idea where to begin with a problem, write down what you do and don't know—this may give you a clue for where to start. And if it doesn't, when you return to the problem, you'll know exactly what you're looking for and where you left off.

Math 36 Strategy 2 ⟋ *Draw a picture*

This is the graphical counterpart to Math 36 Strategy 1. Drawing a picture is critical to solving some problems, especially those that involve graphs or shapes.

Be sure to write down all of the information given, such as angles, side lengths, and area. Label unknowns with variable names, such as x, y, and z. Using the facts and data that you're given, quickly calculate unknown values and write these on your picture; for example, if you're given the measure of two angles of a triangle, quickly determine the measure of the third angle and write it in. Mark vertical angles and angles that you know to be congruent with parallel lines.

If you know that two angles or side lengths are the same but you don't know their measure, indicate this fact by marking them with a single line, as in the diagram on the right.

Drawing a picture helps you organize your thoughts—and makes returning to a problem easier and more efficient.

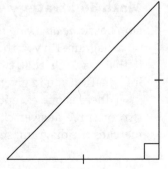

Math 36 Strategy 3 ⌐ *Perform a sanity check*

The ACT exam writers are aware of the most common errors students make in answering particular types of problems, and they include incorrect answer choices that result from these errors. Don't be overcome by a rush of joy when your answer matches one of the choices; you should still perform a quick sanity check on your answer.

Here are common errors to watch for:

- **Swapped positives and negatives.** Are your signs correct? When working with lengths, areas, or volumes, values should never be negative. If your answer is negative, does it make sense that it is?
- **Order of magnitude.** A question may ask you to calculate the number of ice cream cones sold by a certain creamery over the course of a year, and your calculation yields an answer of 47. Don't be fooled by the fact that 47 appears as an answer choice—if it doesn't make sense, it's probably not correct. Unless this is the world's worst creamery, your number should be much higher. What if, instead, your calculation yields 56,684,000 cones? That would be far too many, and you should eliminate that answer as well. Be sure that your answer fits the scale of the question.
- **Specificity.** A question may ask you to determine the number of people in a store at a certain time, and your calculation yields an answer of 134.68008. The order of magnitude may seem correct, but the level of specificity should raise a red flag: .68008 of a person? Unless the question specifically tells you to round to the nearest person, pound, or cent, you should be wary of answers with several decimal places when the items being measured are usually whole items.
- **Units.** If you are asked for a temperature but your answer is in inches, review your calculations. Keep units with their numbers throughout the problem-solving process; if your units aren't correct, chances are your numbers aren't either.

These checks, which won't take more than a few seconds, will help you catch careless mistakes that can lower your ACT Math score.

Math 36 Strategy 4 ⌐ *Don't trust your eyes*

Don't assume *anything* that is not explicitly stated in the question or included on a diagram. Do you think a triangle is equilateral because the diagram shows it that way? Or that two lines look parallel? Don't be fooled—use only the information you're given.

There is one exception: when you're forced to guess. If you've eliminated two or three answer choices and recognize that only one remaining choice matches the diagram, select that choice.

Math 36 Strategy 5 ⟋ *Target the unknown*

Even before you finish reading a question, you should be asking yourself, "What do I need to solve for?" Circle the unknown in the question, and make sure that your calculations help you solve for it. Often, students solve for a quantity that isn't asked about.

Another common error is not solving a problem entirely. For example, a question may ask you to determine the average number of hours, but you don't perform the final step of division—and your answer is the total number of hours instead. The ACT exam writers anticipate such an error, and they'll have an answer choice waiting for you. By checking that your answer is consistent with what the question is asking for, you won't forget to perform the last step in the solution.

Math 36 Strategy 6 ⟋ *Use your calculator—last*

Your calculator is an extremely valuable tool in ACT Math, and it will help you solve quite a few problems. By using your calculator too soon, however, you are prone to make two errors: (1) careless keystroke errors and (2) failure to write down your work. Manipulate equations and make basic calculations with a pencil in your exam booklet. Use your calculator to perform a step that would otherwise be time-consuming (for example, multiplying 3,475 by 451).

If you don't write down any of your steps and get an incorrect result, you must start over. If you work a problem with paper and pencil first, then use your calculator to crunch numbers at the end, you're less likely to make a mistake—and if you do make one, it will be easier to spot.

Math 36 Strategy 7 ⟋ *Don't be afraid to take the first step*

Imagine that you have absolutely no clue how to work an ACT Math problem. You've memorized an equation that may apply, but you're not sure how or where to use it. You realize what the first step of the solution is, but you don't know how to proceed after that. If you skip the question without putting pencil to paper, you would be making a big mistake.

Take the first step. Even if you're not sure where to go from there, writing down the first step and mulling it over may give rise to a clue to the problem's solution. The first step often leads to a second step, and a third. As you ponder the first step, fiddle with the numbers and variables: factor if you can factor, expand if you can expand, simplify, move expressions around. Using this approach, you may find that the solution reveals itself.

Math 36 Strategy 8 ⟋ *When in doubt, test it out*

If you are staring at an algebraic equation with no clue how to solve it, try entering answer choices in the equation to see if one works. Because this can be time-consuming, it shouldn't be your first approach; sometimes, however, quickly testing choices may be faster than struggling through lengthy calculations.

If you can eliminate one or more answer choices, testing the other choices becomes more attractive—you don't have five potential choices to test.

A word of caution: if you've tested and rejected all but one of the answer choices, don't automatically assume that the last one is correct. Test that choice, too. If it doesn't work, you will know that you need to change your approach to the problem.

Equations to memorize

You should memorize all of the following equations. I recommend making a set of flashcards and quizzing yourself until you know them by heart. In addition to memorizing each equation, you must know what each variable signifies, how to recognize when the equation should be applied, and how to apply it.

Intermediate algebra

The quadratic formula

$$x = \frac{-b \pm \sqrt{b^2 - 4ac}}{2a}$$

where a, b, and c are constants

Arithmetic sequences

$$a_n = a_1 + (n-1)d$$

where a_n is the nth term of a sequence with a first term a_1 and a difference d

$$\Sigma_n = \frac{n(a_1 + a_n)}{2}$$

where Σ_n is the partial sum of the first n terms of a sequence with a first term a_1 and an nth term a_n

Geometric sequences

$$a_n = a_1(r^{n-1})$$

where a_n is the nth term of a sequence with a first term a_1 and a common ratio r

$$\Sigma_n = \frac{a_1(1 - r^n)}{1 - r}$$

where Σ_n is the partial sum of the first n terms of a sequence with a first term a_1 and a common ratio r

Complex numbers

$$i = \sqrt{-1}$$

where i is an imaginary number

$$i^2 = -1$$

Logarithms

Log form	$\log_m(x) = n$
Exponential form	$m^n = x$

where n is the exponent to which m must be raised to produce x

Coordinate geometry

Slope

$$\text{Slope} = \frac{(y_2 - y_1)}{(x_2 - x_1)}$$

where (x_1, y_1) and (x_2, y_2) are points in the coordinate plane

Slope-intercept form

$$y = mx + b$$

where m is the slope of the line and b is the y-intercept (the y-coordinate of the point where the line crosses the y-axis)

Distance between two points in 2-D

$$\text{Distance} = \sqrt{(x_2 - x_1)^2 + (y_2 - y_1)^2}$$

where (x_1, y_1) and (x_2, y_2) are points in the coordinate plane

Midpoint

$$\text{Midpoint} = \left(\frac{x_1 + x_2}{2}, \frac{y_1 + y_2}{2} \right)$$

where (x_1, y_1) and (x_2, y_2) are points in the coordinate plane

Parabola

Vertex located at $\left(-\dfrac{b}{2a}, \dfrac{4ac - b^2}{4a} \right)$

where a, b, and c are constants

Axis of symmetry is the vertical line $x^2 = -\dfrac{b}{2a}$

Ellipse

$$1 = \frac{(x - h)^2}{a^2} + \frac{(y - k)^2}{b^2}$$

where h and k are the x- and y-coordinates of the center of the ellipse, respectively, a is the length of the horizontal axis, and b is the length of the vertical axis

Center $= (h,k)$

Plane geometry

Circle

$$C = 2\pi r$$
$$A = \pi r^2$$

where C is the circumference of the circle, r is its radius, and A is its area

Triangle

$$A = \frac{1}{2} bh$$

where A is the area of the triangle, b is the length of its base, and h is its height

The Pythagorean theorem

$$a^2 + b^2 = c^2$$

where a and b are the lengths of the two shorter sides and c is the length of the hypotenuse

Square

$$A = s^2$$
$$P = 4s$$

where A is the area of the square, s is the length of one of its sides, and P is its perimeter

Rectangle

$$A = w \times h$$
$$P = 2w + 2h$$

where A is the area of the rectangle, w is its width, h is its height, and P is its perimeter

Parallelogram

$A = \text{base} \times \text{altitude}$

$P = 2w + 2h$

where A is the area of the parallelogram, P is its perimeter, w is its width, and h is its height

Other polygons

Sum of interior angles $= 180°(n - 2)$

where n is the number of sides of the polygon

Volume of 3-D solids

Rectangular solid

$V = l \times w \times h$

where V is the solid's volume, l is its length, w is its width, and h is its height

Sphere

$V = \dfrac{4}{3}\pi r^3$

where V is the sphere's volume and r is its radius

Cylinder

$V = \pi r^2 h$

where V is the cylinder's volume, r is its radius, and h is its height

Cone

$V = \dfrac{1}{3}\pi r^2 h$

where V is the cone's volume, r is its radius, and h is its height

Surface area of 3-D solids

Rectangular solid

$SA = 2lw + 2wh + 2lh$

where SA is the solid's surface area, l is its length, w is its width, and h is its height

Sphere

$SA = 4\pi r^2$

where SA is the sphere's surface area and r is its radius

Cylinder

$$SA = 2\pi rh + 2\pi r^2$$

where SA is the cylinder's surface area, r is its radius, and h is its height

Cone

$$SA = \pi rs + \pi r^2$$

where SA is the cone's surface area, r is its radius, and s is the hypotenuse of the triangle created by r and h ($s = \sqrt{r^2 + h^2}$)

Trigonometry

Trigonometric ratios

$$\sin \theta = \frac{\text{opposite}}{\text{hypotenuse}}$$

$$\cos \theta = \frac{\text{adjacent}}{\text{hypotenuse}}$$

$$\tan \theta = \frac{\text{opposite}}{\text{adjacent}}$$

where θ is the angle of the triangle (not the right angle) and opposite, adjacent, and hypotenuse are the sides

Trigonometric identities

$$\tan x = \frac{\sin x}{\cos x}$$

$$\sin^2 x + \cos^2 x = 1$$

Prepare for ACT Reading

It's exam day, and you've successfully made it through English and Math. You've had a short drink-and-snack break, and now it's back in your seat for the second half of the test.

For some students, ACT Reading triggers trepidation and dread. If reading isn't easy for you, reading four 750-word passages can be daunting in and of itself, not to mention answering the accompanying questions. I've developed key strategies that will help you overcome this fear. If you're a good reader, these strategies can help you gain a few points and score a 36.

Even if you wouldn't describe yourself as a bookworm or a voracious reader, you can ace this section of the ACT if you know what to focus on. ACT Reading does *not* test the following:

- ◄ Recall of facts not explicitly stated in the passage
- ◄ Mastery of long vocabulary lists
- ◄ Rules of formal logic

Unlike the SAT, the ACT doesn't test your familiarity with isolated vocabulary words. It tests you only on vocabulary in context, making rote memorization of vocabulary lists unnecessary.

Stats

Time allowed	35 minutes
Number of questions	40 questions
Time allowed per question	52.5 seconds

⬆ Breaking down ACT Reading

""The ACT Reading Test measures your reading comprehension. You are asked to read four passages and answer questions that show your understanding of what is directly stated as well as statements with implied meanings."

—ACT.org

The ACT Reading section includes four passages, each of which is accompanied by ten questions. Each of the four passages is worth 25% of your total ACT Reading score and covers one of four categories of writing:

◄ **Social studies**

This passage concerns a topic in anthropology, archaeology, biography, business, economics, education, geography, history, political science, psychology, or sociology.

◄ **Natural sciences**

This passage concerns a topic in anatomy, biology, botany, chemistry, ecology, geology, medicine, meteorology, microbiology, natural history, physiology, physics, technology, or zoology.

◄ **Prose fiction**

This passage is based on a short story or is an edited excerpt from a short story or novel.

◄ **Humanities**

This passage is excerpted from a memoir or personal essay and concerns a topic in architecture, art, dance, ethics, film, language, literary criticism, music, philosophy, radio, television, or theater.

Before you complain that you're not even sure what the difference between anthropology and sociology is, or that merely hearing the word "microbiology" makes your head hurt, don't panic! You don't have to know anything about any of the subjects in the lists above. You might be reading a passage about one of them, but you'll only be asked questions that test your ability to understand what you read—not your knowledge of the entire subject.

Your strategies in tackling ACT Reading will be the same for the four types of passages listed above. As an additional aid, I've included a few subject-specific strategies at the end of the chapter.

Your ACT Reading score is a composite of two subscores, each worth 18 points. One subscore is the score on the social studies and natural sciences passages; the other is the score on the prose fiction and humanities passages. In the past, students have typically done equally well on the two sections, although you may have a personal preference for one or the other. Regardless, the two subscores are added to determine your final score.

General strategy

Some experts advocate going straight to the questions (as you should in ACT Science), while others insist that you read and fully understand the entire passage before tackling the questions. I recommend that you quickly read the passage before answering the questions, and I'll tell you why.

Let's say you read the questions first—all 10 of them—and then read the passage with those questions in mind. By the time you start reading the passage, you have probably forgotten half the questions. You stumble across a line in the passage that you think might be related to one of the questions, but when you flip back to the question, you realize that you had the wrong line number. You continue flipping back and forth from the passage to the questions, never developing a sense of the main idea of the passage or understanding the flow of ideas. When it comes time to answer the main idea and voice/tone questions, you have to reread the entire passage. When you finally finish the first 10 questions, you sigh with relief, only to realize that you've spent 20 minutes on the first passage and you have only 15 minutes left for the remaining three passages . . . not a happy story!

As an alternative, let's say you read the entire passage very carefully, making a mental note of each detail and example. You underline and make notes in the margin. When you're not sure about a detail, you reread the sentence so that you can answer what you hope will be a question that refers to that sentence. Eight minutes later, you've carefully read through the first passage and you charge into the questions, only to realize that you've already spent all the time that you should have allotted to read the first passage *and* answer all 10 questions . . . another unhappy ending!

How about a happy story? I've said that the best way to approach ACT Reading is to quickly read the passage, then move on to the questions. Let's say you start reading and finish the passage in three minutes. You set to work on the questions with a sense of the main idea of the passage, knowing that any specific details that you're asked about are indicated by line numbers in the questions—you didn't waste time trying to memorize details the first time around. You have plenty of time to finish answering all the questions, even after looking back to the passage a few times, and you flip to the next passage confidently and within your eight-minute passage limit.

This third method is the best approach to ACT Reading. If you read all of the questions first, as in the first method, you will end up reading most of them twice. If you read the passage too closely in the beginning, as in the second method, you will waste time trying to remember details that may not even be tested (and besides, if a question refers to a specific detail in the passage, it provides the line number for easy reference).

You should read quickly through the passage so you can answer all the "big idea" questions and only have to flip back to the passage to answer the specific questions. You can try this yourself: Go to ACT.org, which has a set of practice questions for each of four passages. Using the three strategies discussed above, complete three passages (timing yourself—eight minutes per passage) and see the difference for yourself.

Timing

You have only 35 minutes to read 360 lines of text (about 3,000 words!) and answer 40 questions, so managing your time well is of the utmost importance. A low score in ACT Reading often results from not having enough time to read all of the passages. To avoid this problem, you'll need to follow the timing guidelines set out here:

- Use a maximum of 8 minutes per passage.
- Use up to 3½ minutes to read through each passage the first time.
- Use the remaining time (4½-plus minutes) to answer the questions.

This strategy leaves 3 minutes of "cushion" at the end of the exam—in case you had to spend extra time on a particularly difficult passage, or to check that you've bubbled the answer sheet correctly.

Go to ACT.org and locate a Reading section practice passage. Read it from start to finish, timing yourself. If it takes you longer than 3½ minutes to read the passage, you need to increase your baseline reading speed. This may sound harsh, but if you can't read a passage in 3½ minutes or less, there's no way you'll have enough time to answer the questions.

If you can read the passage in 3½ minutes, great! Skip the next section on increasing your reading speed.

If it takes you longer than 3½ minutes, read on.

Increasing your reading speed

The average reading speed in the United States is 200 words per minute; for a 750-word passage on the ACT, that's 3½ to 4 minutes of reading. This is good news: in order to read fast enough to score a 36 in ACT Reading, you only need to be able to read slightly faster than the average American. Being a student gives you an advantage, since you're used to reading textbooks, literature, and homework assignments.

Before you study the reading tips below, you should determine your reading speed, using one of several online reading speed tests (search on "reading speed test" and pick one). Once you know your baseline speed, check your progress by testing your speed about once a week, using the same online tool. The following tips and tricks will help you increase your speed.

- **Don't subvocalize.** "Subvocalization" means pronouncing each word out loud in your head as you read. Almost all readers are guilty of this to some degree, but subvocalization can markedly decrease your reading speed—it forces you to read as slowly as you would say the words out loud. As you read, listen for that voice in your head that is "saying" all the words out loud. If you can hear it, try to read the same passage without letting your mind "speak" the words. Keep practicing. Although it may take getting used to, eliminating subvocalization will help you improve your reading speed dramatically.

- ◀ **Read in chunks.** Reading words one by one can really slow you down. Instead of reading and digesting each word as an independent unit, try to read the words as "chunks" that have meaning. Pay attention to your eye movement as you read a line. If you're stopping at each word, try to stop every two words, then every three words. Reading in chunks of three to five words will help you increase your reading speed.
- ◀ **Don't reread.** One of the most common problems that plague slow readers is unintentional rereading of material. These readers jump back to read words or phrases that they've already read. Not only does this slow you down, it also hinders your ability to develop a sense of the flow of the passage. To correct this common reading error, use your finger or a pencil to maintain your place. Keep it moving smoothly across each line, and don't jump back to something you've already read.
- ◀ **Stay focused.** Concentrate on what's being said in the passage. Don't let your mind wander and be forced to reread several lines because you were thinking about something else.

These tips should help you achieve a reading speed of 200 to 250 words per minute, which will guarantee that you have enough time to read the passage and answer the questions in eight minutes. One of the most important keys to increasing your reading speed is practice—you have to read and read and read until you have mastered these tips and are using them automatically. If you're still having trouble reading more than 200 words per minute, consider an online speed-reading course.

Be sure to practice one passage at a time and always time yourself, checking that you can read each passage and answer its ten questions in eight minutes.

The high school difference

The ACT Reading section tests very different skills than your high school English classes. If you use the same strategies that you've been using in the classroom, you won't score very well on the ACT. The reason? The ACT is written to test, among other things, your ability to *infer* the answer by drawing conclusions from information in a passage. High school English tests, on the other hand, usually ask you to *analyze* a passage; in order to do that, you need to *assume* information about characters, plots, or the author's writing style.

What's the difference between inference and assumption? As tools for analyzing literature, *inference* requires that you draw a conclusion based directly on evidence in the text, while *assumption* requires that you draw a conclusion that isn't based on evidence in the text. *Never assume on the ACT Reading section.* The assumption strategy may have helped you score high on English tests, but ACT exam writers are aware that many students do this, and they purposefully include incorrect answers to catch these students. Making the transition from assumption to inference is critical to scoring well in ACT Reading.

Literal vs. critical thinking

The ACT expects you to think both literally and critically.

With *literal thinking,* you find exact words or phrases in the passage that will help you answer a question. Think about a computer using a search function to find information online; there is no interpretation or complex thinking required. The ACT tests literal thinking, because being able to read literally is critical to reading well. If you don't understand what a passage says literally, you won't be able to progress to the interpretation and inference that characterizes more sophisticated readers and that you'll need to ace ACT Reading. Having made it through most of high school, you should be able to think literally quite well. Thus, you should succeed on questions of detail and sequence, as well as on many comparison and main-idea questions—they test literal thinking.

Critical thinking goes beyond your ability to understand the words and phrases that you are reading; it is required to synthesize, compare, contrast, analyze, and infer, based on what you've read. You use critical thinking on questions of cause-and-effect, point of view, contextual vocabulary, and inference. You identify relationships among events and characters, and draw conclusions from the information in the passage.

Skills tested

According to the ACT, the Reading section measures your ability to perform the following tasks:

- Locate and interpret significant events.
- Determine the main idea.
- Understand sequences of events.
- Comprehend cause-and-effect relationships.
- Determine the meaning of context-dependent words, phrases, and statements.
- Make comparisons.
- Analyze the author's/narrator's voice and stylistic approach.
- Make generalizations.

Each question on the Reading section falls into one of eight categories, listed below in order of difficulty, using a scale of 1 to 5.

- **Details.** You pick out details verbatim from the passage. These questions are the easiest. (DIFFICULTY = 1)
- **The main idea.** You summarize the main point of a paragraph or passage in your own words. (DIFFICULTY = 2)
- **Sequence.** You determine the sequence of several events in the passage. Little or no interpretation is required. (DIFFICULTY = 2)

◂ **Cause-and-effect.** You identify cause-and-effect relationships among events in the passage. The level of difficulty depends on the proximity of the events in the passage and the subtlety of their relationship. (DIFFICULTY = 2, 3, or 4)

◂ **Contextual vocabulary.** You determine the meaning of a specific word based on its context in the passage. The question, which directs you to a specific line, requires you to decide which of several meanings is most appropriate in the context. (DIFFICULTY = 3)

◂ **Comparison.** You identify similarities or differences between parts of the passage. (DIFFICULTY = 3)

◂ **Point of view/character.** You analyze the tone, voice, or identity of the author or character, based on evidence in the passage. This question, which relates to the passage as a whole, appears at the end of the question set. (DIFFICULTY = 4)

◂ **Inference.** You draw conclusions based on information suggested—but not plainly stated—in the passage. These are the trickiest questions of all. (DIFFICULTY = 5)

A practice passage is presented below, interspersed with questions that test your skill in these categories. On the actual ACT exam, the passage is presented in its entirety, followed by the 10 questions. Read the passage, then answer the question.

Inference

NATURAL SCIENCE: This passage is adapted from chapter 4 of Charles Darwin's *On the Origin of Species* (ed. 6).

How will the struggle for existence act in regard to variation? Can the principle of selection, which we have seen is so potent in the hands of man, apply under nature?

5   The variability which we almost universally meet with in our domestic productions is not directly produced by man; he can neither originate varieties nor prevent their occurrence; he can only preserve and accumulate such as do occur.

  1. From this passage it can reasonably be inferred that Charles Darwin would argue that the variability that he sees among individual domestic plants and animals:

    A. has been enhanced by man's efforts to select the optimal specimens to breed.

    B. has decreased over time due to man's interference.

    C. arises because of God's role in generating diverse specimens.

    D. arises independently of man's activity.

Nearly all of the inference questions in ACT Reading contain the word "infer," alerting you to be prepared to extrapolate from the material in the passage. In this case, you're asked to infer how Charles Darwin believes that the variability mentioned in the passage comes about.

This is a fairly straightforward inference question—you scan the passage quickly for the words "variable," "variation," and "variability" and determine what the passage says about variability. Lines 5–7 state, "The variability . . . is not directly produced by man." This eliminates answer choices A and B, which mention man as having a role in the process, as well as choice C, which mentions God, who is not mentioned in the passage at all. If you had chosen C, you would have been making the assumption (oh no!) that because man didn't create the variability, then God must have. This dangerous, incorrect assumption illustrates why you need to stick closely to the text and not draw conclusions without proper evidence.

Having ruled out choices A, B, and C, you are left with choice D, which closely matches the sentiment expressed by Darwin about the negligible impact of man on variability.

Details

10   Can it be thought improbable that other variations useful in some way to each being in the great and complex battle of life, should occur in the course of many successive generations? If such do occur, can we doubt that individuals having any advantage,
15 however slight, over others, would have the best chance of surviving and procreating their kind? This preservation of favourable individual differences and variations, and the destruction of those which are injurious, I have called Natural Selection, or the Sur-
20 vival of the Fittest. When we see leaf-eating insects green, and bark-feeders mottled-grey; the alpine ptarmigan white in winter, the red-grouse the colour of heather, we must believe that these tints are of service to these birds and insects in preserving them
25 from danger.

    2. Which of the following is NOT given as an example of the effects of natural selection?

    F. Green-colored insects that eat leaves
    G. Grey-colored insects that feed on bark
    H. White birds that live on snowy mountaintops
    J. Birds whose feathers turn white in the winter

Because the question includes the word "NOT," you must identify the answer choice that is not supported by the passage. Lines 20–23 refer to "leaf-eating insects green, and bark-feeders mottled-grey; the alpine ptarmigan white in winter, the red-grouse the colour of heather." Green insects that eat leaves are mentioned, so choice F is ruled out. Grey, bark-feeding insects are mentioned, so choice G is eliminated. Only choices H and J remain. Ask yourself: Is Darwin saying that the ptarmigan is always white or that it turns white in winter? Line 22 notes the "ptarmigan white in winter," implying that this is not always the case. Thus, choice J is eliminated, and choice H is correct—which makes sense: the fact that the ptarmigan lives in the mountains has little to do with why Darwin includes it in his argument for natural selection.

Cause-and-effect

Several writers have misapprehended the term Natural Selection. Some have imagined that natural selection induces variability, whereas it implies only the preservation of such variations as arise and are
30 beneficial to the being under its conditions of life. Others have objected that the term selection implies conscious choice in the animals which become modified. It has been said that I speak of natural selection as an active power; but who objects to an author
35 speaking of the attraction of gravity as ruling the movements of the planets? I mean by nature, only the aggregate action and product of many natural laws, and by laws the sequence of events as ascertained by us.

40 We shall best understand the probable course of natural selection by taking the case of a country undergoing some slight physical change, for instance, of climate. The proportional numbers of its inhabitants will almost immediately undergo a change, and
45 some species will probably become extinct. If the country were open on its borders, new forms would certainly immigrate. But in the case of an island, into which new and better adapted forms could not freely enter, we should then have places in the economy of
50 nature which would assuredly be better filled up if some of the original inhabitants were in some manner modified. In such cases, slight modifications, which in any way favoured the individuals of any species, by better adapting them to their altered conditions,
55 would tend to be preserved.

3. Which of the following is NOT implied by the illustration of natural selection given in the fifth paragraph (lines 40–55) of the passage?

- **A.** A change in the climate of an island could almost immediately lead to increased variability in the types of plant and animal life found there.
- **B.** A change in the climate of an island could almost immediately lead to the deaths of many of its native plants and animals.
- **C.** After a change in climate, the populations of some types of plants or animals on an island might increase.
- **D.** If climate change were to cause a country to become warmer in certain regions, new kinds of animals might move into that territory.

You must determine the nature of the cause-and-effect relationship between two ideas or events in the passage. The answer choices indicate that you must identify the one incorrect "effect" caused by climate change.

The paragraph mentions the following possible effects: a change in the proportion of animals, as some become extinct and some thrive; new animals immigrating to the new climate; and existing species evolving to adapt to the new climate. You can eliminate choice B (line 45: "some species will probably become extinct"), choice C (lines 43–44: "The proportional numbers of its inhabitants will almost immediately undergo a change"), and choice D (lines 45–47: "If the country were open on its borders, new forms would certainly immigrate"). Choice A remains—although climate change may lead to variability over time, this is not an immediate change.

The main idea

As man can produce a great result with his domestic animals and plants by adding up in any given direction individual differences, so could natural selection, but far more easily from having incomparably longer time for action. Man can act only on external and visible characters; Nature can act on every internal organ, on the whole machinery of life. Man selects only for his own good; Nature only for that of the being which she tends.

4. The main idea of the sixth paragraph (lines 56–64) is best summarized by which of the following sentences?

F. Man is better at making changes than Nature is, because Man's changes are intentional.

G. The changes that man has made in livestock have been only for his own good.

H. Unlike man, nature can make changes that affect both the inside and outside of organisms.

J. Just as man can make small changes over a short time period, nature can make evolutionary changes with more breadth and scope over a much longer time period.

Questions about the main idea often include the words "main idea" or "main argument." These questions ask you to summarize the entire passage, or perhaps only a paragraph. It is an easy, but serious, mistake to select a detail as the main idea. Such a choice is tempting, because it often closely follows the exact wording of the passage; you want to select it because it sounds right! Don't be fooled. The main idea is usually not stated explicitly, so you should be wary of choices that too closely resemble phrases or sentences in the passage.

Choice F, which is a subjective statement about whose changes are "better," is clearly not the correct answer. Choices G and H can be ruled out, because each one, although true, is a detail that appears in only one sentence. Choice J is correct, because it summarizes several ideas from the passage in one sentence.

Comparison

65　　Man feeds a long and a short-beaked pigeon on the same food; he exposes sheep with long and short wool to the same climate; he does not rigidly destroy all inferior animals, but protects during each varying season, as far as lies in his power, all his productions.
70　He often begins his selection by some half-monstrous form, or at least by some modification prominent enough to catch the eye or to be plainly useful to him.

5. Which of the following statements would be inconsistent with the beliefs expounded in this passage?

   A. If one specimen differs from the rest of its kind, it will have an advantage over the others.

   B. Natural variability is important to the survival of a species.

   C. Man can exploit naturally occurring variability to improve the quality of domestic livestock through careful breeding.

   D. Naturally occurring variations can have harmful as well as helpful consequences for individual specimens.

This question asks you to compare the answer choices to the views presented in the passage, then decide which contradicts one of those views. The process of elimination is useful here; you rule out choices that match an idea expressed in the passage.

The statement in choice A doesn't reflect any of the ideas expressed in the passage, so you move on. (Any of the choices could be the answer, so if you can't find the idea within a short time, it is best to move on to the next choice.) Choice B reflects the idea in lines 16–19: "This preservation of favourable individual differences and variations . . . I have called Natural Selection." Choice B can be ruled out, because it can be reasonably inferred that these differences are important to the survival of the species. Choice C reflects the idea in the paragraph directly before this question, where Darwin says that man uses selection to breed animals "to be plainly useful to him" (lines 70–72). Thus, choice C can be eliminated. Choice D can be ruled out; not all variation is good, because some species become extinct (line 45) while others thrive (lines 46–47). Only choice A remains—which is inconsistent with the beliefs of the passage, notably with line 68's reference to "inferior animals," which implies that some variation is bad.

Contextual vocabulary

6. As it appears in line 68, the word "inferior" most nearly means:

   F. of a lower quality.

   G. cheaper.

   H. less evolutionarily viable.

   J. sickly.

A vocabulary question doesn't test whether you know the definition of a word as much as it tests whether you can figure out what the word means in the context of its use. This is great news for you as a test taker, because you don't have to memorize lists of vocabulary words like you do for the SAT.

Depending on context, "inferior" could have any of the meanings in the answer choices. Replace "inferior" with each choice, so that you can identify which choice preserves the meaning of the sentence. Choice F doesn't make sense, since there is no suggestion that the animals are of a lower quality. Choice G doesn't make sense, since price isn't mentioned in the passage. Choice H could be correct—it has to do with evolution and how likely each animal is to survive given the different variations it has. Choice J can be eliminated, because sickness and disease are not mentioned in the neighboring sentences. Thus, choice H is the correct answer.

Note that you didn't need to know what "inferior" means; you just had to know which of the choices suggests the same idea as "inferior" in the context.

Sequence

It has been asserted, that of the best short-beaked tumbler-pigeons a greater number perish in the egg
75 than are able to get out of it; so that fanciers assist in the act of hatching. Now, if nature had to make the beak of a full-grown pigeon very short for the bird's own advantage, the process of modification would be very slow, and there would be simultaneously the
80 most rigorous selection of all the young birds within the egg, which had the most powerful and hardest beaks, for all with weak beaks would inevitably perish: or, more delicate and more easily broken shells might be selected. We see nothing of these slow
85 changes in progress, until the hand of time has marked the long lapse of ages, and then so imperfect is our view into long-past geological ages that we see only that the forms of life are now different from what they formerly were.

7. Which of the following happens first in the passage?
   A. Darwin uses the artificial selection made by man as proof of evolution by natural selection.
   B. Darwin discusses how evolutionary changes would occur differently on islands.
   C. Darwin mentions the opinions held by others on the topic of Natural Selection.
   D. Darwin asserts that there is variation present in the natural world and discusses the significance of this variability.

Sequence questions, which appear at or near the end of the question set, ask you to order the events of a passage as they occurred. Sometimes, ACT exam writers try to be tricky by using flashbacks or by choosing passages that relate events out of order. Because of this, you can't answer sequence questions based only on the location of an idea in the passage; you need to make a mental time line and plot each event asked about in chronological order. If the last paragraph in the passage mentions a flashback to the time when the narrator got her first doll, you may need to place that event at the beginning of the sequence rather than at the end. This problem occurs most often in prose fiction passages.

Since this passage is in the category of natural sciences, there probably aren't any tricks of this nature. All you need to do is look back at the passage and locate where each of the events mentioned in the answer choices occurs. Once you have identified the sequence, simply choose the event that comes first—in this case, choice D: Darwin's discussion of variation and variability, which appears in the second paragraph.

Point of view/character

8. Darwin's tone throughout the passage most closely resembles one of:
   F. unbridled disdain.
   G. curious skepticism.
   H. blatant confidence.
   J. scholarly inquiry.

In passages of prose fiction, you may be asked about the character traits of one or more characters. In other categories, you may be asked about the author and his or her voice. Success on these types of questions varies tremendously from student to student: some students are very good at identifying voice and attitude, while others struggle with these concepts.

This question asks you to classify Darwin's tone as he explains his theory of natural selection. Is he disdainful, skeptical, confident, or scholarly? You should immediately eliminate disdainful and skeptical (choices F and G); as a proponent of natural selection, Darwin is arguing for, not against, this theory. Is Darwin's tone one of blatant confidence or scholarly inquiry? Throughout the passage, Darwin asks questions and explores different sides of an idea. He doesn't come across as trying to force his beliefs on the reader, and he maintains a scholarly attitude. Thus, choice D is the correct answer.

Reading 36 Strategies

There are eight Reading strategies; together, they will increase your chances of scoring a 36 on this section of the ACT exam. You will learn these strategies one by one, then you'll read a full-length passage and answer questions about it. Finally, you will check your answers against my analysis of each question.

1 · Write your own answer down first
2 · Skim it to win it
3 · Read actively
4 · Don't defend the choices—attack
5 · Don't assume
6 · Avoid extremes
7 · Choose general over specific
8 · Mark it up

Reading 36 Strategy 1 *Write your own answer down first*

One of the most helpful ACT strategies is to write down your own personal answer before you look at the answer choices. Although you can't use this strategy on every single question (some questions require you to read all of the choices in order to know what the question is asking you to do), this strategy will make it a lot easier to answer many questions. Here's how you do it:

- ◂ **Cover the answer choices.** Use one hand to cover the four choices. If you find that you can't answer the question without reading the choices, remove your hand. Otherwise, keep the choices covered.
- ◂ **Jot down your own answer.** Next to the question, scribble down a general idea of what you think the answer should be. Don't spend a lot of time doing this; use abbreviations and just a few words to record your idea. In this way, you'll avoid being tricked by the answer choices before you formulate your own idea about an answer. Keep your idea simple; it doesn't have to be complex or sophisticated.

ACT exam writers know the most common mistakes that students make, and they slip in answer choices that take advantage of these mistakes. They include correct-sounding choices meant to entice you to guess wrong. Don't be fooled! If you write down your own answer before looking at any of the choices, you're much less likely to be fooled. If one of the choices contradicts what you've jotted down, you're much less likely to be tricked into selecting that choice.

Although you may think you will lose time by writing your own answer down, you'll actually gain points by using this technique to avoid being swayed by devious choices.

Reading 36 Strategy 2 *Skim it to win it*

Write the main idea of each paragraph down right after you've read it the first time. At the end of the passage, jot down the passage's main idea. As discussed earlier, reading the passage slowly and painstakingly wastes time. Instead, read it quickly to get a sense of the main ideas—and write them down. In this way, you won't have to reread whole paragraphs to figure out what the main idea is—you'll already have it in the margin. Keep your summaries brief and to the point. They should take you only a few seconds. Be sure to use abbreviations and symbols.

Writing down the main idea of each paragraph as you read it the first time also ensures that you really understand what the main idea is. It's easy to passively read a paragraph without absorbing the information; stopping to write down the main idea will keep you focused on what you're reading.

When writing down the main idea, be sure not to steal words or phrases from the passage itself. Rewriting the topic sentence in the margin won't help you at all. By using your own words, you're forcing yourself to understand and interpret. Besides, an incorrect main-idea answer choice often mimics the text, and a plagiarized summary can tempt you to select such a choice.

After reading through all the paragraphs, write down the main idea of the passage itself. Try to reduce the main idea to one or two short phrases or sentences.

Reading 36 Strategy 3 ◢ *Read actively*

Reading passively can limit your understanding of the passage—you've read each word but haven't extracted the big ideas.

You're more likely to lose interest and read passively when you're bored, and the passages in the ACT Reading section, especially the prose passages, can be one big snooze fest. In order to keep yourself interested and engaged, whether you're reading about dining etiquette in Victorian England or social reform in France following World War II, try to read actively. There are several ways to do this:

- ◂ **Question.** Constantly ask questions as you read. Do you have an annoying classmate who won't stop asking questions in class? As you read a passage, be that person. Ask why certain things happen the way they do. Ask about cause-and-effect relationships. Ask why the author chose to write about the subject the way she did. Don't answer your questions—just formulate them as you read. You'll stay interested in the topic, and you'll be ready for the questions when you finish the passage.

- ◂ **Comment.** Take time to comment on parts of the passage. Does something stand out as odd? Is there an interesting word choice? A twist in the plot? Comment on these as you read to keep yourself engaged and focused on the passage.

- ◂ **Anticipate.** Try to guess what will happen next. Will a new character be introduced? Will the author present a counterpoint? Provide a list of examples? By anticipating what's next, you'll stay focused on the passage and make predictions that may come in handy when answering the questions.

Experienced and enthusiastic readers do this naturally, and you can use it as a tool to read a passage more closely and stay focused.

Reading 36 Strategy 4 *Don't defend the choices—attack*

One of the biggest mistakes in ACT Reading is to defend the answer choices:

> I guess that could be right if you looked at it this way . . .
> Maybe the passage could be talking about this . . .
> I probably just didn't see that relationship the first time . . .
> Now that I think about it, I guess this choice could be true if . . .

Stop! Such thoughts will lure you into picking a tempting but incorrect choice that the ACT exam writers like to sneak in. Don't be tricked! Instead of considering how each choice could be correct, try to convince yourself how each choice could be wrong.

Attack, rather than defend—eliminate choices by thinking like this:

> There's no way this answer could be right, because . . .
> The passage is definitely not focused on that idea . . .
> That relationship is not implied by the text . . .
> The author surely doesn't have that point of view, because . . .

This attack strategy helps you quickly rule out choices that you know are wrong, and it will prevent your being tricked by a choice that "sounds good now that you think about it." On the ACT, only the correct answer will be able to stand up to the attack, and this strategy will swiftly narrow your choices.

Reading 36 Strategy 5 *Don't assume*

Many students allow themselves to make unwarranted assumptions about the passage. ACT exam writers know that your English classes have conditioned you to make assumptions, and they'll test you on it. To avoid falling into this trap, always ask yourself, "Can I find specific evidence supporting this statement in the text?" If your response is no, cross out the answer choice.

Make sure that every answer you choose has a clear link to the passage. Don't be fooled by a choice that only sounds like it would make sense.

Reading 36 Strategy 6 *Avoid extremes*

Beware of extremes. It is much harder to support extreme answers than moderate ones. If an answer choice includes any of the following extreme words, you can probably eliminate it unless you can find the same word used in the passage:

all	never
every	prove
universal	refute
only	absolute
unique	impossible
always	inevitable
forever	

Answer choices that contain extreme words are much more likely to be incorrect than those with moderate words, such as "relatively," "somewhat," "occasionally," and "to some degree." If you are considering a choice with an extreme word, make sure you can find the same level of certainty in the passage. If you can't, select a more moderate choice.

When a question asks about the tone or attitude of the author, it's unlikely that the author is displaying any of the following moods:

apathy	perturbation
disregard	bewilderment
indifference	confusion
unconcern	

Finally, if you need to guess, never pick an extreme choice.

Reading 36 Strategy 7 ⏤ *Choose general over specific*

General answer choices are much more likely to be correct than specific choices. The more specific and detailed the choice, the less likely it is to be supported by the passage.

Similarly, the more material included in a choice, the more likely it is that there is a contradiction between a part of the choice and the passage. Since it takes only one contradiction for the choice to be incorrect, even if the rest of the choice's details are correct, you can eliminate it.

The following examples show increasing specificity:

Margaret felt disheartened.
Margaret felt disheartened when she was with Mark.
Margaret felt disheartened when she was with Mark, because their discussion about the future depressed her.
Margaret felt disheartened when she was with Mark, because their discussion about the future depressed her and she was worried that she wouldn't get the job that she applied for.

As the choices become narrower and narrower, it becomes less likely that every single one of the details is supported by the passage.

Reading 36 Strategy 8 ⏤ *Mark it up*

A blank ACT exam booklet is a sad ACT exam booklet—the more you jot down, underline, and circle, the better! When you read through the passage the first time, underline the topic sentences and main ideas of each paragraph. In this way, when you need to refer to the passage to answer a question about the main idea or argument of a paragraph, you will know exactly where to look. Likewise, mark an asterisk or an "X" next to specific details or lists of details that you may need to refer to.

Don't go overboard with the marking—you still need to be able to read the text clearly. Plus, if everything is marked up, nothing will stand out when you return to the passage, which defeats the whole purpose of marking.

Subject-specific strategies

For each of the four categories, there are tips that will help drive your ACT Reading score up.

Prose fiction

The fiction passage is unique; unlike the other passages, this subsection of the test asks you to analyze characters. You are expected to digest a lot of information about a character and devise a "character summary" that describes the character in a collection of words or phrases. When you jot down the main idea of the passage before tackling the questions, write down one or two keywords that describe the main character. This will provide a starting place when you encounter statements about the character in the questions.

Social sciences

This passage is more likely to be accompanied by detail-oriented and sequence questions than by character or inference questions. Point-of-view questions in this subsection usually ask you to analyze the author's tone or to determine whether or not the author supports the views being presented.

Natural sciences

Since this passage is likely to be fact-based, there will be a predominance of cause-and-effect, detail, main-idea, comparison, and sequence questions. Point-of-view questions for this passage may ask you to determine whether the author supports the conclusion he or she makes, or thinks that the data are irrelevant. For cause-and-effect questions, pay close attention to which events or phenomena in the passage are dependent on others. For main-idea questions, focus on where the facts presented seem to be pointing.

Humanities

This subsection will probably contain more inference, point-of-view, and contextual vocabulary questions. Comparison questions are likely to concern figurative language, such as simile or metaphor. For point-of-view questions, focus on the author's commentary about individual topics.

The solutions follow the problem set.

HUMANITIES: This passage is adapted from the book *The Works of William Hogarth; In a Series of Engravings: With Descriptions, and a Comment on Their Moral Tendency* by John Trusler (1833).

William Hogarth is said to have been the descendant of a family originally from Kirby Thore, in Westmorland. His grandfather was a plain yeoman, who possessed a small tenement in the vale of
5 Bampton, a village about fifteen miles north of Kendal; and had three sons. The eldest assisted his father in farming, and succeeded to his little freehold. The second settled in Troutbeck, a village eight miles north west of Kendal, and was remarkable for his
10 talent at provincial poetry. Richard Hogarth, the third son, who was educated at St. Bees, and had kept a school in the same county, appears to have been a man of some learning. He came early to London, where he resumed his original occupation of
15 a schoolmaster, in Ship-court in the Old Bailey, and was occasionally employed as a corrector of the press.

Mr. Richard Hogarth married in London; and our artist, and his sisters, Mary and Anne, are
20 believed to have been the only product of the marriage. William Hogarth was born November 10, and baptised Nov. 28, 1697, in the parish of St. Bartholomew the Great, in London.

HOGARTH'S WORKS. INDUSTRY AND IDLENESS.

25 As our future welfare depends, in a great measure, on our own conduct in the outset of life, and as we derive our best expectations of success from our own attention and exertion, it may, with propriety, be asserted, that the good or ill-fortune of mankind is
30 chiefly attributable to their own early diligence or sloth; either of which becomes, through habit in the early part of life, both familiar and natural. This Mr. Hogarth has made appear in the following history of the two Apprentices, by representing a series of such
35 scenes as naturally result from a course of Industry or Idleness, and which he has illustrated with such texts of scripture as teach us their analogy with holy writ.

Now, as example is far more convincing and persuasive than precept, these prints are, undoubtedly, an excellent lesson to such young men as are brought up to business, by laying before them the inevitable destruction that awaits the slothful, and the reward that generally attends the diligent, both appropriately exemplified in the conduct of these two fellow-'prentices; where the one, by taking good courses, and pursuing those purposes for which he was put apprentice, becomes a valuable man, and an ornament to his country; the other, by giving way to idleness, naturally falls into poverty, and ends fatally, as shown in the last of these instructive prints. In the chamber of the city of London, where apprentices are bound and enrolled, the twelve prints of this series are introduced, and, with great propriety, ornament the room.

Plate I. The Fellow-'Prentices At Their Looms

The first print presents us with a noble and striking contrast in two apprentices at the looms of their master, a silk-weaver of Spitalfields: in the one we observe a serene and open countenance, the distinguishing mark of innocence; and in the other a sullen, down-cast look, the index of a corrupt mind and vicious heart. The industrious youth is diligently employed at his work, and his thoughts taken up with the business he is upon. His book, called the "'Prentice's Guide," supposed to be given him for instruction, lies open beside him, as if perused with care and attention. The employment of the day seems his constant study; and the interest of his master his continual regard. We are given to understand, also, by the ballads of the London 'Prentice, Whittingham the Mayor, &c. that hang behind him, that he lays out his pence on things that may improve his mind, and enlighten his understanding. On the contrary, his fellow-'prentice, with worn-out coat and uncombed hair, overpowered with beer, indicated by the half-gallon pot before him, is fallen asleep; and from the shuttle becoming the plaything of the wanton kitten, we learn how he slumbers on, inattentive alike to his own and his master's interest. The ballad of Moll Flanders, on the wall behind him, shows that the bent of his mind is towards that which is bad; and his book of instructions lying torn and defaced upon the ground, manifests how regardless he is of any thing tending to his future welfare.

1. Which of the following can be inferred about William Hogarth?

    A. He was born in Kirby Thore, Westmorland.
    B. He had two brothers.
    C. He had two sisters.
    D. He had three sons.

2. In which of these places did William Hogarth's ancestors NOT live?

    F. Westmorland
    G. Bampton
    H. Troutbeck
    J. London

3. The point of view from which the paragraph beginning on line 25 was written can best be described as:

    A. that of William Hogarth, explaining his philosophy on industry and idleness.
    B. that of a narrator, describing William Hogarth's philosophy on industry and idleness.
    C. that of a narrator, describing his own philosophy on industry and idleness.
    D. that of William Hogarth's son, describing his father's philosophy on industry and idleness.

4. William Hogarth's work is described as promoting the idea that:

    F. a person's ultimate success in life depends on early good fortune.
    G. good fortune comes from maintaining consistent habits in life.
    H. good fortune comes from maintaining familiar and natural habits.
    J. those who work hard throughout life are rewarded with greater success than those who do not.

5. As it is used in line 49, the word *ornament* most nearly means:

    A. a decorative item.
    B. a leader and pioneer.
    C. a source of honor and pride.
    D. something beautiful but possessing no practical purpose.

6. William Hogarth's work "Industry and Idleness" can best be described as:

F. a treatise on the importance of hard work.

G. a series of drawings that tell a story.

H. illustrations in a book of holy scripture.

J. a set of twelve bound pamphlets used to explain lessons to young men.

7. Which characteristics does William Hogarth NOT use to differentiate the hard-working youth from the lazy one in plate 1?

A. Their facial expressions and clothing

B. The activities that they are engaged in

C. The nature of the reading material that surrounds them, and the care with which they treat it

D. The amount of interest that their master takes in each of them

8. Which of the following can be inferred from this passage?

F. William Hogarth was one of the most accomplished artists of London in the early 1800s.

G. William Hogarth was one of the most accomplished artists of London in the early 1700s.

H. William Hogath's art was primarily focused on teaching young people how to conduct themselves in life.

J. The twelve prints in William Hogarth's series "Industry and Idleness" had a strong moral focus.

9. Which of the following best represents the causal relationship implied by Hogarth's prints?

A. Misfortune causes laziness, which in turn leads to ruin.

B. Idleness leads to failure, while hard work is rewarded with success.

C. Failure leads to idleness, and success creates hard work.

D. Idleness leads to hard work, just as failure is eventually replaced by success.

10. Which of the following correctly orders these four items as they appear in the passage?

    I. Plate 1 is described in detail.

    II. Hogarth's background is explained.

    III. The narrator expresses his philosophy on what leads to success in life.

    IV. The location of the prints is revealed.

    F. I, II, III, IV

    G. II, I, IV, III

    H. II, III, IV, I

    J. III, II, IV, I

Solutions for the practice problem set • *ACT Reading*

1. C. (Inference/detail) Using Reading 36 Strategy 4 (Don't defend the choices—attack), you can rule out answer choice A, because the passage states that William Hogarth descended from a family that originally came from Kirby Thore (line 2); in fact, it is implied in lines 21–23 that William was born in London. Since the passage says nothing about the existence of brothers or sons, choices B and D can be eliminated. Line 19 refers to "our artist [William Hogarth], and his sisters, Mary and Anne," so choice C is the correct answer.

2. H. (Detail) If you are working quickly, you could easily be tricked into selecting answer choice F, but that would be incorrect. The passage states that William Hogarth's family originally lived in Westmorland (line 3), his grandfather lived in Bampton (line 5), his uncle lived in Troutbeck (line 8), and his father lived in London (lines 13–14). Each of these individuals is an ancestor of Hogarth's except his uncle, so choice H is the correct answer. If you answered this question incorrectly, make sure that you consider each choice carefully, and leave time to double-check your answers for sense.

3. C. (Point of view) It is important to realize that the point of view and the philosophy presented are the narrator's, not Hogarth's. Reading 36 Strategy 1 (Write your own answer down first) is helpful here. After reading the question (while covering the answer choices with your hand) and rereading the paragraph, you should be able to write down your own answer—that the narrator mentions the example of Hogarth to support his point of view. In this way, you wouldn't be tricked by choices that wrongly indicate that the point of view belongs to Hogarth.

4. J. (The main idea) This question asks you to identify the main idea of Hogarth's work, as described in lines 25–52. Reading 36 Strategy 1 (Write your own answer down first) is helpful again. After reading the question (while covering the answer choices with your hand) and rereading the paragraph, you should be able to pick out the main idea. Lines 41–44 refer to Hogarth's prints as "an excellent lesson to such young men as are brought up to business, by laying before them the inevitable destruction that awaits the slothful, and the reward that generally attends the diligent." Thus, you can postulate that the main idea is, roughly, "hard work gets rewarded." Choice J most closely resembles this idea. The narrator does not mention habits, so choices G and H can be ruled out. Since the narrator's point contradicts the idea that success in life comes from luck, you can eliminate choice F.

5. **C.** (Contextual vocabulary) Lines 48–49 state that one apprentice "becomes a valuable man, and an ornament to his country." Outside the context of this sentence, you would assume that "ornament" is a decorative item, like one placed on a Christmas tree. That definition makes no sense in the context of the passage, so answer choice A can be eliminated. Similarly, you can rule out choice D, since "ornament," as used here, is a positive descriptor of the hard-working apprentice. This leaves choices B and C. Using Reading 36 Strategy 4 (Don't defend the choices—attack), you can rule out choice B—nowhere in the passage does it indicate that the apprentice's hard work makes him a leader or pioneer. Never assume anything; the apprentice's hard work does not automatically make him a pioneer. Being a source of honor and pride, however, is directly suggested by lines 48–49, and this makes sense before the phrase "to his country."

6. **G.** (Detail) Using Reading 36 Strategy 1 (Write your own answer down first), flip back to the passage and determine what exactly Hogarth's works are. In line 40, they are described as prints. Lines 53–55 indicate that "the twelve prints of this series" adorn a room. The description of plate 1 depicts a pictorial scene. You can conclude that Hogarth's works are a set of 12 prints illustrating the importance of hard work by showing the story of two apprentices. After you jot this down, you can look at the answer choices. Only choice G matches your personal answer.

7. **D.** (Comparison) The process of elimination is useful here. Consider the characteristics in each answer choice, and try to find them in the passage. For choice A, lines 60–62 mention an "open countenance" and a "sullen, downcast look," and line 75 refers to one apprentice's "worn-out coat," so facial expressions and clothing can be ruled out. For choice B, the passage states that "the industrious youth is diligently employed at his work" (lines 63–64) and "his fellow-'prentice . . . is fallen asleep" (lines 75–77), so their activities can be ruled out. For choice C, lines 65–68 state that the good apprentice's "book, called the ' 'Prentice's Guide,' . . . lies open beside him, as if perused with care and attention," and lines 83–84 report the other apprentice's "book of instructions" as "lying torn and defaced upon the ground," so choice C can be eliminated. Choice D, the only remaining option, can be verified by making sure that no mention is made in the passage of the amount of attention that the master gives to each apprentice.

8. **J.** (Inference/the main idea) Using Reading 36 Strategy 4 (Don't defend the choices—attack), examine each of the answer choices. Choices F and G are fairly specific, and both use the extreme description "most accomplished"; these choices can be eliminated when you take into consideration Reading 36 Strategy 7 (Choose general over specific) and Reading 36 Strategy 6 (Avoid extremes). This is confirmed by the fact that there is no evidence in the passage that Hogarth was one of the most accomplished artists of any time period. Choice H appears to be correct at first glance. It's important to realize, however, that you've only been exposed to one piece of Hogarth's artwork; it would be dangerous to assume that all of his artwork has the same focus. This leaves choice J. Lines 40–46 state that "these prints are . . . an excellent lesson to such young men . . . by laying before them the inevitable destruction that awaits the slothful, and the reward that generally attends the diligent, both appropriately exemplified in the conduct of these two fellow-'prentices." This statement implies that the prints had a strong moral focus.

9. **B.** (Cause-and-effect) This question asks you to make clear the nature of the cause-and-effect relationship suggested by Hogarth's prints of the apprentices. Using Reading 36 Strategy 1 (Write your own answer down first), review the passage before looking at the answer choices and determine the nature of the relationship Hogarth is emphasizing. Even before the in-depth description of plate 1, you should recognize that the goal of Hogarth's work is to demonstrate the benefits of working hard and the consequences of laziness. In causal terms, you could jot down "hard work → success, laziness → ruin." Once you uncover the answer choices, you will discover that only choice B correctly matches the relationship you identified. Given the main idea of Hogarth's prints, none of the other choices makes sense.

10. **H.** (Sequence) The key to solving a sequence question is to find the line number(s) of each of the items in the answer choices. This information will determine the order of the items (unless flashbacks are involved). In random order, here are the items with line numbers assigned:

    1. Plate 1 is described in detail. (lines 56–85)
    2. Hogarth's background is explained. (lines 1–23)
    3. The narrator expresses his philosophy. (lines 25–52)
    4. The location of the prints is revealed. (lines 52–55)

    Clearly, the correct order is 2, 3, 4, 1, and choice H is the correct answer.

Prepare for ACT Science

The science section of the ACT exam creates anxiety for a lot of students. Confronted with a vast range of topics and two dozen graphs and tables to analyze in 35 minutes, even experienced test takers may flounder. After all, the science section is unique to the ACT, and many students have never taken this kind of test before.

With an understanding of how ACT Science works, however, and with practice, success is within reach. Using the strategies outlined below, I improved my score by 6 points!

Stats

Time allowed	35 minutes
Number of questions	40 questions
Time allowed per question	52.5 seconds

When I first read the description of ACT Science in the boxed material below, my heart sank. While I had taken chemistry and physics, I had just started biology and hadn't thought about any of the Earth sciences since the middle of eighth grade. As I explored the ACT website, I became even more worried—especially when I stumbled on a list of 45 possible topics, ranging from photo-

⏎ Breaking down ACT Science

"The content of the Science Test includes biology, chemistry, physics, and the Earth/space sciences (for example, geology, astronomy, and meteorology). Advanced knowledge in these subjects is not required, but background knowledge acquired in general, introductory science courses is needed to answer some of the questions. The test emphasizes scientific reasoning skills over recall of scientific content, skill in mathematics, or reading ability."
    —ACT.org

synthesis to magnetism to weathering and erosion. I knew little about these topics, and I certainly wasn't ready to be tested on them!

When I took the ACT the first time, however, I learned that ACT Science doesn't test your knowledge and understanding of science; in fact, it's not a science test at all.

In reality, ACT Science tests how well—and how quickly—you can read tables and graphs. Notice the ACT's description of the test: "background knowledge acquired in general, introductory science courses is needed to answer *some* of the questions." In my experience (taking the test three times and researching it thoroughly), "some" means one question, or maybe two, out of forty. You could nearly ace the test without getting any "background knowledge" questions correct. Furthermore, the background knowledge required to answer these questions doesn't exceed what most of us know after taking a single science class.

For example, here's a "background knowledge" question, straight from an online ACT practice exam:

> Scientist 2 explains that ice sublimes to water vapor and enters Europa's atmosphere. If ultraviolet light then broke those water vapor molecules apart, which of the following gases would one most likely expect to find in Europa's atmosphere as a result of this process?
>
> **A.** Nitrogen
> **B.** Methane
> **C.** Chlorine
> **D.** Oxygen

"Ice sublimes," "ultraviolet light," "water vapor molecules"? You might take one look at this question, decide there's no way you could answer it, and skip to the next one. Instead, take a deep breath and read the question again. Do you know the molecular formula for water? If you're like 99% of students taking the test, you know that H_2O means water. Even if you know nothing about splitting molecules, what could result from breaking H_2O apart? Glancing at the answer choices, you should be able to see that only one of them seems plausible—oxygen.

The background knowledge necessary to answer such a question is usually common knowledge among high school students. And remember: even if you don't have the background knowledge, there are only one or two of these questions in the entire section.

The key to success in ACT Science? Come prepared to read graphs and tables quickly and efficiently.

Science 36 Strategies

There are three types of questions in the ACT Science section.

	NO. OF QUESTIONS	PERCENT OF TOTAL
Data representation	15	38%
Research summaries	18	45%
Conflicting viewpoints	7	17%

The test is divided into seven passages, with five to seven questions each. A "passage" consists of text, graphics, and questions with answer choices.

Six of the passages present graphs, tables, and summaries of experiments, then ask questions that test your comprehension of the material; the questions are a mix of data representation and research summaries. One of the passages presents two conflicting viewpoints on a particular subject, then asks questions that test how well you grasp each author's argument and understand the similarities and differences between the arguments.

To conquer ACT Science, I've developed specific strategies for each type of question. Keep in mind that it takes time to improve your skills in reading graphs and interpreting data. Begin early and practice often.

Data representation

Data-representation questions account for 38% of the ACT Science test. Here's how the ACT describes these questions:

> This format presents graphic and tabular material similar to that found in science journals and texts. The questions associated with this format measure skills such as graph reading, interpretation of scatterplots, and interpretation of information presented in tables, diagrams, and figures.

And here's my translation: You're going to be looking at a lot of graphs and tables, and you'll be expected to recognize trends and patterns in the data they contain.

The questions ask you to draw conclusions or make predictions from the data in these graphs and tables. A question typically refers to only one graphic, but sometimes you'll be asked to compare data in two or more graphics.

Every data-representation question requires only one thing: an understanding of the information in the graphic(s). No "background knowledge" or special scientific skill is necessary.

Science 36 Strategy 1 · *Go straight to the questions in data representation*

The first time I took the ACT, I read through all of the experiments carefully, taking the time to understand what each was testing and what the results were, before tackling the first question. At the five-minute warning, I was working on the fifth passage, and I barely had enough time to randomly bubble the answers for the last passage. I learned the hard way that I needed a different approach if I wanted to finish the test on time. Speed is one of the keys to success in ACT Science.

There are two reasons why this strategy—going straight to the questions—works:

1. Not all experiments and graphics are referred to in the questions.
2. You don't have to thoroughly understand the experiments and graphics to answer the questions.

You can save a lot of time by going straight to the questions in order to figure out what you need to know, instead of wasting time reading and trying to understand experiments that may not even be asked about.

To appreciate how effective this strategy is, time yourself on a sample passage. Record how long it takes you to read and understand the passage, including the tables and graphs. It will probably take a minute to a minute and a half to read the passage, perhaps longer. If you have only 52.5 seconds to answer each question in the section, reading the passage will have consumed one or two questions' worth of time. Repeat that for five more experiment-based passages, and it means losing time to answer between six and twelve questions!

Reset your stopwatch and start over with a different passage. Read the questions first, and observe how many of them direct you to specific elements of the passage and graphics. You won't waste time trying to understand and interpret data trends that aren't even asked about. Sometimes, entire graphics and paragraphs are completely useless for answering *any* of the questions.

Going straight to the questions is the No. 1 time-saver in ACT Science.

Science 36 Strategy 2 — *Look for trends*

Data in ACT graphs and tables usually follow easy-to-recognize trends. A *trend* is a pattern showing a simple and straightforward relationship among the data. To identify a data trend, try to compose a sentence that summarizes what is happening in the graphic. Here's an example:

> As VARIABLE 1 goes up / down, VARIABLE 2 goes up / down / up, then down / down, then up.

A word of caution, however: there might not be a trend. Most graphics have a trend, but some don't. It's important not to impose a trend on data where there isn't one.

The speed with which you can identify trends impacts how quickly you're able to understand a passage and answer the questions.

The seven most common trends

1. Both variables increase (direct variation)—for example, as caffeine intake increases, so does heart rate.
2. Both variables decrease (direct variation)—for example, as rainfall decreases, so does average plant height.
3. One variable increases, the other decreases (inverse variation)—for example, as volume increases, pressure decreases.
4. One variable increases, the other increases, then decreases—for example, as mean temperature increases, plant biomass increases, then decreases.
5. One variable increases, the other decreases, then increases—for example, as the grades in a class increase from F to A, teacher attention decreases, then increases.
6. One variable increases, the other increases, then plateaus—for example, as time increases, the number of bacteria in a culture increases, then levels off.
7. One variable increases, the other decreases, then plateaus—for example, as the frequency of drought conditions increases, the variety of plant life decreases, then levels off.

You don't need to memorize this list of trends; it's enough to be able to recognize these patterns in the tables and graphs on the ACT.

In the areas of biology and population growth, you may encounter two types of curves:

◂ **Exponential growth** Sometimes referred to as a "J curve," exponential growth begins increasing slowly, then increases more and more quickly:

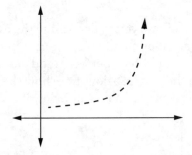

This type of curve is common in unchecked population growth—when a population is growing without restraints in food or habitat supply. Human population growth, for example, is roughly exponential.

◄ **Logistic growth** Sometimes referred to as an "S curve," logistic growth resembles exponential growth in the beginning, but then encounters limits to growth and levels off:

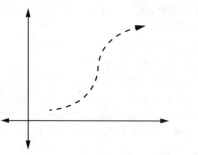

A colony of bacteria on a petri dish, for example, grows rapidly at first, but then runs out of food and the population levels off.

Other important data elements

The following elements are often useful in answering questions like "What was the maximum temperature of the sample in Experiment 1?" and "At what point did the temperature in Experiment 2 change from increasing to decreasing?"

◄ Extremes (maximums and minimums)
◄ Critical points (points of change)

Recognizing these elements can save a few seconds on almost every question in ACT Science; over the course of the section, these seconds add up.

Generalizing

This important trend-recognition skill allows you to determine the overall pattern in the data, without being distracted by small discrepancies in the trend. Tiny variations from what otherwise would be a perfect trend shouldn't distract you from the overall pattern. In the graphs below, note how the trendline fits the data, even though some data points fall above or below it:

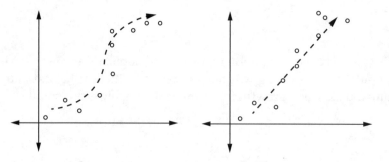

Generalizing allows you to see the "big picture" without being sidetracked by small deviations and minor inconsistencies. In ACT Science, it's the overall trend that counts. Being able to recognize the general relationship in a set of data points is an essential skill in this section of the exam.

Science 36 Strategy 3 ⸱ *Know your graphs*

The ability to quickly identify the most important features of a graph can save a tremendous amount of time. These features include the following:

- ◄ The type of graph
- ◄ What the graph represents (what each axis stands for)
- ◄ Patterns in the data

Common graph types

- ◄ **Line graph.** A line graph typically shows the relationship between two variables, one on the *x*-axis (the bottom line) and one on the *y*-axis (the line at the left). The *x*-axis represents the independent variable, which the researcher purposefully changes, while the *y*-axis represents the dependent variable, which may be changed by the independent variable. A solid line is used to show the data.

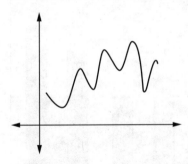

Time is frequently represented on the *x*-axis. For many experiments, time is the independent variable; the other variable changes as time goes on.

◄ **Scatterplot.** A scatterplot is similar to a line graph in terms of the axis and variables; the data, however, are not shown by a solid line, but as points scattered throughout the graph, with each point representing one trial in an experiment. Sometime, a "line of best fit" (shown as a dotted line in the graph below) is used to trace the general path of the data. This line doesn't connect the points on the graph; in fact, it may not pass directly through any points.

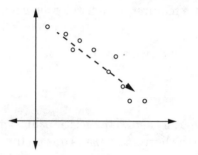

◄ **Bar graph.** While a bar graph uses the same axes and independent/dependent variables as a line graph, it portrays each trial with a bar.

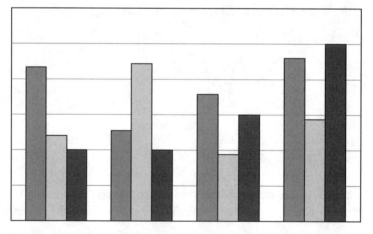

Bar graphs are much less common on the ACT than line graphs and scatterplots.

◄ **Pie chart.** A pie chart is a circle divided into segments that show relative percentages of several elements. A pie chart doesn't show variables; instead, it reflects the relative sizes of the components of a whole.

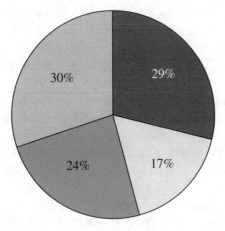

While a pie chart itself cannot show a trend, a series of pie charts can.

What a graph represents

For scatterplots and line and bar graphs, the two axes indicate what the graph is depicting. For example, if the x-axis represents temperature and the y-axis represents pressure, the graph shows the relationship between temperature and pressure. For a pie chart, the whole and the segments are labeled so that they can be quickly identified.

Some ACT Science graphs use the same set of axes and variables to plot several sets of data. For example, a graph may plot four different gases with respect to temperature on one axis and pressure on the other; this graph displays four sets of data—four potential trends—instead of one.

Independent and dependent variables

Understanding variables is not only critical for solving science problems on the ACT, but also valuable in comprehending how science explores the natural world. Scientists often ask questions like "How does this work?" and "Where did that come from?" It's difficult to answer such questions without breaking them down into smaller questions.

A grade-school scientist may want to explore what makes certain plants grow taller than others. To design an experiment, she first needs to select a single variable to test—say, the amount of water that each plant gets. The variable that the scientist chooses to change is the *independent variable*, and it usually varies in logical, progressive increments (for instance, 25 mL, 50 mL, and 100 mL of water daily).

The scientist could measure two variables: the effects of both water and fertilizer on the growth of plants. She could apply no water and no fertilizer to the first plant, a little water and a little fertilizer to the second plant, and a lot of water and a lot of fertilizer to the third plant. She may learn that the first plant dies, the second plant grows a little, and the third plant grows quite tall.

For the first plant, how can she determine if it was the lack of water or the lack of fertilizer that killed the plant? She might guess that it was the lack of water, but she wouldn't know for sure unless she *isolated* the variable—that is, tested only the effect of water while applying the same amount of fertilizer.

This hypothetical account demonstrates the importance of *constants,* or fixed values, in scientific experiments. In the plant experiment, constants could be the size of pot, the type and amount of soil in the pot, the light to which the plants are exposed, and the amount of fertilizer. By keeping these values constant, any differences observed in the height of the plants would be due to the different amounts of water the plants get, and not to another variable.

The *dependent variable* (plant growth, based on the height of the plants) measures the impact of the *independent variable* (the varying amount of water). The dependent variable, which is almost always plotted on the y-axis of a graph, is the variable that the scientist is unsure of: Will plant height increase with an increase in the amount of water applied?

For practice, identify the independent and dependent variables in the following hypothetical experiments:

1. John wants to see how the amount of food he gives his caterpillars will affect how long they become.

   Independent variable _____

   Dependent variable _____

2. Priyanka wants to explore whether there is a relationship between the grade a student receives in a certain class and the number of hours he spent studying.

   Independent variable _____

   Dependent variable _____

3. Timmy wants to see if the temperature of the water in the fish tank affects the heart rate of his fish.

   Independent variable _____

   Dependent variable _____

4. Allison wants to learn how the growth of a plant changes over its first 15 days.

   Independent variable _____

   Dependent variable _____

The answers are in the footnote on the following page.

Patterns in the data

There are many forms of data representation beyond the common graph types described above. You will probably encounter at least one unfamiliar type of diagram or model in the course of the ACT Science section. Don't try to understand the entire graphic at once; read the question first, so that you can begin a targeted search for the necessary information. In this way, you'll save time as well as mental energy.

A graphic may include multiple data sets, such as several lines on a graph or several columns in a table. In addition to understanding how two variables are related, you may need to determine how the data sets differ with regard to those variables. Here is a line graph in which several data sets are presented:

1. *Independent variable:* amount of food; *dependent variable:* length of caterpillars.
2. *Independent variable:* hours spent studying; *dependent variable:* grade in the class.
3. *Independent variable:* temperature of the water; *dependent variable:* heart rate of the fish.
4. *Independent variable:* time measured in days; *dependent variable:* plant height.

Each data set is represented by a different style of line. In general, the graph shows that as time goes on, wave height increases, then decreases. The wave height of molasses changes most drastically, the wave height of water at 40°F changes much less, and that of water at 100°F changes least. The key to understanding graphics with multiple data sets is to recognize not only the overall trends, but also the similarities and differences among the data sets themselves.

The following sample passage involves interpretation of a graphic:

Fossils found in a certain mountainous part of the Western United States have been uncovered at varying regions on hillsides. Fossils (imprints of ancient plants and animals made by being buried in sediment, mud, or other minerals and compacted for hundreds of thousands of years) are primarily found in the sedimentary limestone that is common in the area. The different parts of the hillsides where fossils have been found are marked on the following diagram.

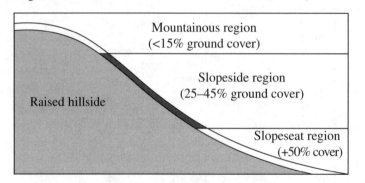

The diagram shows the 3 regions of the hillside where fossils have been discovered. The regions are differentiated based on the percentage of floral ground cover (plants, shrubs, trees, etc.) that exists at that particular height. The mountainous region is highest, but has the lowest percentage of ground cover. In the middle is the slopeside region, which has a moderate amount of ground cover, and at the base of the hill is the slopeseat region, which has an abundance of ground cover.

1. A fossil found in the region discussed above has been found in an area with 27% ground cover. What region has it been found in?

   A. The mountainous region
   B. The slopeside region
   C. The slopeseat region
   D. Not enough information is given.

2. According to the graph above, what is the cutoff height between the mountainous region and the slopeside region?
   F. +15 feet in height
   G. 25 feet in height
   H. 45 feet in height
   J. Regions are defined by ground cover percentage, not height.

Don't be intimidated by the irregular nature of the graphic; using the strategies described above, you will be able to extract data from the graphic quickly and efficiently. First, go straight to the questions. The first question asks you to identify a region with 27% ground cover. The slopeside region (25–45% ground cover) clearly meets this requirement, so the correct answer is B.

The second question asks you to determine the cutoff height between the mountainous and slopeside regions. Since the regions are defined by ground cover percentage, not by height in feet, you quickly decide that the correct answer is J.

As you can see from this example, unfamiliar types of graphics aren't more difficult than the standard graphics. You can recognize the same variables, trends, and critical points, just in a different way.

Data-representation problems generally require nothing more than reading a piece of data in a graph or table and, perhaps, extrapolating or generalizing from that data.

Research summaries

Research-summary questions account for 45% of the ACT Science test. Here's how the ACT describes these questions:

> This format provides descriptions of one or more related experiments.
> The questions focus on the design of experiments and the interpretation of experimental results.

And here's my translation: instead of analyzing graphs and tables as you did in data-representation questions, you'll read short descriptions of experiments and determine what each one is trying to test and how it is similar to or different from the other experiments.

The key to success on research-summary questions is to understand what each experiment seeks to test and how it works. It's important to understand the concept of independent and dependent variables, as well as how scientific inquiry uses experiments to test hypotheses about the relationships between the variables. These questions ask you to identify the variables that each experiment is testing, to identify similarities and differences between experiments, and to synthesize an overall conclusion, based on data from the experiments.

Since research-summary questions contribute to nearly half of the ACT Science score, it is critical to know and apply the best approach to answering these questions. The strategies described below, plus lots of practice, will improve your score. As with data-representation questions, no background knowledge is required to answer research-summary questions.

Science 36 Strategy 4 ⁄ *Go straight to the questions in research summaries*

Like data-representation questions, research-summary questions often ask you to examine only certain parts of a passage. Even if you eventually must sift through all of the experiments, you will be more efficient in pinpointing the object of your search if you have already read the questions. Furthermore, only certain aspects of an experiment may be of interest, and confining your focus to these will save you time.

It's important to read—or at least scan—the answer choices as well as the questions. Having possible answers in mind can be helpful as you inspect a passage for your answer.

Science 36 Strategy 5 ⁄ *Look for keywords in research summaries*

As you read a question and its answer choices, arm yourself with keywords to look for in the passage. These will help you spot the answer sooner than reading (and rereading) the entire passage. Important keywords focus on the following:

- ◄ Variables (for example, temperature or distance)
- ◄ Trends (for example, increasing or decreasing)

Keywords are homing signals in the passage: they will quickly draw you to the answer—and save you time.

Science 36 Strategy 6 ⁄ *Focus on similarities and differences in research summaries*

Many research-summary questions ask you to identify similarities and differences among the experiments presented. This is good news, because these questions are among the easiest and fastest to answer correctly.

Experiments can be different in two key areas:

- ◄ **Variables.** Variables change from experiment to experiment, or rather, one variable changes while the other stays the same. For example, one experiment may test temperature vs. pressure, while another tests temperature vs. rate of diffusion.
- ◄ **Trends.** When variables change among experiments, it is likely that data trends will change, too. For example, one experiment may show direct variation (as one variable increases, so does the other), another

experiment may show inverse variation (as one variable increases, the other decreases), and still another experiment may show no trend at all.

It is crucial to be able to zero in on the similarities and differences among experiments. With this strategy in mind as you answer other types of questions, you will be better prepared to answer similarity/difference questions, perhaps without looking back at the passage.

Conflicting viewpoints

Conflicting-viewpoint questions account for 17% of the ACT Science test. Here's how the ACT describes these questions:

> This format presents expressions of several hypotheses or views that, being based on differing premises or on incomplete data, are inconsistent with one another. The questions focus on the understanding, analysis, and comparison of alternative viewpoints or hypotheses.

And here's my translation: You'll read two paragraphs that present conflicting viewpoints on the same topic, then answer questions about the similarities, differences, and details of these arguments.

The conflicting-viewpoint passage is very different from the other six passages in ACT Science. Hopefully, you will save enough time in the other passages (by going straight to the questions, recognizing patterns, and using keywords) so that you have enough time to read both arguments and answer the questions.

That's right. In the conflicting-viewpoint passage, *don't* go straight to the questions. Instead, before you tackle the questions, read both arguments completely so that you understand their points of view.

Conflicting-viewpoint questions resemble reading-comprehension questions more than they do scientific-reasoning questions; it is for this reason that they're separated from data-representation and research-summary questions. Consequently, you will approach this passage as you would approach a passage in ACT Reading. Don't let the scientific jargon and complicated theories fool you—to answer these questions, you must understand the arguments, not the complex processes behind them.

Science 36 Strategy 7 ⚊ *Mark the passage*

Be an active reader—one who interacts with the material, making mental notes as you read. Or, as I recommend, physical notes. It's not in your best interest to waste time writing notes in the margins of the Science test, but I suggest that you underline words and phrases that strike you as important. These highlights will serve to orient you when you refer to the passage for an answer to a question.

In the first practice exams you take, you may not underline all the words and phrases that pertain to the questions. As you continue to practice, however, you will become more familiar with the types of questions asked in this part of ACT Science. By the time you take the actual ACT exam, you'll be able to quickly home in on each author's most important points. One further advantage: You don't waste time doing this. You're reading the passage anyway, and it takes no extra time to underline important words and phrases.

Conflicting-viewpoint questions fall into three categories:

◄ **Specifics.** These questions refer to an argument and ask about particular details. The first questions in this passage are of this type and are relatively straightforward.

◄ **Compare/contrast.** These questions ask you to identify points on which the scientists agree and disagree.

◄ **Extension/prediction.** These questions often take the form "Based on _____, predict/explain _____." They ask you to use information in one or both of the arguments to predict a future event or to explain the reasons for a given occurrence. These questions are rare, and they can be quite challenging.

Keep these three question types in mind when marking the passage.

Science 36 Strategy 8 ⁓ *Look for keywords in conflicting viewpoints*

Looking for keywords is an important strategy for research-summary questions. The same principle applies here: keywords save time and help you reference the passage efficiently. You'll be able to quickly home in on important words and phrases and find the answer without wasting time sifting through the entire passage. Here's how the strategy works:

1. As you read a question and its answer choices, pick out one or two important words to look for in the passage.
2. Keep the word(s) in mind when you return to the passage.
   Instead of having to reread the whole paragraph, you should be able to go straight to the part that answers the question.

Science 36 Strategy 9 ⁓ *Focus on similarities and differences in conflicting viewpoints*

This strategy differs from the similarity/difference strategy in research summaries. Since the data aren't presented in an accessible visual format, more work is required to determine where the arguments agree and diverge.

You should be on the lookout for similarities and differences even as you read the arguments the first time. As you read the second argument, circle parts that contradict the first argument. The ability to recognize similarities and differences improves with practice; you may reach the point where you don't even find it necessary to mark them in the exam booklet.

Science 36 Strategy 10 ⁄ *Don't be intimidated*

The arguments in the passage will probably contain jargon and sophisticated vocabulary and will refer to complex processes or phenomena. Just remember: you don't have to understand either argument. It doesn't matter if you have no idea how the Big Bang happened or what cosmic background radiation is. The questions test your understanding of and ability to compare different viewpoints, not your understanding of the science behind them.

Don't waste time trying to make sense of parts of the passage that aren't referenced in the questions. Instead, focus on the three other strategies (mark the passage, look for keywords, and focus on similarities and differences) to answer the questions that are being asked.

Additional tips

Timing

These 10 strategies should save you quite a lot of time, so that you will finish all seven passages and have a few minutes to review your answers.

Even with these strategies, however, the situation can quickly disintegrate if you spend more time on the first passages than you realize, and have a couple of passages left when the five-minute warning is given. This happened to me the first time I took the ACT.

To prevent this from happening to you, it is essential that you time your practice. In ACT Math, where the questions are unrelated, you have a sense of how long it should take to answer one question. ACT Science is different: it is divided into seven passages, in which the questions are often interrelated, and it isn't possible to know how much time you should spend on a single question.

The solution is to practice individual passages. Since you have 35 minutes to complete the seven passages (and the conflicting-viewpoint passage usually takes longer than the other six), I suggest that you allow yourself five minutes to complete each passage. Set your stopwatch for five minutes and try to finish just one passage. You may only get partway through when the alert sounds—don't worry, just complete the passage and try again. After some practice, you should be able to finish most passages in less than five minutes. Obviously, variation between passages means that some will take more time to complete and some less, but this practice will provide a sense of the pace required to finish the test on time.

At the end of this chapter, there are seven sample ACT Science passages. Try to work each of the passages in five minutes before tackling the science sections on practice exams. In this way, you'll have a better sense of the pace at which you need to work through each passage. By tackling practice passages in five-minute sessions, you will also avoid frustration and exhaustion.

ACT 36 General Strategy

Don't forget to guess! If, despite rigorous preparation, you find yourself running out of time, guess at the remaining questions. Guessing is not penalized on the ACT.

Quickly eliminate choices you know are wrong. This can save you time (you are looking for fewer keywords and trends), and your chance of guessing correctly improves.

Keep an eye on the clock. Skip questions that can't be answered quickly, so that you can maintain the pace required. It's better to return to difficult questions in the final few minutes than to fail to reach entire passages that may contain several questions that you could have answered easily.

The "not enough information" choice

If a question seems especially tricky and you have no idea how you would set about finding the answer, check to see if there's an answer choice similar to "It is impossible to determine the answer from the data given." If, after examining the data, you conclude that there is no way to determine the answer, select this option—there's a reason that it's offered. It is as important to know that you *can't* draw a conclusion because of insufficient data as it is to know that you *can* draw a conclusion from adequate data.

When to skip a passage

Should you tackle the passages in order, or should you skip around? Since your goal is to answer all 40 questions in ACT Science, you probably should work straight through the passages, one through seven. If you encounter a passage whose topic is completely unfamiliar or whose graphics look exceptionally complicated, you may decide to skip to the next passage and return later. Decide *quickly*! If you run out of time before finishing the science section and you've skipped a difficult passage, it is likely that you wouldn't have done particularly well on it anyway. A reminder: if you've skipped a passage, be sure to return to it if time permits.

Work these seven passages in five-minute sessions. The solutions appear at the end of the chapter.

Passage I

Large vertical tunnels have recently been discovered on the surface of Mars. These tunnels lead hundreds of miles to massive underground chambers that scientists believe once housed millions of cubic kilometers of trapped gas. The scientists theorize that, for reasons yet unknown, the volumes of gas that have been collecting under Mars' surface were suddenly released, spewing tons of rock and debris into the atmosphere and leaving these empty tunnels behind.

Study 1

A diagram of a gas-escape tube was created using a theoretical model and aided by surface maps of Mars. It is hypothesized that trapped gas, once released, escaped the tubes with such force that the tunnels were worn smooth by the intense blast. Upon reaching the surface of the planet, the gases expanded and dispersed into the atmosphere and out into space. Figure 1 details the smooth escape tube, the direction of gas escape, and the dispersal of the gas into the atmosphere.

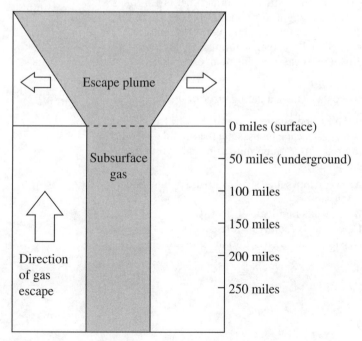

Figure 1

Study 2

Four gas-escape tubes (A–D) were studied. The volume of gas held within each tube, the rate at which that gas accumulated, and the amount of time that it took for that gas to accumulate were all estimated and can be found in Table 1. Also listed is the approximate age at which the accumulated gas violently escaped each tube, or "erupted."

Table 1				
Gas-escape tube	Approx. eruption age (Myrs)	Est. volume (km³)	Est. accumulation rate (km³/year)	Est. length of accumulation (years)
A	55	32,000,000	1,000	32,000
B	45	60,000,000	300	200,000
C	72	61,000,000	250	244,000
D	60	39,000,000	1,300	30,000

Study 3

Scientists have found 3 cratered sites around certain gas-escape tubes that appear to have been formed by exceptionally violent escape-plume phenomena. The first site has a crater 5 miles in diameter and is roughly 70 million years old; the second site has a diameter of 3.5 miles and is thought to be 50 million years old; the third site has a crater that is 1.5 miles across and is thought to be 45 million years old. It is hypothesized that these craters were created by either (A) exceptionally large quantities of gas escaping over time or (B) gas escaping at an exceptionally fast rate.

(All listed dates have a dating error of ±5%.)

1. If the escape plume shown in Figure 1 is typical of all gas-escape tubes, scientists could generally say that, after emerging from underground, the gas plume:

   A. stays the same size as it did while underground.
   B. expands rapidly as it rises.
   C. contracts rapidly as it rises.
   D. slowly sinks back into the ground.

2. Based solely on the information found in Study 3, can you determine which of the two hypotheses found in Study 3 for explaining how the craters are formed is correct?

   F. Yes: hypothesis A is correct.
   G. Yes: hypothesis B is correct.
   H. Yes: both hypotheses A and B are correct.
   J. No: it is impossible to tell, based on the information found in Study 3.

3. Based on the information found in the table attached to Study 2, what trends can be inferred from the quantitative estimations and approximations of the 4 gas-escape tubes (A–D)?

   A. A higher rate of gas accumulation seems necessary to form the largest-volume tubes.
   B. A lower rate of gas accumulation seems necessary to form the largest-volume tubes.
   C. There seems to be a direct correlation between volume and age.
   D. The largest-volume tubes seem to form most quickly.

4. According to information found in Study 2, what is the relation between the ages of the tubes and their volumes?

   F. The older the tube, the larger its volume.
   G. The younger the tube, the larger its volume.
   H. All tubes are the same age and have the same volume.
   J. There seems to be no direct relation between age and volume.

5. Which graph most accurately represents data found in the table in Study 2?

A.

B.

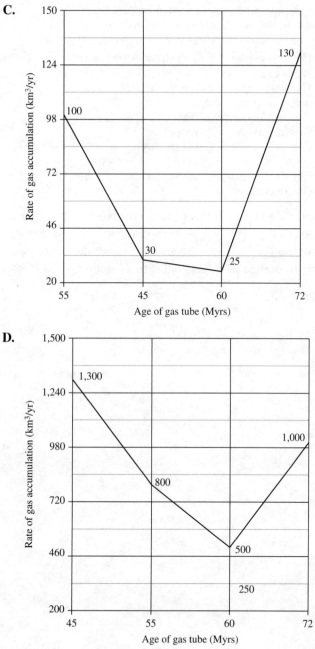

C.

D.

6. Considering information found in Studies 1 and 2, what hypothesis from Study 3 seems to be the most likely cause of the observed cratering?

   F. The data suggest that more voluminous stores of gas caused the craters.
   G. The data suggest that more violent explosions caused the craters.
   H. The data suggest that craters have nothing to do with gas-escape phenomena.
   J. Craters have been found in varying ages of tubes, and rates of gas escape are not given; there is not enough evidence to make a conclusive decision.

Were you able to finish the passage in five minutes? On the actual ACT exam, some passages take less time than others. If this passage took you six minutes to complete, there may be another that takes only four minutes. Still, it's important to realize that the goal is to average no more than five minutes per passage.

Passage II

Table 1				
Plant species	500,000 BCE (Length: 50,000 years)	450,000 BCE (Length: 150,000 years)	300,000 BCE (Length: 50,000 years)	200,000 BCE (Length: 100,000 years)
Solar era dates →				
Sun intensity →	High	Medium	Low	Medium2
Calamovilfa longifolia (G)	▓	▓	▓	
Andropogon gerardii (G)	▓	▓	▓	▓
Poa alpina (G)	▓	▓	▓	▓
Sorghastrum nutans (G)		▓	▓	▓
Physocarpus capitatus (S)		▓	▓	
Spiraea douglasii (S)		▓		
Lonicera involucrata (S)		▓		
Ribes sanguineum (S)			▓	▓
Berberis aquifolium (S)	▓	▓	▓	
Baccharis pilularis (S)			▓	▓
Alnus rubra (T)			▓	▓
Populus tremuloides (T)			▓	▓
Pseudotsuga menziesii (T)				▓

Note: Shaded areas indicate the species was numerous enough to be consider prevalent at the time.

Legend: G—grass, S—shrub, T—tree.

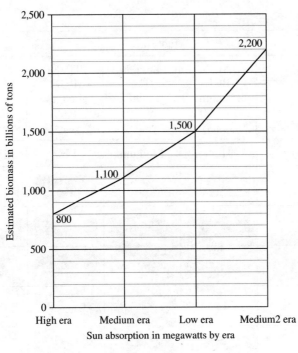

Figure 1

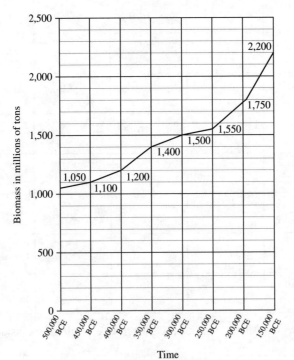

Figure 2

7. According to Figure 1, what was the estimated biomass of the high era?

   A. 800 million tons
   B. 800 billion tons
   C. 1100 billion tons
   D. 1500 billion tons

8. Based on the information found in Figures 1 and 2, what conclusions can the researchers make about the increase in biomass over time?

   F. Biomass increased linearly (evenly) through all time periods and eras.
   G. Biomass increased randomly, without regard to time frame or the solar era.
   H. Biomass increased fastest between 200,000 and 150,000 BCE.
   J. Biomass increased fastest during the high era.

9. According to Table 1, what type of flora is dominant in all 4 eras?

   A. Grasses only
   B. Shrubs only
   C. Trees only
   D. Shrubs and grasses only

10. According to Table 1, what types of flora were dominant during the high era?

   F. Grasses only
   G. Grasses and shrubs
   H. Grasses and trees
   J. Trees and shrubs

11. A student is asked what type of plant life is most likely to be dominant during the low era. Based on the information found in Table 1, what should her answer be?

   A. Grasses are most likely to be dominant.
   B. Shrubs are most likely to be dominant.
   C. Grasses and shrubs are equally likely to be dominant.
   D. Trees are most likely to be dominant.

12. Which of the following is NOT a key difference between Figure 1 and Figure 2?

F. Figure 2 has more data points.
G. Figure 1 ends at 100,000 BCE while Figure 2 ends at 150,000 BCE.
H. Figure 2 is a scatterplot, while Figure 1 is a line graph.
J. The range of data in the two figures is different.

This passage is probably easier than any you'll encounter on the ACT. Hopefully, you were able to finish it in less than five minutes.

Passage III

The following tables give the results of an experiment where 3 rows of sensors were continuously exposed to sunlight filtered through 3 different filters. Each row used the same filter for each of the 6 days the experiment ran, and the filters were not changed or swapped out. The changes in sunlight intensity recorded in Table 1 attest to how the filters performed, on average, throughout each of the 6 days of use. Table 2 records the average air temperature above the sensors in each row.

Table 1			
Average daily sunlight intensity (arbitrary units)			
Day	Row A	Row B	Row C
1	48.9	40.1	52.4
2	51.2	41.1	54.5
3	52.4	42.0	56.8
4	68.8	42.2	59.4
5	81.3	42.1	62.3
6	91.1	42.5	63.0

Table 2			
Average daily air temperature (in °C)			
Day	Row A	Row B	Row C
1	19.2	17.2	20.1
2	20.3	17.5	20.9
3	20.9	17.8	21.5
4	24.1	17.8	22.0
5	28.9	17.7	22.3
6	30.1	17.9	23.1

13. What was the highest average sunlight intensity during the 6 days of the study?

  A. 91.1
  B. 42.5
  C. 63.0
  D. 30.1

14. According to Table 2, the accuracy of the daily average air temperatures were recorded to the nearest:

F. 1°C.
G. 0.1°C.
H. 0.01°C.
J. 10°C.

15. Which of the following graphs most accurately depicts the average daily sunlight intensity for Row C?

A.

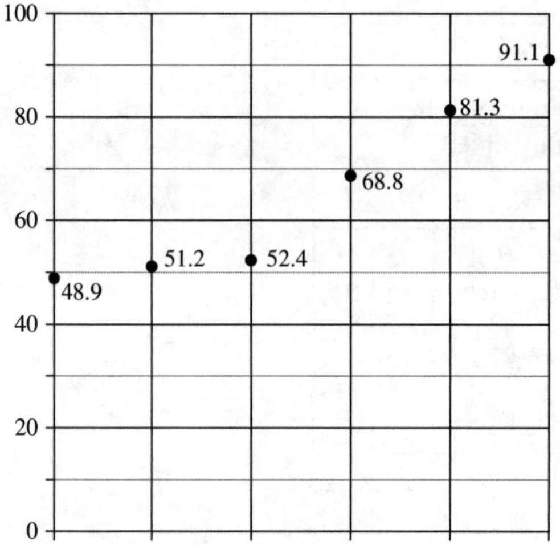

B.

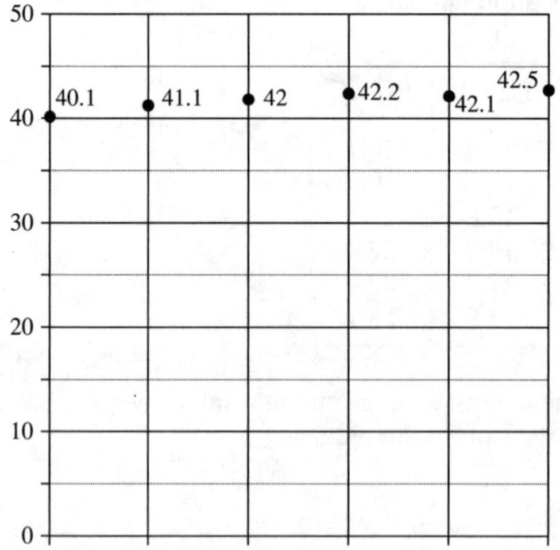

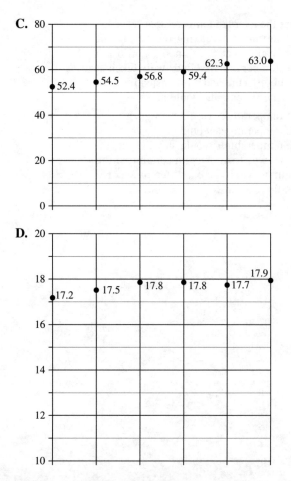

C.

D.

16. Which of the following statements most accurately describes the temperature trend as recorded in Table 2?

   F. Temperature rose in all 3 rows from Days 1 to 3 and fell from Days 4 to 6.
   G. Temperature fell in all 3 rows from Days 1 to 3 and rose from Days 4 to 6.
   H. Temperature fell in all 3 rows from Day 1 to Day 6.
   J. Temperature rose in all 3 rows from Day 1 to Day 6.

17. Suppose that the average temperatures recorded in Table 2 were made by taking the average of temperature readings at 6 am, noon, and 6 pm every day. If temperature readings were taken at 6 am, 9 am, noon, 3 pm and 6 pm instead, which of the following statements would be true?

A. Average temperatures would be higher.
B. Average temperatures would be lower.
C. Average temperatures would stay the same.
D. There is no way to know with certainty if the new readings would give a different average than the old readings.

Passage IV

The following tables show the results of 2 different trials of 4 different models of Farnsworth Oxygen Converters, which are complex machines used to turn nonbreathable gases found on most nonhabitable planets in the solar system into a breathable oxygen mixture. In each trial, the converters are started and run continuously. Their efficiencies (measured in arbitrary units) are measured every 24 hours, as shown. Table 1 records the measurements of a trial undertaken at $-100°C$, while Table 2 records the same 4 converters operating at $+100°C$. Values are given in percentages (%).

Experiment 1

Table 1			
Efficiency (in %) of Farnsworth Oxygen Converters at $-100°C$			
Time after starting (hours)	3000 CE model	3001 CE model	3002 model	3003 model
24	50	55	60	65
48	55	60	62.5	67.5
72	60	62.5	65	69
96	62.5	65	67.5	70
120	65	67.5	69	71.5
144	67.5	69	69.5	71.5
168	70	70	70	70

Experiment 2

Table 2			
Efficiency (in %) of Farnsworth Oxygen Converters at $+100°C$			
Time after starting (hours)	3000 CE model	3001 CE model	3002 model	3003 model
24	50	55	60	61
48	51	60	62.5	63
72	52	61	65	65.5
96	53	62	65.1	67.6
120	54	63	65.2	67.7
144	55	64	65.3	67.8
168	56	65	65.5	70

18. Based on the data found in Tables 1 and 2, do Farnsworth converters seem to work more efficiently in hotter or colder conditions?

    F. All converters seem to work more efficiently in hotter conditions.
    G. All converters seem to work more efficiently in colder conditions.
    H. Most, but not all, converters seem to work more efficiently in colder conditions.
    J. There is not enough information to answer this question accurately.

19. The planet Uranus needs a converter that reaches >70% conversion efficiency as soon as possible. Based on the information available in Tables 1 and 2, which converter should they use?

    A. The 3000 CE model
    B. The 3001 CE model
    C. The 3002 model
    D. The 3003 model

20. What factor varied between Experiments 1 and 2?

    F. Time
    G. Detection method
    H. Temperature of operation
    J. Models tested

21. Which model of converter reaches peak efficiency and then declines to subpeak efficiency within the time frame of the experiments, and under what conditions?

    A. The 3003 model at $-100°C$
    B. The 3003 model at $+100°C$
    C. The 3000 CE model at $-100°C$
    D. No model operates as described under any measured conditions.

22. What model converter would probably take the longest amount of time to reach an operating efficiency of 70% at $+100°C$, assuming that the average increase in efficiency vs. time found in Table 2 holds true indefinitely?

    F. The 3000 CE model
    G. The 3001 CE model
    H. The 3002 model
    J. The 3003 model

Passage V

Nuclear radiation

There are three types of radiation typically associated with nuclear power, weapons, and other sources of high-energy interactions: alpha, beta, and gamma radiation. Different types of radiation have different properties, different uses, and different dangers. The following study explains each in more detail.

Study 1

Radiation can be stopped by solid objects via absorption, but some types of radiation penetrate more easily than others. Table 1 lists the amount of a particular material required to completely absorb a moderate amount of a given radiation.

Table 1
Penetrating properties of radiation types

Alpha	Can be stopped by a single sheet of paper
Beta	Can be stopped by a thin sheet of aluminum
Gamma	Can be stopped by several inches of lead or feet of concrete

Table 2 presents some practical uses for the three types of radiation discussed.

Table 2
Practical uses for various radiation types

Alpha	Smoke detectors
Beta	Medical imaging, industrial-material thickness monitoring
Gamma	Sterilizing medical equipment, "gamma knife" cancer treatments, shipyard container inspection

Table 3 lists some of the dangers of the various types of radiation discussed.

Table 3
Dangers of various radiation types

Alpha	Cannot penetrate skin, but can be absorbed into the body through the soil and into plants, food, or drink, causing DNA damage
Beta	Can penetrate skin, but is much less damaging to DNA than alpha radiation; can also be taken into the body via breathing beta-radiated particles
Gamma	Is much harder to shield against and avoid, but much less damaging than alpha or beta particles

23. When you are given an X-ray in a dental office, you are required to wear a special protective apron made of lead. Assuming this apron is to protect you from one or more of the radiation types discussed above, what type(s) of radiation do you think the protective garment is meant to absorb?

    A. Alpha radiation
    B. Beta radiation
    C. Gamma radiation
    D. Alpha and beta radiation

24. What type of radiation exposure would pose the most serious risk to human life in the middle of a wheat field?

    F. Alpha
    G. Beta
    H. Gamma
    J. X-rays

25. What types of radiation could penetrate every-day clothing?

    A. Only alpha and beta
    B. Only beta and gamma
    C. Only alpha and gamma
    D. Only gamma

26. What type of radiation could be used to search for treasure buried under several feet of dirt?

    F. Alpha
    G. Beta
    H. Gamma
    J. None of the above

27. Why would a smoke detector using beta radiation instead of alpha be a bad choice?

    A. Beta radiation would pass through the smoke and could make it radioactive.
    B. Beta radiation would not have the range needed to detect smoke inside the home.
    C. Beta radiation would pass through the concrete in the foundation and irradiate the groundwater.
    D. It would not be a bad choice: beta radiation is used in smoke detectors.

Passage VI

Two students explain why water is a better medium than air for transporting heat away from the CPU (central processing unit) housed inside a modern computer and into the outside air. They also discuss how the use of a radiator (a series of winding pipes designed to optimize airflow over its surface to help cool the heated water within) and fan (a series of blades, attached to a central rotating hub, designed to push air) increases the efficiency of heat transfer from the CPU to the air.

Student 1

Water is a better medium for transporting heat than air because it has a much higher *thermal conductivity* than air does: 0.58 for water as opposed to 0.024 for air. (Thermal conductivity is the amount of heat transmitted through a given thickness of a given medium.) Because water is over 20× more thermally conductive than air, it can hold more than 20× the heat of air in exactly the same volume. This higher amount of conductivity means that water does not have to be circulated as often as air, because it takes longer to heat up.

A fan and radiator increase the efficiency of heat transport of a water-based cooling system by allowing heat to radiate from the water into the outside air without the complexities of exposing the heated water to air. Because the hot water stays within the radiator piping at all times, it is not exposed to pressure changes or influenced by outside current, and its flow can be regulated with ease.

Student 2

Water is a better medium for transporting heat than air because it has a much higher *specific heat capacity* than air. (Specific heat capacity is the amount of heat required to raise the temperature of 1 gram of a particular substance 1 degree Celsius.) Water has a specific heat capacity of 4.18, as opposed to a capacity of 1.0035 for air. What this means is that it will take more than 4× the amount of heat to increase 1 gram of water 1 degree Celsius than it would 1 gram of air.

A fan-and-radiator setup increases the efficiency of heat transport of a water-based cooling system by increasing the surface area of the hot water by running it through a radiator. Once in the radiator, the fan will push air over the surface of the hot radiator tubes, drawing out heat quickly (remember that air heats much faster than water) and expelling it outside the computer.

28. According to Student 1, why is a radiator helpful in dispersing heat?

   F. The piping keeps the hot water flowing and is easily regulated.
   G. The fan removes the heat by pushing air over the pipes.
   H. Air heats faster than water.
   J. Surface area is increased via the radiator.

29. Assume that instead of water, a much denser liquid was used that absorbed heat much more slowly than water, but was able to retain much more energy before becoming hotter. What would each student say would happen to the heat transportation efficiency if this denser liquid were used?

   A. Student 1 would say that the efficiency would be lower; Student 2 would say that the efficiency would be higher.
   B. Student 2 would say that the efficiency would be lower; Student 1 would say that the efficiency would be higher.
   C. Both students would say that the efficiency would be lower.
   D. Both students would say that the efficiency would be higher.

30. Which student(s) would claim that if air were used instead of water to transport heat, heat transportation would be more efficient?

   F. Both students would say that it would be more efficient.
   G. Neither student would say that it would be more efficient.
   H. Student 1 would say that it would be more efficient.
   J. Student 2 would say that it would be more efficient.

31. Suppose an unknown liquid was used instead of water to transport heat. The liquid seemed to be much more efficient than water. What would Student 1 assume was making the liquid more efficient?

   A. A higher thermal conductivity in the liquid
   B. A lower thermal conductivity in the liquid
   C. A higher specific heat capacity in the liquid
   D. A lower specific heat capacity in the liquid

32. According to Student 2, what would be a disadvantage of removing a fan from a radiator-and-fan setup?

   F. There would be no disadvantage.
   G. Water would no longer be pushed through the radiator.
   H. Air would no longer be pushed over the outside of the radiator and draw heat away.
   J. Air would get inside the radiator tubes and interrupt the flow of water.

33. What would Student 1 and Student 2 probably NOT agree on?

   A. Water is a better medium for transporting heat than air.
   B. Water's thermal conductivity is what makes it better at transporting heat.
   C. Fans and radiators increase the efficiency of heat transport.
   D. Water is an important cooling agent in the CPUs of modern computers.

Passage VII

Monosodium glutamate (MSG) is a substance regularly added to food products as a flavor enhancer and/or salt substitute. Though MSG has been in commercial production and use for over 100 years, its use in food remains controversial. Students conducted a taste test using various MSG concentrations to estimate what concentration of MSG tasted best to the participants. Table 1 shows each participant's weight for use in estimating dosage of MSG by body weight.

Experiment 1

Four solutions of MSG (diluted in water) were added to 3.5-ounce (100-gram) cooked steaks to determine how the MSG affected the participants' perceptions of the taste of the steak. One steak, as a control, did not have an MSG solution applied to it. Each of the 5 participants tasted each of the 5 steaks. The results are reported in Figure 1.

Table 1	
Participants' weights	
Participant	Weight (in lbs.)
1	160
2	185
3	200
4	150
5	115

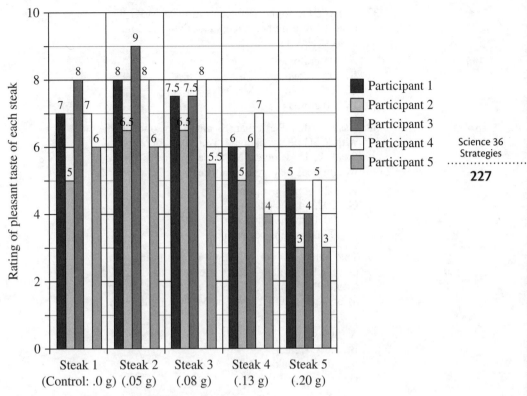

Figure 1

34. How many participants rated the control steak (Steak 1) higher than the steak with the smallest application of MSG (Steak 2)?

F. 5
G. 4
H. 1
J. 0

35. What steak was rated highest?

A. Steak 1
B. Steak 2
C. Steak 3
D. Steak 4

36. What steak was rated lowest?

F. Steak 1
G. Steak 2
H. Steak 4
J. Steak 5

37. What is the highest concentration of MSG that resulted in a higher-rated steak than the control steak (Steak 1)?

A. .05 grams
B. .08 grams
C. .13 grams
D. .20 grams

38. Assume that Participant 3 eats only one meal with MSG per week and it is a steak identical to Steak 2. How much MSG per pound of body weight does he consume a week?

F. .025 grams per pound
G. .0025 grams per pound
H. .0050 grams per pound
J. .00025 grams per pound

39. The lethal dosage of MSG is 7.5 grams per pound. How many steaks identical to Steak 2 would Participant 3 have to eat in one sitting to achieve a lethal dose of MSG for his body weight?

A. 300 steaks
B. 3,000 steaks
C. 30,000 steaks
D. 30 steaks

40. Which of the following would NOT have been an important control to have in the experiment?

F. Constant appearance and temperature of steak
G. Portion size and texture of steak
H. Tenderness and freshness of steak
J. Person serving the steak

Step 4
Prepare for
ACT Science

228

Solutions for the practice problem set • ACT Science

1. **B.** The arrows in Figure 1 indicate that as the gas rises from the escape tube, it expands. The large arrow indicates that the gas is traveling upward, while the two small arrows indicate that the plume is getting wider as it rises.

2. **J.** You may only consider the information in Study 3. There is no way to determine which of the hypotheses is correct, even if data from the other studies provided evidence (they don't).

3. **B.** The key here is recognizing the trends. Even though the data aren't presented in graphical form, where the pattern would be easy to recognize, you should notice that as the rate of gas accumulation increases, the volume of the tube decreases.

4. **J.** You're seeking the relationship between age and volume. The table doesn't reveal a pattern with regard to age and volume: from youngest to oldest, the volumes are 60,000,000 km³, 32,000,000 km³, 39,000,000 km³, and 61,000,000 km³. Since there is no pattern, the correct answer is J.

5. **A.** All of the graphs plot the rate of accumulation with respect to the age of the gas tubes, so these are the two variables you should look for in the table. The differences in the answer choices arise from what is displayed on each axis: the numbers 45, 55, 60, and 72 should be on the x-axis and a range from 250 to 1,300 km³/yr on the y-axis. You can immediately rule out choice B (the values on the y-axis are incorrect), choice C (the rates are incorrect by a factor of 10), and choice D (the lowest value is not 250). Thus, the correct answer is A.

6. **J.** The information in Studies 1 and 2 doesn't indicate which hypothesis is correct. Sometimes, there just aren't enough data to make a decision.

7. **B.** You can read the answer on the graph, being careful to note that the label for the y-axis means that it is 800 *billion* tons, not 800 million tons.

8. **H.** Both graphs indicate that biomass increased fastest between the low and medium2 eras (roughly 200,000 BCE to 150,000 BCE).

9. **A.** The two species that were present in all four eras are grasses, as indicated by the "(G)" next to their name and the legend.

10. **G.** There are three dominant grasses and one dominant shrub.

11. **C.** Since there are four dominant grasses and four dominant shrubs, they are equally likely to be dominant.

12. **H.** Both are line graphs, and all of the other differences are valid.

13. **A.** The highest average in Table 1 was 91.1 for Row A on Day 6.

14. **G.** This question tests your knowledge of decimal places. Since all of the data in Table 2 is reported to one decimal place, this is equivalent to 0.1°C.

15. **C.** The data in Row C in Table 1 should be compared to the graphs. The only graph with a data range of 52.4 to 63.0 is that in answer choice C.

16. **J.** Although the temperature decreased from Day 3 to Day 5 in Row B, the general trend was that the temperature rose over the course of the experiment. Don't let minor fluctuations distract you from the overall data trend in an experiment.

17. **D.** Since the values at those times of day aren't given, it is impossible to know what the new averages would be.

18. **G.** All of the converters either have higher efficiencies at $-100°C$ than at $+100°C$, or there is no difference (for the 3003 model at 168 hours after starting).

19. **D.** The 3003 model reaches 70% efficiency most quickly.

20. **H.** The difference in the two experiments is the temperature at which the converters were operated.

21. **A.** The 3003 model at $-100°C$ reaches 71.5% efficiency before declining to 70% efficiency; it is the only model whose efficiency increases, then decreases.

22. **F.** The 3000CE model's efficiency increases most slowly; if the trend continues, this model will take the longest amount of time to reach 70% efficiency.

23. **C.** Because you are required to wear a lead apron, you are being protected from gamma radiation. If you needed to be protected from alpha or beta radiation, a much simpler shield (paper or aluminum) would be required.

24. **F.** In a wheat field, the most serious concern would be alpha particles, which can't penetrate skin but can be absorbed into the body via edible plants (like wheat).

25. **B.** Alpha particles can be absorbed by only a single sheet of paper, and clothing is thicker and denser than that. It would take aluminum or lead, however, to shield a person from beta or gamma particles.

26. **H.** Only gamma radiation could be used to search for treasure, because it would take several feet of concrete (which is much denser than dirt) to stop gamma radiation.

27. **A.** The process of elimination can be used to solve this problem. Answer choice B is ruled out, because the range of particles isn't discussed in the passage. Choice C is ruled out, based on the information in Table 1. Choice D is ruled out, based on the information in Table 2. Choice A makes sense, because beta radiation would not be stopped by the smoke and can be damaging when inhaled (as it would be if it made the smoke radioactive in a fire).

28. **F.** In the second paragraph of Student 1's explanation, it is stated that a radiator is helpful because it controls the hot-water flow and allows it to be regulated.

29. **B.** Because Student 2 believes specific heat capacity to be a critical factor in heat-transportation efficiency, the fact that the denser liquid took much longer to heat up would make it less efficient than water. Student 1, on the other hand, would think that the ability of the denser liquid to hold more heat (due to thermal conductivity) would make it more efficient than water.

30. **G.** Air has a lower thermal conductivity and a lower specific heat capacity than water, so neither of the students would think it would be more efficient at heat transportation.

31. **A.** Since Student 1 attributes the heat-transportation efficiency of water to its high thermal conductivity, Student 1 would assume that a liquid that transports heat even more efficiently than water would have a higher thermal conductivity.

32. **H.** Student 2 states that "the fan will push air over the surface of the hot radiator tubes, drawing out heat quickly."

33. **B.** Student 1 believes that the thermal conductivity of water is the critical factor, while Student 2 believes that the specific heat capacity of water is the critical factor.

34. **J.** Everyone except Participant 5 rated Steak 1 lower than Steak 2, and Participant 5 rated the two steaks the same.

35. **B.** Steak 2 had the highest average rating.

36. **J.** Steak 5 had the lowest average rating.

37. **B.** Steak 3 had the highest concentration of MSG among steaks whose average rating was above that of the control.

38. **J.** Participant 3 weighs 200 pounds and consumes .05 grams of MSG per week (the amount in Steak 2). Divide .05 grams by 200 pounds; the result is .00025 grams per pound.

39. **C.** Since Participant 3 weighs 200 pounds, multiply 7.5 grams by 200; the result is 1,500 grams of MSG. Since Steak 2 has a concentration of .05 grams per pound, divide 1,500 by .05; the result is 30,000 steaks.

40. **J.** While all of the other factors may have had an impact on the perceived taste of the steak, the person serving a steak probably wouldn't affect the rating given to it.

Prepare for ACT Writing

The optional ACT Writing section is your last stop on exam day—meaning you should be warmed up and ready to go. Unlike the SAT, which forces you to write your essay at the beginning of the exam, the ACT makes sure that you're in full test mode before tackling this part of the exam.

ACT Writing tests your ability to write an organized, coherent, and convincing essay on a prescribed topic. Like every other part of the ACT, the writing section is predictable, and it rewards students for using the cookie-cutter, five-paragraph essay format. Fortunately, it's not like writing a creative story or an inspiring speech. To churn out a top-scoring ACT essay, all you must do is learn and follow a set formula.

The essay may be the easiest ACT section to prepare for. While you won't know the topic of the essay before exam time, you will be able to produce a polished essay no matter what the topic is. You will choose examples suited to the topic, of course, but everything else—the structure, the format, the style— will remain the same, regardless of what you are writing about. You'll see what I mean when you learn what kinds of essays score well on the ACT.

Stats

Time allowed	30 minutes
Number of questions	1 essay
Time allowed per question	30 minutes

⤵ Breaking down ACT Writing

"The ACT Writing Test complements the English Test. The combined information from both tests tells postsecondary institutions about students' understanding of the conventions of standard written English and their ability to produce a direct sample of writing."

—ACT.org

Scoring the ACT essay

After you've written your essay in your answer booklet, it will be photocopied and placed in front of two ACT essay readers. Working independently, each reader will read your essay and assign it a score of 0 to 6, based on its organization, clarity, and effectiveness. The two readers' scores will be added together for a composite ACT Writing score.

To comprehend the mental state of essay readers, imagine that you are being paid a meager fee to sit in a stuffy room filled with other people, reading essay after essay from dawn to dusk. Sounds torturous, doesn't it? Although the very first essays of the day may be read with energy and enthusiasm, by the time your essay hits the readers' desks, they will probably be exhausted and sick of looking at mediocre essay after mediocre essay. They're not going to

⊡ ACT Writing score sheet

Essay score of 1

- Is 0–1 pages long
- Lacks a coherent argument
- Hardly supports claims
- Has no organization of ideas
- Displays a poor use of vocabulary
- Contains many grammatical errors

Essay score of 2

- Is 0–1 pages long
- Lacks a sufficient argument
- Offers general or personal evidence to support claims
- Has poorly organized ideas
- Displays a mediocre use of vocabulary
- Contains many grammatical errors

Essay score of 3

- Is 1–2 pages long
- Presents an argument
- Offers general or personal evidence to support claims
- Has fairly organized ideas
- Displays a fair use of vocabulary
- Contains some grammatical errors

want to spend any longer than necessary to decide what score you deserve before moving on to the next essay in their seemingly endless stack.

Each reader will spend no more than three or four minutes with your essay; there's no time for you to start slowly and build. Not only must you write convincingly and well, you must demonstrate from the start that your essay is deserving of a 6. First impressions are extremely important, and a strong introduction will convince the reader that you're a serious contender.

The readers don't know or care who you are. They have no idea how smart you are, how nice you are, or how well you could communicate if you were allowed just a few more minutes. You have 30 minutes to earn their respect, and only three or four pages in which to do it. Make your move, and make it quickly!

Essay score of 4
- ◄ Is 2–3 pages long
- ◄ Presents a logical argument
- ◄ Offers academic evidence to support claims
- ◄ Has well-organized ideas
- ◄ Displays a good use of vocabulary
- ◄ Contains some grammatical errors

Essay score of 5
- ◄ Is 2–3 pages long
- ◄ Presents a logical and persuasive argument
- ◄ Offers strong academic evidence to support claims
- ◄ Has well-organized ideas
- ◄ Displays a proficient use of vocabulary
- ◄ Contains few grammatical errors

Essay score of 6
- ◄ Is 3–4 pages long
- ◄ Presents a logical and compelling argument
- ◄ Offers substantial, strong academic evidence to support claims
- ◄ Has superbly organized ideas
- ◄ Displays a masterful use of vocabulary
- ◄ Contains few or no grammatical errors

Familiarize yourself with the requirements of a "6" essay in the boxed material on the previous two pages—these are the characteristics your essay must have to score a 12 on the Writing section.

The essay topic

The ACT wants you to write a well-organized five-paragraph essay that takes a stand on a certain issue. An introductory statement presents an issue relevant to a high school student's life, and you are asked to take a position on the issue. Take a look at a sample prompt:

> Online school has been growing in popularity over the last few years. As computers and access to the Internet become increasingly common across the country, online school is becoming more and more a viable option for many students. Some educators are in favor of online school, because they feel it allows increased flexibility to students who otherwise may have dropped out of school to pursue work or extra-curricular activities. However, many educators have reservations about online learning, asserting that school is more than the academic content covered— it's about making connections with teachers and peers, developing social skills, and gaining hands-on experience. In your opinion, should online schools become the new method for K–12 instruction?
>
> In your essay, take a position on this question. You may write about either one of the two points of view given, or you may present a different point of view on this question. Use specific reasons and examples to support your position.

The second paragraph is worded exactly like the instructions on the actual ACT.

Unlike the SAT, whose essay prompts pose philosophical questions like "Is innovation always positive?" or "Is cheating always wrong?", the ACT focuses on topics that relate to a high school student's life. Here are some prompts that the ACT has used in the past:

> Should high school be extended to five years?
> Should more schools adopt a dress code?
> Should a core curriculum be required for high school students?
> Should there be a curfew for high school students?
> Should Internet use in schools be regulated?

Writing 36 Strategies

To conquer the ACT essay, you'll need to adopt the following eight Writing 36 strategies:

---

1 · Master the five-paragraph essay format
2 · Pace yourself
3 · Use vocabulary to your advantage
4 · Fill the space
5 · Stay active
6 · Transition smoothly
7 · Don't get personal
8 · Plan, plan, plan

Writing 36 Strategy 1 ⁄ *Master the five-paragraph essay format*

Many high school English courses teach the basics of writing a five-paragraph essay. If you haven't been exposed to this type of essay writing, don't worry! I'll teach you everything you need to know about your essay structure.

Although some writers feel that the five-paragraph format limits their creative expression, it is what your ACT readers will be looking for. I'm not exaggerating: *Correct format is the most important part of your essay.* It is more important than which side of the argument you take and what examples you use to support your claims.

The good news is that the five-paragraph essay format is easy to learn, and once you grasp it, you'll find that writing ACT-style essays is relatively straightforward.

Here's how your essay should be structured:

- ◄ Paragraph 1   **Introduction** (3–4 sentences)
- ◄ Paragraph 2   **First body paragraph** (5+ sentences)
- ◄ Paragraph 3   **Second body paragraph** (5+ sentences)
- ◄ Paragraph 4   **Third body paragraph** (5+ sentences)
- ◄ Paragraph 5   **Conclusion** (3–4 sentences)

Introduction

Your first sentence should provide a "hook" that pulls the readers into your essay and makes them want to continue reading just to find out what interesting things you have to say. Your essay can begin with a real-world example, a personal anecdote, a quote, or a rhetorical question—we call this the *lead*. The lead should never be more than two sentences long.

Next is a sentence that explicitly relates your lead to your thesis. This sentence is known as the *link* and will be immediately followed by your thesis. Here are examples of very good lead/link duos (with the lead in roman type and the link in italics):

> I've always felt that societal restrictions are becoming tighter and tighter as civilization advances. As individuals become more and more powerful due to technology, they are increasingly fettered by regulations and rules, limiting their ability to explore and develop. *In our schools, strict Internet restrictions are having this effect on students.* [THESIS]

> My Mexican grandmother used to smile and shake her head when I told her what we were learning about in school: "When are you going to use that in real life?" she would ask, leaving me scrambling for a way to relate my geometry class to the cluttered kitchen around us. *While her question was meant mostly in jest, it is important to ask ourselves whether or not we should continue to require all students to pursue a core curriculum when they have already decided on a career path in which those skills will be useless.* [THESIS]

Notice how the lead creates interest in your essay, while the link connects the lead to the thesis? For practice, write lead/link combinations for the following essay prompts:

> Should more schools have school pets?

> Should more high schools create "teaching assistant" programs in which some students are paid to help instruct other students?

> Should schools remove unhealthy food choices from their menus or allow students to choose what they eat?

Now, review the leads and links you've written. Does the first sentence pull the readers in or demand their attention? Does the link effectively tie the lead to the thesis you are about to present? If so, great job! If not, keep practicing. Think of a possible essay topic, then write a lead/link combination for it. Being able to generate a lead/link combination quickly (within one or two minutes) will be extremely valuable on exam day.

The last sentence of your introduction is the *thesis*. You may already know what a thesis is and how to write one. If you do, great! Keep reading to make sure that what you've learned is consistent with ACT expectations. If you're not sure what a thesis is or how to use one, have no fear! I'm about to tell you.

The thesis is arguably the most important sentence in your essay. It should tell the reader exactly what you're going to talk about for the next few pages. It presents your argument for the first time and sets the stage for the rest of your essay.

Your thesis statement must do two very important things:

- **Make an argument.** To make an argument, answer the essay question. The prompt writer is asking you whether or not something should happen. Decide whether you want to answer yes or no, then state your position. For example:

  > More schools should adopt school pets, because . . .
  > High schools should not create "teaching assistant" programs, since . . .
  > School menus should offer only healthy eating options, because . . .

  Some students think that arguing the middle ground rather than taking sides will show the ACT readers how sophisticated and complex their arguments are. Wrong! ACT readers expect you to state and support a point of view; arguing both sides makes your essay exponentially weaker. The ACT isn't testing how complex or interesting your argument is—it's testing your ability to write an organized five-paragraph essay.

  Don't use "I think," "I feel," or "In my opinion" in your thesis. Personal information is allowed only in the lead. The ACT readers want you to argue as if your point is correct, so don't sound wishy-washy by prefacing your argument with an "I" statement. State your argument like it is the absolute truth, then proceed to convince the readers that you're right.

- **Introduce provable parts.** These are the reasons you'll use to convince the readers that your argument is correct. Each provable part will become the topic of one of three body paragraphs. You declare your position on the topic, then provide the three reasons why you've taken that position. For example:

  > More schools should adopt school pets, because interaction with animals increases the empathy and compassion of students, teaches students important lessons about responsibility and chores, and provides a feeling of purpose that unites the classroom community.

  Each of the three body paragraphs will discuss one of these points in detail; they are stated in the thesis so that the readers are aware of the key points of your argument and know what to expect in the rest of the essay.

  The order of provable parts matters. You should create a "sandwich effect" by placing your two best points at the beginning and end, and your weakest point in the middle. The order of provable parts in your thesis should mirror the order in which they appear in the body paragraphs.

Body paragraphs

Each body paragraph should be organized as follows:

- ◄ Topic sentence
- ◄ Supporting detail 1
- ◄ Supporting detail 2
- ◄ Supporting detail 3
- ◄ Link to the thesis/conclusion

The *topic sentence,* which restates one of your provable parts, tells the reader what the paragraph is going to be about. Continuing the example of pets in schools, here is the first topic sentence:

> Having animals in the classroom helps foster empathy and compassion among the students.

One of the key principles of the five-paragraph essay is that you always return to the same ideas. Your topic sentence should clearly restate one of the provable parts of your thesis—that's all it has to do.

The *supporting details* back up the topic sentence. Like a good debater, you should use factual evidence to support your claims. While the ACT doesn't expect you to memorize facts and statistics, it is very helpful to include real-world, concrete evidence in your arguments. Because you won't know the ACT Writing prompt ahead of time, you can't research the subject before you write your essay. This means that you must rely on knowledge and examples from your own life for supporting details. Fortunately, the ACT Writing prompt is relevant to high school students, so you should have plenty of relevant life experience to draw from.

Compare the following two supporting details, which are meant to bolster an argument for a four-year physical education requirement in high school:

> For example, my friend Diana, who was slightly overweight, would often skip exercise until her doctor recommended that she take gym classes. The mandatory classes helped her lose weight and improve her health, which led to long-term benefits such as lower blood pressure and lower cholesterol.

> For example, students whose health is at risk due to their weight often fail to comply with voluntary diet and exercise plans. By participating in mandatory physical education, however, they can achieve long-term health benefits such as lower blood pressure and lower cholesterol.

The second paragraph is better, because it states the argument inspired by Diana in a general, objective way, rather than as an anecdote.

The ability to quickly generate supporting details and examples improves tremendously with practice. Take advantage of a few idle minutes by choosing a random prompt and thinking up details and examples that support an argument for or against it.

If you have background knowledge in a particular area, don't be afraid to use it. For example, if you've written a paper on the benefits of language immersion for elementary students and that topic appears in the ACT Writing prompt, incorporate your knowledge into your argument.

The ACT readers are more interested in how you organize your arguments and evidence than in whether you can produce highly detailed evidence. Most importantly, use details that clearly support your thesis.

Include three supporting details in each body paragraph, and explain each detail in one or two sentences. Make sure that your ideas are relevant and that they relate directly to your topic sentence.

◰ **Template for the five-paragraph essay**

Introduction (3–4 sentences)
    Lead (1–2 sentences)
    Link (1 sentence)
    Thesis and provable parts (1 sentence)

Body paragraph 1 (5+ sentences)
    Topic sentence (1 sentence)
    Supporting detail 1 (1–2 sentences)
    Supporting detail 2 (1–2 sentences)
    Supporting detail 3 (1–2 sentences)
    Concluding sentence (1 sentence)

Body paragraph 2 (5+ sentences)
    Topic sentence (1 sentence)
    Supporting detail 1 (1–2 sentences)
    Supporting detail 2 (1–2 sentences)
    Supporting detail 3 (1–2 sentences)
    Concluding sentence (1 sentence)

Body paragraph 3 (5+ sentences)
    Topic sentence (1 sentence)
    Supporting detail 1 (1–2 sentences)
    Supporting detail 2 (1–2 sentences)
    Supporting detail 3 (1–2 sentences)
    Concluding sentence (1 sentence)

Conclusion (3–4 sentences)
    Argument summary
    Rebuttal (optional)
    Restatement of thesis

End each of your body paragraphs with a concluding sentence that sums up the main idea of the paragraph and links directly to your thesis. Here's an example:

> In summary, it's clear that the positive impact on student compassion and empathy is a compelling argument for why pets should be incorporated into the classroom.

Conclusion

A strong concluding paragraph restates your provable parts, as well as your thesis. If you reach this point in your essay and you still have five minutes left, consider adding a rebuttal to your thesis. A rebuttal anticipates a point that an opponent might make and shows why the point is invalid or incorrect. Introduce your rebuttal with "Opponents of _____ claim that _____, but . . .". A rebuttal adds sophistication to your argument and tells the ACT readers that you have already thought about how to defend yourself against counterarguments. Here's an example of a rebuttal in the theoretical "pets in school" essay:

> While some opponents of school pets argue that allergies can prevent some students and classrooms from being able to enjoy the benefits of these animals, there are plenty of hypoallergenic animals that make excellent class pets, such as lizards, geckos, and snakes.

If you decide to include a rebuttal, put it in the middle of your conclusion. A rebuttal is a bonus, not a necessity, so don't worry if you don't have time to include one.

The last sentence of your conclusion should restate your thesis for the final time.

Writing 36 Strategy 2 *Pace yourself*

Make sure that you have enough time to write your essay. If you're still writing your second body paragraph when time is called, you won't score well. Half an hour is a surprisingly short period of time, and it can fly by when you're writing an essay.

To avoid nasty surprises on exam day, practice writing complete essays in the 30-minute time frame. Here's my recommendation for time allotment by task:

Brainstorming and outlining	5–7 minutes
Introduction	5 minutes
Body paragraph 1	5 minutes
Body paragraph 2	5 minutes
Body paragraph 3	5 minutes
Conclusion	3 minutes
Proofreading and review	0–2 minutes

As you can see, you have to write fairly quickly in order to finish in 30 minutes. The most important part of the essay process is the first five to seven minutes, in which you decide your position on the topic and select your key points. If you don't plan well, your essay will be weak and your score will suffer.

Practice writing strong outlines until you can consistently crank them out in five to seven minutes. When writing a 30-minute practice essay, wear a watch and keep track of how much time you spend on each component. If you exceed the 30-minute limit, you'll be able to determine where you need to speed up.

On the day of the exam, check your watch as you write. If you're falling behind, it's better to recognize it before the proctor calls the five-minute warning. Don't panic. One way to save time is to reduce the number of details in each body paragraph from three to two. As with other sections of the ACT, practice makes perfect: you can't expect to write a beautiful, organized, five-paragraph essay without practice.

Writing 36 Strategy 3 ⟋ *Use vocabulary to your advantage*

I'm sure you know that using big words is not the key to good writing. Still, the ACT readers have only a few minutes to judge your writing ability, and one way to impress them is to use complex vocabulary. Long words don't necessarily signify quality, so don't use big words just for the sake of using big words. Instead, use advanced vocabulary—one or two words in each paragraph, and at least two in your introduction. Try to incorporate some of the following words in your essay:

abhor	erratic	pragmatic
acclaim	flourish	pristine
adept	frivolous	prosperity
adversity	heed	quell
affluent	hinder	refute
apprehensive	impetuous	reproach
augment	indifferent	resilient
benign	innate	scorn
candid	jaded	succinct
chronic	keen	terse
concede	laconic	trivial
curtail	lament	veiled
denounce	lucid	vigilant
disparity	mollify	waver
dour	novel	zealous
elusive	ominous	
enhance	pliable	

An easy way to improve your vocabulary is to read educated books and magazines, including classic novels and readings assigned in English classes.

If you're unsure whether a word is appropriate in a particular context, don't use it. It is better to use a less sophisticated word correctly than a more sophisticated word incorrectly.

Writing 36 Strategy 4 ⁄ *Fill the space*

You may think that the ACT readers will only be concerned about what you write and how well you write it, but it matters a lot how *much* you write. Regardless of the size of your handwriting or the spacing you use between words, aim to fill four pages (both sides of two sheets of paper). If your handwriting is small, try to write larger; not only will you fill a page faster, but your handwriting will be easier to read. You can make the ACT readers happier by making your handwriting neat, large, and easy to read. If you want to score a perfect 6 in ACT Writing, you should fill *at least* four pages.

Writing 36 Strategy 5 ⁄ *Stay active*

The ACT readers will score your essay higher if you use the active voice. The verb is in the *active voice* when the subject of the sentence is performing the action.

> John caught the ball.
> Sarah cooked a delicious meal.
> The dog ate the biscuits.

In the *passive voice*, the subject is the receiver of the action.

> The ball was caught by John.
> A delicious meal was cooked by Sarah.
> The biscuits were eaten by the dog.

Because ACT readers strongly prefer the active voice, it's very important to "stay active."

Writing 36 Strategy 6 ⁄ *Transition smoothly*

Use transitions between ideas in your essay. Transitions make your sentences and ideas flow smoothly, and make your writing sound organized and well thought out. Here's a list of transition words and phrases you can use:

TO INTRODUCE AN IDEA
to start (with),
to begin (with),
initially,
primarily,
first and foremost,

TO TRANSITION BETWEEN SIMILAR IDEAS

furthermore,
moreover,
additionally,
in addition,
similarly,
in the same way,
likewise,

TO TRANSITION BETWEEN CONTRASTING IDEAS

on the other hand,
in contrast,
however,
nevertheless,
yet
even so,
despite that,

TO SUMMARIZE

thus,
in essence,
in conclusion,
in summary,
finally,

Writing 36 Strategy 7 ✒ *Don't get personal*

When you're stressed or running short on time, it's easy to resort to personal examples and narratives. Don't! Avoid at all costs the following words and phrases:

I	I think
me	I feel
myself	I feel like
mine	in my opinion,
you	the way I see it,
your	
yourself	
we	
us	
ourselves	
our	

Keep your writing impersonal. The only time it is acceptable to use a personal example in your writing is in the lead.

Writing 36 Strategy 8 *Plan, plan, plan*

The most important part of the essay process is the first five to seven minutes, when you plan your approach to the essay.

Take a deep breath. When the proctor calls time, open the exam booklet and read the question slowly, then read it again. Make sure you understand exactly what the ACT exam writers want you to answer. As quickly as possible, decide which position feels right to you. Some experts recommend taking the side that you think the readers will agree with, while others suggest taking the side that you think most students *won't* take.

My personal advice is to choose the position that you have the best examples for. The strongest essays are centered around solid evidence, so adopt the position that you know how to support.

In reality, it doesn't matter which side you choose. It's much worse to waste valuable time deliberating between the two sides. Pick a side, and start planning!

Jot down a thesis. (You can edit it later if necessary.) Once you have decided on your thesis and three provable parts, write out the topic sentences for your three body paragraphs. Now, you're ready to begin writing in earnest. Simply follow the five-paragraph template described earlier in the chapter.

Practice problem set **ACT Writing**

Write a thesis statement and three topic sentences for each of the following prompts:

Should all schools move to using a weighted GPA?

Should schools be separated by gender?

Should high school students have to fulfill a volunteering requirement in order to graduate?

Should high school teachers have to pass yearly examinations to make sure they are keeping their knowledge up-to-date?

Should high school students be required to spend a year abroad before going to college?

Practice a full-length ACT exam

Now that you've learned the ACT 36 strategies and worked dozens of example problems, it's time to practice an entire exam. On the following pages is a full-length ACT exam, and you should take it as if it's the real deal. Gather all your materials, including a timer, in a quiet space, sit down, and press START. Bubble your answers on the answer sheets on the next two pages.

After you've finished the exam, be sure to compare your answers to the solutions in Step 7, which contains the explanation for the answer to every one of the 215 problems on the practice exam. Make entries in your 36 Review notebook as recommended in the WORK TOGETHER section at the beginning of the book.

Good luck!

Answer sheets

Step 6
Practice a
full-length
ACT exam

248

Section 1 English

1 Ⓐ Ⓑ Ⓒ Ⓓ	21 Ⓐ Ⓑ Ⓒ Ⓓ	41 Ⓐ Ⓑ Ⓒ Ⓓ	61 Ⓐ Ⓑ Ⓒ Ⓓ
2 Ⓕ Ⓖ Ⓗ Ⓙ	22 Ⓕ Ⓖ Ⓗ Ⓙ	42 Ⓕ Ⓖ Ⓗ Ⓙ	62 Ⓕ Ⓖ Ⓗ Ⓙ
3 Ⓐ Ⓑ Ⓒ Ⓓ	23 Ⓐ Ⓑ Ⓒ Ⓓ	43 Ⓐ Ⓑ Ⓒ Ⓓ	63 Ⓐ Ⓑ Ⓒ Ⓓ
4 Ⓕ Ⓖ Ⓗ Ⓙ	24 Ⓕ Ⓖ Ⓗ Ⓙ	44 Ⓕ Ⓖ Ⓗ Ⓙ	64 Ⓕ Ⓖ Ⓗ Ⓙ
5 Ⓐ Ⓑ Ⓒ Ⓓ	25 Ⓐ Ⓑ Ⓒ Ⓓ	45 Ⓐ Ⓑ Ⓒ Ⓓ	65 Ⓐ Ⓑ Ⓒ Ⓓ
6 Ⓕ Ⓖ Ⓗ Ⓙ	26 Ⓕ Ⓖ Ⓗ Ⓙ	46 Ⓕ Ⓖ Ⓗ Ⓙ	66 Ⓕ Ⓖ Ⓗ Ⓙ
7 Ⓐ Ⓑ Ⓒ Ⓓ	27 Ⓐ Ⓑ Ⓒ Ⓓ	47 Ⓐ Ⓑ Ⓒ Ⓓ	67 Ⓐ Ⓑ Ⓒ Ⓓ
8 Ⓕ Ⓖ Ⓗ Ⓙ	28 Ⓕ Ⓖ Ⓗ Ⓙ	48 Ⓕ Ⓖ Ⓗ Ⓙ	68 Ⓕ Ⓖ Ⓗ Ⓙ
9 Ⓐ Ⓑ Ⓒ Ⓓ	29 Ⓐ Ⓑ Ⓒ Ⓓ	49 Ⓐ Ⓑ Ⓒ Ⓓ	69 Ⓐ Ⓑ Ⓒ Ⓓ
10 Ⓕ Ⓖ Ⓗ Ⓙ	30 Ⓕ Ⓖ Ⓗ Ⓙ	50 Ⓕ Ⓖ Ⓗ Ⓙ	70 Ⓕ Ⓖ Ⓗ Ⓙ
11 Ⓐ Ⓑ Ⓒ Ⓓ	31 Ⓐ Ⓑ Ⓒ Ⓓ	51 Ⓐ Ⓑ Ⓒ Ⓓ	71 Ⓐ Ⓑ Ⓒ Ⓓ
12 Ⓕ Ⓖ Ⓗ Ⓙ	32 Ⓕ Ⓖ Ⓗ Ⓙ	52 Ⓕ Ⓖ Ⓗ Ⓙ	72 Ⓕ Ⓖ Ⓗ Ⓙ
13 Ⓐ Ⓑ Ⓒ Ⓓ	33 Ⓐ Ⓑ Ⓒ Ⓓ	53 Ⓐ Ⓑ Ⓒ Ⓓ	73 Ⓐ Ⓑ Ⓒ Ⓓ
14 Ⓕ Ⓖ Ⓗ Ⓙ	34 Ⓕ Ⓖ Ⓗ Ⓙ	54 Ⓕ Ⓖ Ⓗ Ⓙ	74 Ⓕ Ⓖ Ⓗ Ⓙ
15 Ⓐ Ⓑ Ⓒ Ⓓ	35 Ⓐ Ⓑ Ⓒ Ⓓ	55 Ⓐ Ⓑ Ⓒ Ⓓ	75 Ⓐ Ⓑ Ⓒ Ⓓ
16 Ⓕ Ⓖ Ⓗ Ⓙ	36 Ⓕ Ⓖ Ⓗ Ⓙ	56 Ⓕ Ⓖ Ⓗ Ⓙ	
17 Ⓐ Ⓑ Ⓒ Ⓓ	37 Ⓐ Ⓑ Ⓒ Ⓓ	57 Ⓐ Ⓑ Ⓒ Ⓓ	
18 Ⓕ Ⓖ Ⓗ Ⓙ	38 Ⓕ Ⓖ Ⓗ Ⓙ	58 Ⓕ Ⓖ Ⓗ Ⓙ	
19 Ⓐ Ⓑ Ⓒ Ⓓ	39 Ⓐ Ⓑ Ⓒ Ⓓ	59 Ⓐ Ⓑ Ⓒ Ⓓ	
20 Ⓕ Ⓖ Ⓗ Ⓙ	40 Ⓕ Ⓖ Ⓗ Ⓙ	60 Ⓕ Ⓖ Ⓗ Ⓙ	

Section 2 Mathematics

1 Ⓐ Ⓑ Ⓒ Ⓓ Ⓔ	16 Ⓕ Ⓖ Ⓗ Ⓙ Ⓚ	31 Ⓐ Ⓑ Ⓒ Ⓓ Ⓔ	46 Ⓕ Ⓖ Ⓗ Ⓙ Ⓚ
2 Ⓕ Ⓖ Ⓗ Ⓙ Ⓚ	17 Ⓐ Ⓑ Ⓒ Ⓓ Ⓔ	32 Ⓕ Ⓖ Ⓗ Ⓙ Ⓚ	47 Ⓐ Ⓑ Ⓒ Ⓓ Ⓔ
3 Ⓐ Ⓑ Ⓒ Ⓓ Ⓔ	18 Ⓕ Ⓖ Ⓗ Ⓙ Ⓚ	33 Ⓐ Ⓑ Ⓒ Ⓓ Ⓔ	48 Ⓕ Ⓖ Ⓗ Ⓙ Ⓚ
4 Ⓕ Ⓖ Ⓗ Ⓙ Ⓚ	19 Ⓐ Ⓑ Ⓒ Ⓓ Ⓔ	34 Ⓕ Ⓖ Ⓗ Ⓙ Ⓚ	49 Ⓐ Ⓑ Ⓒ Ⓓ Ⓔ
5 Ⓐ Ⓑ Ⓒ Ⓓ Ⓔ	20 Ⓕ Ⓖ Ⓗ Ⓙ Ⓚ	35 Ⓐ Ⓑ Ⓒ Ⓓ Ⓔ	50 Ⓕ Ⓖ Ⓗ Ⓙ Ⓚ
6 Ⓕ Ⓖ Ⓗ Ⓙ Ⓚ	21 Ⓐ Ⓑ Ⓒ Ⓓ Ⓔ	36 Ⓕ Ⓖ Ⓗ Ⓙ Ⓚ	51 Ⓐ Ⓑ Ⓒ Ⓓ Ⓔ
7 Ⓐ Ⓑ Ⓒ Ⓓ Ⓔ	22 Ⓕ Ⓖ Ⓗ Ⓙ Ⓚ	37 Ⓐ Ⓑ Ⓒ Ⓓ Ⓔ	52 Ⓕ Ⓖ Ⓗ Ⓙ Ⓚ
8 Ⓕ Ⓖ Ⓗ Ⓙ Ⓚ	23 Ⓐ Ⓑ Ⓒ Ⓓ Ⓔ	38 Ⓕ Ⓖ Ⓗ Ⓙ Ⓚ	53 Ⓐ Ⓑ Ⓒ Ⓓ Ⓔ
9 Ⓐ Ⓑ Ⓒ Ⓓ Ⓔ	24 Ⓕ Ⓖ Ⓗ Ⓙ Ⓚ	39 Ⓐ Ⓑ Ⓒ Ⓓ Ⓔ	54 Ⓕ Ⓖ Ⓗ Ⓙ Ⓚ
10 Ⓕ Ⓖ Ⓗ Ⓙ Ⓚ	25 Ⓐ Ⓑ Ⓒ Ⓓ Ⓔ	40 Ⓕ Ⓖ Ⓗ Ⓙ Ⓚ	55 Ⓐ Ⓑ Ⓒ Ⓓ Ⓔ
11 Ⓐ Ⓑ Ⓒ Ⓓ Ⓔ	26 Ⓕ Ⓖ Ⓗ Ⓙ Ⓚ	41 Ⓐ Ⓑ Ⓒ Ⓓ Ⓔ	56 Ⓕ Ⓖ Ⓗ Ⓙ Ⓚ
12 Ⓕ Ⓖ Ⓗ Ⓙ Ⓚ	27 Ⓐ Ⓑ Ⓒ Ⓓ Ⓔ	42 Ⓕ Ⓖ Ⓗ Ⓙ Ⓚ	57 Ⓐ Ⓑ Ⓒ Ⓓ Ⓔ
13 Ⓐ Ⓑ Ⓒ Ⓓ Ⓔ	28 Ⓕ Ⓖ Ⓗ Ⓙ Ⓚ	43 Ⓐ Ⓑ Ⓒ Ⓓ Ⓔ	58 Ⓕ Ⓖ Ⓗ Ⓙ Ⓚ
14 Ⓕ Ⓖ Ⓗ Ⓙ Ⓚ	29 Ⓐ Ⓑ Ⓒ Ⓓ Ⓔ	44 Ⓕ Ⓖ Ⓗ Ⓙ Ⓚ	59 Ⓐ Ⓑ Ⓒ Ⓓ Ⓔ
15 Ⓐ Ⓑ Ⓒ Ⓓ Ⓔ	30 Ⓕ Ⓖ Ⓗ Ⓙ Ⓚ	45 Ⓐ Ⓑ Ⓒ Ⓓ Ⓔ	60 Ⓕ Ⓖ Ⓗ Ⓙ Ⓚ

Section 3   Reading

1 (A) (B) (C) (D)   11 (A) (B) (C) (D)   21 (A) (B) (C) (D)   31 (A) (B) (C) (D)
2 (F) (G) (H) (J)   12 (F) (G) (H) (J)   22 (F) (G) (H) (J)   32 (F) (G) (H) (J)
3 (A) (B) (C) (D)   13 (A) (B) (C) (D)   23 (A) (B) (C) (D)   33 (A) (B) (C) (D)
4 (F) (G) (H) (J)   14 (F) (G) (H) (J)   24 (F) (G) (H) (J)   34 (F) (G) (H) (J)
5 (A) (B) (C) (D)   15 (A) (B) (C) (D)   25 (A) (B) (C) (D)   35 (A) (B) (C) (D)
6 (F) (G) (H) (J)   16 (F) (G) (H) (J)   26 (F) (G) (H) (J)   36 (F) (G) (H) (J)
7 (A) (B) (C) (D)   17 (A) (B) (C) (D)   27 (A) (B) (C) (D)   37 (A) (B) (C) (D)
8 (F) (G) (H) (J)   18 (F) (G) (H) (J)   28 (F) (G) (H) (J)   38 (F) (G) (H) (J)
9 (A) (B) (C) (D)   19 (A) (B) (C) (D)   29 (A) (B) (C) (D)   39 (A) (B) (C) (D)
10 (F) (G) (H) (J)   20 (F) (G) (H) (J)   30 (F) (G) (H) (J)   40 (F) (G) (H) (J)

Section 4   Science

1 (A) (B) (C) (D)   11 (A) (B) (C) (D)   21 (A) (B) (C) (D)   31 (A) (B) (C) (D)
2 (F) (G) (H) (J)   12 (F) (G) (H) (J)   22 (F) (G) (H) (J)   32 (F) (G) (H) (J)
3 (A) (B) (C) (D)   13 (A) (B) (C) (D)   23 (A) (B) (C) (D)   33 (A) (B) (C) (D)
4 (F) (G) (H) (J)   14 (F) (G) (H) (J)   24 (F) (G) (H) (J)   34 (F) (G) (H) (J)
5 (A) (B) (C) (D)   15 (A) (B) (C) (D)   25 (A) (B) (C) (D)   35 (A) (B) (C) (D)
6 (F) (G) (H) (J)   16 (F) (G) (H) (J)   26 (F) (G) (H) (J)   36 (F) (G) (H) (J)
7 (A) (B) (C) (D)   17 (A) (B) (C) (D)   27 (A) (B) (C) (D)   37 (A) (B) (C) (D)
8 (F) (G) (H) (J)   18 (F) (G) (H) (J)   28 (F) (G) (H) (J)   38 (F) (G) (H) (J)
9 (A) (B) (C) (D)   19 (A) (B) (C) (D)   29 (A) (B) (C) (D)   39 (A) (B) (C) (D)
10 (F) (G) (H) (J)   20 (F) (G) (H) (J)   30 (F) (G) (H) (J)   40 (F) (G) (H) (J)

Section 5   Writing (optional)

Guidelines for scoring your essay are provided in the box "ACT Writing score sheet" at the beginning of Step 5.

SECTION 1
ENGLISH

45 minutes — 75 questions

> **DIRECTIONS:** In the passages that follow, some words and phrases are underlined and numbered. In the answer column, you will find alternatives for the words and phrases that are underlined. Choose the alternative that you think is best and fill in the corresponding bubble on your answer sheet. If you think that the original version is best, choose "NO CHANGE," which will always be either answer choice A or F.
>
> You will also find questions about a particular section of the passage, or about the entire passage. These questions will be identified by either an underlined portion or by a number in a box. Look for the answer that clearly expresses the idea, is consistent with the style and tone of the passage, and makes the correct use of standard written English. Read the passage through once before answering the questions. For some questions, you should read beyond the indicated portion before you answer.

Passage I

Minneapolis and St. Paul, dubbed "the Twin Cities," is a conjoined metropolis in the southeastern part of Minnesota. The history of the urban area began in the early 19th century with the arrival of the settlers; who began building a fort in the area in the year 1819.

Within only a few decades, the city has already grown to a remarkable size, and today Minneapolis has the largest population of any city in the state of Minnesota. [2] The city's name supposedly comes from *mni,* Dakota for "water," and *polis,* Greek for "city." The combined populations of Minneapolis and St. Paul make the metropolitan area the 16th larger in the United

1. **A.** NO CHANGE
   B. is
   C. are a
   D. are

2. **F.** NO CHANGE
   G. settlers. Who
   H. settlers, whom
   J. settlers, who

3. **A.** NO CHANGE
   B. had already grown
   C. will have already grown
   D. have already grown

4. **F.** NO CHANGE
   G. largest in
   H. largest of
   J. larger of

States, with close to 4 million residents. [5]

Residents of the Twin Cities have always been especially passionate about the outdoors: Minneapolis boasts the largest amount of land

dedicated to public parks between cities of similar densities. The city is also a great place for cultural

enthusiasts to visit an opera, to see a play, eating a variety of ethnic food, or to tour a museum. The Twin Cities is also a great place to watch sports—between the Twins, the Saints, the

Vikings, and the Gophers, its almost guaranteed there will be something to watch in a given week.

Minneapolis and St. Paul, although very near to one another, is still able to maintain their individual personalities and quirks. Anyone who

visits both cities is likely to find themselves surprised at how different the two are despite being so close to one another.

5. Sentence 2 of this paragraph:
   A. fits well where it is, because it has to do with the population of the city.
   B. fits well where it is, because it discusses the history of the city and its name.
   C. doesn't fit well where it is, because it doesn't have to do with the population of the city.
   D. doesn't fit well where it is, because it doesn't discuss the history of the city and its name.

6. F. NO CHANGE
   G. outdoors;
   H. outdoors—
   J. outdoors.

7. A. NO CHANGE
   B. between all the
   C. of
   D. among

8. F. NO CHANGE
   G. see a play, eat a variety of ethnic food, or tour a museum.
   H. seeing a play, eating a variety of ethnic food, or touring a museum.
   J. to see a play, to eating a variety of ethnic food, or to tour a museum.

9. A. NO CHANGE
   B. its' almost
   C. it's almost
   D. it was almost

10. F. NO CHANGE
    G. one another, were
    H. one another, was
    J. one another, are

11. A. NO CHANGE
    B. theirselves
    C. himself or herself
    D. him or her selves

If you get a chance to talk to a Minnesotan about the Twin Cities. Chances are they'll be pretty open about their love for the area.

As a former resident of the Twin Cities metro myself, I am keenly aware of the wealth of opportunities offered by the city. From theater productions to art shows to attending authentic

global cuisine, theres something for everyone. [15]

12. **F.** NO CHANGE
    G. Cities: chances
    H. Cities—chances
    J. Cities, chances

13. **A.** NO CHANGE
    B. attended
    C. attend
    D. DELETE the underlined portion.

14. **F.** NO CHANGE
    G. there's
    H. they'res
    J. theirs

Question 15 asks about the passage as a whole.

15. Suppose the writer had intended to write a persuasive essay convincing readers that they should move to the Twin Cities. Would this essay successfully fulfill the writer's goal?
    A. Yes, because the essay contains many reasons that living in the Twin Cities would be good.
    B. No, because the essay has no reasons why living in the Twin Cities might be nice.
    C. Yes, because the essay mentions many of the attractions that the Twin Cities have to offer.
    D. No, because while the essay lists some positive aspects of living in the Twin Cities, it is not designed to convince someone to move there.

Passage II

Synthetic biology is a fascinating new area of science that brings together the fields of biology or engineering. Research in synthetic biology

hope to design and build new biological systems that aren't already found in nature, such as

organisms capable of producing biofuels or to digest pollutants.

This exciting new field is relatively young in comparison to it's sisters in the engineering and pure sciences, largely due to the fact that the technologies that enable the field to make progress (DNA sequencing and fabrication, advanced modeling of proteins, and precise measures of gene activity) have only recently been developed. The term "synthetic biology" which was coined in the early 20th century has become somewhat of a buzzword in the scientific community as of

late; the number of students declaring majors in fields such as Systems Biology, Biosystems Engineering, and Bioengineering has risen exponentially across the country.

16. **F.** NO CHANGE
    G. together the fields of biology and engineering
    H. together: the fields of biology, or engineering
    J. together, the fields of biology and engineering

17. **A.** NO CHANGE
    B. hopes
    C. has hoped
    D. has been hoping

18. **F.** NO CHANGE
    G. producing biofuels, or to digest
    H. producing biofuels, or digesting
    J. producing biofuels or digesting

19. **A.** NO CHANGE
    B. its
    C. their
    D. DELETE the underlined portion.

20. **F.** NO CHANGE
    G. biology," that was coined in the early 20th century, has
    H. biology," which was coined in the early 20th century, has
    J. biology" that was coined in the early 20th century has

21. **A.** NO CHANGE
    B. late—the
    C. late. The
    D. late, the

Synthetic biology is somewhat of a conglomeration field, with approaches and technologies being integrated from biology, chemistry, computer science, and engineering. As such, a scientist who wants to succeed in the field must make sure to include in their education a wide variety of classes across different

disciplines. Someone who does good across a wide field of sciences and has strong creative intuition would be a great candidate for a career in synthetic biology.

However, synthetic biologists hail from a wide variety of backgrounds, including biology, chemistry, chemical engineering, computer science, and more. Thus, undergraduate students interested in synthetic biology when choosing they're classes, need not be too concerned about exactly which classes to take. As long as they

select from among the myriad offerings in science, chemistry, biology, and computer science, they are setting themselves up for success.

However, the new field is not without challenges. There are many important bioethical questions that still need answers. The backlash against genetically modified organisms (GMOs) currently used in agriculture have demonstrated

22. **F.** NO CHANGE
    G. conglomerate
    H. conglomorated
    J. conglomater

23. **A.** NO CHANGE
    B. in they're
    C. in there
    D. in his or her

24. **F.** NO CHANGE
    G. who do good across a
    H. who does well across a
    J. who do well across a

25. **A.** NO CHANGE
    B. As such,
    C. In contrast,
    D. Surprisingly,

26. **F.** NO CHANGE
    G. undergraduate students
        interested in synthetic biology,
        when choosing their classes,
    H. undergraduate students
        interested in synthetic biology.
        When choosing their classes,
    J. undergraduate students,
        interested in synthetic biology,
        when choosing they're classes,

27. **A.** NO CHANGE
    B. selects from among
    C. selects from between
    D. select from between

28. **F.** NO CHANGE
    G. challenges: there
    H. challenges; there
    J. challenges—there

29. **A.** NO CHANGE
    B. has been demonstrating
    C. demonstrates
    D. has demonstrated

that there is still considerable suspicion surrounds
the use of genetic modification in organisms used
for human consumption. A recently appointed
federal commission, the Presidential Commission
for the Study of Bioethical Issues, recently
released a report identifying key areas for federal
oversight in the future. As with any scientific
endeavor, the ability to make fundamental and
powerful changes goes hand in hand with the
responsibility to do so in a safe and humane way.

30. **F.** NO CHANGE
    G. surrounding
    H. that surrounds
    J. that will surround

Passage III

A few days after my sixth birthday, I received
what is probably the most asked-for present of all
<u>time, a pony.</u> Her name was Goldilocks, and from
                31
our very first ride together, we fell in love. Short,

fuzzy, and sweet, she was the <u>cuter</u> little pony
                                    32
anyone had ever seen.

I abandoned the use of a <u>saddle quick,</u> realizing
                          33
that it was far easier to simply swing onto her
broad back than to haul out all the heavy
equipment. I rarely used a saddle, and never
a bridle, <u>and it's likely</u> I took a few more
           34
tumbles from her than I might have. Aside from

<u>fractured</u> the growth plate in my wrist, however,
  35
I never had a bad fall, and would always simply
hop right back on.

<u>Never tiring of carting us children around, my</u>
                          36
<u>best friend and I used Goldilocks</u> in all of our
                          36
games, riding her double bareback through the

woods and fields <u>and we pretended</u> to be knights
                          37
and explorers.

31. A. NO CHANGE
B. time. A pony.
C. time a pony.
D. time: a pony.

32. F. NO CHANGE
G. cutest
H. cuter of the
J. most cutest

33. A. NO CHANGE
B. saddle,
C. saddle soon,
D. saddle quickly,

34. F. NO CHANGE
G. and its' likely
H. and its likely
J. and it was likely

35. A. NO CHANGE
B. a fractured
C. fracturing
D. having had fractured

36. F. NO CHANGE
G. Never tiring of carting us
children around, Goldilocks
was used by my best friend
and I
H. My best friend and I used
Goldilocks, who never tired
of carting us children around,
J. My best friend and I, never
tiring of carting us children
around, used Goldilocks

37. A. NO CHANGE
B. and having pretended
C. and pretending
D. and have pretended

On hot summer days, we would pack up picnics in a bag and carry it with us on our rides, stopping later in the day to break open and enjoy our snacks. Goldilocks always, without fail, tolerated our antics—letting us ride wearing cloaks and costumes and all sorts of odd items.

[1] Each week in first grade one single student was chosen as "star of the week," and got a few minutes at the beginning of the day to show or tell the class something about themselves. I, of course, brought Goldilocks to school so everyone could see the little pony that I was lucky enough to have. The class oohed over her soft nose and fuzzy mane and tail, and many were brave enough to feed her carrots. 42

Even now, when I'm in college, she's still living in the same pasture where I rode her for all those years, probably enjoying the peace and quiet now that I've grown up and moved away. As such, I think part of her might miss the squealing little girls that used to ride her and all the fun we had.

As I moved out of elementary school and into middle school, I rode her less and less as other commitments started draining my time.

38. F. NO CHANGE
G. carried them
H. carried it
J. carry them

39. A. NO CHANGE
B. always would tolerate
C. always, without fail, would tolerate
D. always tolerated

40. F. NO CHANGE
G. one student
H. only one single student
J. some student

41. A. NO CHANGE
B. his or herself.
C. himself or herself.
D. theirselves.

42. For the most effective paragraph structure, the first sentence of this paragraph should be placed:
F. where it is now, because it introduces the context for the rest of the paragraph.
G. where it is now, because it links this paragraph to the one before it.
H. at the end of the paragraph, because it summarizes the main idea.
J. at the end of the paragraph, because it links this paragraph to the one after it.

43. A. NO CHANGE
B. Still,
C. Thus,
D. As a result,

She was always there for me, though. Standing [44]
quietly and letting me hug her tightly when I was
unsure of something, or letting me kiss her soft
nose those nights that I ran out of the house and
down to the barn in the middle of the night to
see her. [45]

44. **F.** NO CHANGE
    G. She was always there for me,
       though, standing
    H. She was always there for me,
       though: standing
    J. She was always there for me,
       though; standing

> Question 45 asks about the passage
> as a whole.

45. For the most logical organization
    of the essay, the final paragraph
    should be placed:
    A. where it is, at the end, because
       it summarizes the main idea
       of the whole essay.
    B. before the second-to-last
       paragraph, so it fits with the
       chronology of the rest of the
       essay.
    C. at the beginning of the essay,
       because it introduces an idea
       that's central to the rest of the
       paragraphs.
    D. It should be removed, since it
       doesn't fit with the rest of the
       essay.

Passage IV

As your teacher drones on and on, you're eyes starts to feel heavy and you let
₄₆
yourself lean your head against the wall next

to you. Before you know it, BANG!, the teacher
₄₇
has slammed his hand down on the desk, catching

you sleeping in class for the third day in a row.

He has frowned and shaken his head, walking
₄₈
away and muttering about "kids these days."

Situations such as the one described are

commonplace in middle and high school

classrooms across the country, as alarming high
₄₉
numbers of students are suffering from sleep

deprivation. In fact, more than half of high school

students in the United States get less then the
₅₀
recommended 8 hours of sleep per night.

Every night that one gets less sleep than
₅₁
the ideal amount contributes to what is called
₅₁

a student's "sleep debt." The more likely you
₅₂
are to suffer both physical and psychological
₅₂
impairments, the larger your sleep debt.
₅₂

46. F. NO CHANGE
G. your eyes starts
H. you're eyes start
J. your eyes start

47. A. NO CHANGE
B. know it—BANG!—the teacher
C. know it. BANG! the teacher
D. know it, "BANG!", the teacher

48. F. NO CHANGE
G. frowned and shook
H. is frowning and shaking
J. frowns and shakes

49. A. NO CHANGE
B. as alarmingly high
C. as alarmingly, surprisingly high
D. alarming highly

50. F. NO CHANGE
G. less than the
H. fewer than the
J. fewer then the

51. A. NO CHANGE
B. , that one gets less sleep than the ideal amount,
C. —that one gets less sleep than the ideal amount—
D. that one gets less sleep than the ideal amount,

52. F. NO CHANGE
G. The more likely you are to suffer both physical and psychological impairments, because of your sleep debt.
H. The larger your sleep debt, the more likely you are to suffer both physical and psychological impairments.
J. Larger sleep debt, more likely to suffer both physical and psychological impairments.

The most debilitating physical effects of sleep deprivation include: light-headedness, headaches, drowsiness, nausea, and fainting. Athletes
₅₃

especially will notice there performance
₅₄
suffering, as muscles need the time when the body is sleeping to repair themselves. Mental affects of sleep deprivation include decreased
₅₅

focus, impaired memory, and reducing mental
₅₆
quickness.
₅₆
  In order to avoid accumulating a sleep debt, try to get at least 8 hours of sleep per night. For every hour less than 8 that you get, you'll be
₅₇
adding to your sleep debt, and you'll have to sleep
₅₇
that much longer than 8 hours to erase those hours from your cumulative sleep debt.

Studies conducted by researchers at Stanford
₅₈
University has shown that there's a "maximum"
₅₈
of 40 hours that you can accumulate as part of your sleep debt. If you know you'll be getting less than the necessary amount of sleep during the

53. A. NO CHANGE
   B. include light-headedness, headaches, drowsiness, nausea,
   C. include: light-headedness; headaches; drowsiness; nausea;
   D. including light-headedness, headaches, drowsiness, nausea,

54. F. NO CHANGE
   G. notice they're
   H. notice their
   J. notice his or her

55. A. NO CHANGE
   B. affects due to sleep
   C. effects due to sleep
   D. effects of sleep

56. F. NO CHANGE
   G. and mental quickness that is reduced.
   H. and reduced mental quickness.
   J. and mental quickness having been reduced.

57. A. NO CHANGE
   B. Every hour fewer than the recommended 8 is added to your sleep debt, and you'll
   C. For every hour fewer than 8 that you get, you'll be adding to your sleep debt and
   D. For every hour less than 8 that you get you'll be adding to your sleep debt and you'll

58. F. NO CHANGE
   G. Studies conducted by researchers at Stanford University have
   H. Studies, conducted by researchers at Stanford University, have
   J. Studies, conducted by researchers at Stanford University, has

week; plan ahead and sleep in during the weekend
59
to make up for those hours. Avoiding sleep

deprivation is a very important part of succeeding
60
as a student, athlete, and to maintain your health.
60

59. **A.** NO CHANGE
    B. week, plan ahead and sleep
    C. week, plan ahead, and sleep
    D. week: plan ahead and sleep

60. **F.** NO CHANGE
    G. of success as a student, athlete, and maintainer of your health.
    H. of succeeding as a student and an athlete, and maintaining your health.
    J. of maintaining your health and succeeding as a student and an athlete.

Passage V

When the Dutch gave the name of Katzbergs
to the mountains west of the Hudson, by reason
of the wildcats <u>and panthers which ranged there,</u>
₆₁
they obliterated the beautiful Indian Ontiora,
"mountains of the sky." In one tradition

<u>of the red men, these</u> hills were bones of a monster
₆₂
that fed on human beings until the Great Spirit
turned <u>it into stone: it was floundering</u> toward the
₆₃
ocean to bathe. The two lakes near the summit

were <u>it's eyes.</u>
₆₄

An Indian <u>witch, living in these peaks,</u>
₆₅
<u>who adjusted</u> the weather for the Hudson Valley
₆₅
with the certainty of a signal service bureau.
It was she who let out the day and night

<u>in blessed alternation, she held</u> back the one
₆₆
when the other was at large, for fear of conflict.

Old moons <u>she cut in to stars</u> as soon as she had
₆₇
hung new ones in the sky, and she was often seen
perched on Round Top and North Mountain,
spinning clouds and flinging them to the winds.

61. A. NO CHANGE
B. and panthers, which ranged there,
C. and panthers that ranged there,
D. and panthers when they ranged there,

62. F. NO CHANGE
G. of the red men these
H. of the Red men, these
J. of the red men, the

63. A. NO CHANGE
B. it into stone as it was floundering
C. it into stone, floundering
D. it into stone. It was floundering

64. F. NO CHANGE
G. was it's eyes.
H. were its eyes.
J. were it's eyes.

65. A. NO CHANGE
B. These peaks were home to an Indian witch, adjusting
C. An Indian witch living in these peaks adjusted
D. An Indian Witch living in these peaks adjusted

66. F. NO CHANGE
G. in blessed alternation that is, she held
H. in blessed alternation, holding
J. in blessed alternation where she held

67. A. NO CHANGE
B. she cut them in to stars
C. she cut into stars
D. she cut from stars

Woe betide the valley residents if they

showed irreverence, then the clouds were black
                                         68
and heavy, and through them she poured floods

of rain and launched the lightning, causing

disastrous freshets in the streams and blasting the

wigwams of the mockers. She would take the form

of a bear or a deer and lead the Indian hunters on

anything but a merry dance, exposing them to fire

and peril, then vanishing or assuming some

terrible shape because they had overtaken her.
                       69
   Sometimes she would lead them to the coves

and would leap into the air with a mocking

"Ho, ho!" just as they stopped with a shudder
                          70
at the brink of an abyss.

   Garden Rock was a spot where she was

often found, and at its foot a lake once spread.

This was held in such awe that the Indians would
                  71
never wittingly pursue their quarry there; but once,

a hunter lost his way and emerged from the forest

at the edge of the pond. Seeing a number of gourds

in crotches of the trees, he took one, but feared the
                                      72
spirit, he turned to leave so quickly that he

stumbled and the gourd fell.

   The water didn't cease running, and in these

times the stream born of the witch's revenge is
                              73
known as Catskill Creek. [2] As it broke, a spring
  73
welled from it in such volume that the unhappy

68. F. NO CHANGE
G. showed irreverence, which then the clouds
H. showed irreverence for then the clouds
J. showed irreverence, for then the clouds

69. A. NO CHANGE
B. terrible shape so they'd think they
C. terrible shape, because they
D. terrible shape when they

70. F. NO CHANGE
G. just as, they stopped with a shudder
H. stopped with a shudder
J. just as they stopped, with a shudder

71. To write the first part of this sentence in the active voice:
A. NO CHANGE
B. Garden Rock was held in such awe that the Indians
C. Held in such awe, the Indians
D. The Indians held this in such awe that they

72. F. NO CHANGE
G. but fearing the
H. and fearing the
J. and feared the

73. A. NO CHANGE
B. witches revenge is known as
C. witch's revenge, is known as
D. witchs' revenge known as,

man was engulfed in its waters, swept to the edge

of <u>Kaaterskill Cove and dashed</u> on the rocks 260
       74

feet below. 75

Step 6
Practice a
full-length
ACT exam
....
264

74. F. NO CHANGE
G. Kaaterskill Cove, and dashed
H. Kaaterskill Cove, and dashing
J. Kaaterskill Cove and dashing

75. The second sentence of this
paragraph should be placed:

A. where it is, because it explains
the reason behind the naming
of the creek.
B. where it is, because it ends
the paragraph with climactic
action.
C. before the first sentence,
because it provides back-
ground for the naming of the
creek.
D. before the first sentence,
because it introduces the topic
of the paragraph.

STOP!
END OF THE ENGLISH TEST

**If you have time left over,
you may check your work on this section only.**

> **DIRECTIONS:** Solve each of the problems in the time allowed, then fill in the corresponding bubble on your answer sheet. Do not spend too much time on any one problem; skip the more difficult problems and go back to them later. You may use a calculator on this test. For this test you should assume that figures are NOT necessarily drawn to scale, that all geometric figures lie in a plane, that the word *line* is used to indicate a straight line, and that the word *average* indicates arithmetic mean.

1. If $x = 3$, what is the value of the expression $y = x(x + 4)^3$?

   A. 21
   B. 27
   C. 1,029
   D. 9,261
   E. 10,296

2. Beanblaster sells 12 pounds of coffee for $39.99, while its competitor, JavaJuice, sells 16 pounds of the same coffee for $54.99. Which distributor sells its coffee cheapest by the pound, and how much does it charge per pound?

   F. Beanblaster, at $0.30 per pound
   G. Beanblaster, at $3.33 per pound
   H. Beanblaster, at $3.44 per pound
   J. JavaJuice, at $0.30 per pound
   K. JavaJuice, at $3.33 per pound

3. A ladder that is 24 feet long is leaning against the top of a wall that is 16 feet high. How many feet is the ladder from the base of the wall?

   A. 8
   B. 16
   C. 24
   D. 32
   E. $\sqrt{320}$

4. Consider the following 3 statements to be true:

All men that are tall play basketball.
Man A does not play basketball.
Man B is tall.

Which of the following statements is necessarily true?

F. Man A is a tall man who does not play basketball.
G. Man A is a short man who does not play basketball.
H. Man A plays basketball.
J. Man B plays basketball.
K. Man B is not tall.

5. The local garbage collector charges its residential customers $20 per month for its basic service and $10 per week for recycling pickup. Which of the following accurately depicts the formula for determining the cost of the basic service plus x recycling pickups, per month, in dollars?

A. $20 + 10x$
B. 20x$ + 10x$
C. $20 + $10
D. 20x$ + $10
E. 200x$

6. What is the value of x that satisfies the equation $x^2 + 3x = x$?

F. -1
G. 1
H. -2
J. 2
K. -2^2

7. In the following diagram, *E* is a point on line *DF*, *H* is a point on line *GI*, *DF* is parallel to *GI*, and *HE* is congruent with *IE*. What is the measurement of *EHG*?

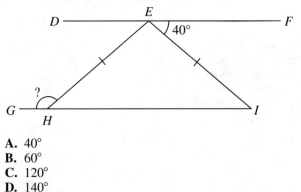

A. 40°
B. 60°
C. 120°
D. 140°
E. 144°

8. What is the least common denominator that can be used to add the following fractions?

$$\frac{e}{2}, \frac{f}{4}, \frac{g}{6}, \frac{h}{8}$$

F. 8
G. 12
H. 16
J. 18
K. 24

9. Which of the following expressions is equivalent to $2x(x^2 + xy - 2xy)$?

A. $-2x^2y + 2x^3$
B. $-2x^2y - 2x^3$
C. $2x^2y + 2x$
D. $-x^2y - x^3$
E. $-2x^2y$

10. A certain type of automobile tire is on sale for $125 each. If you buy 3 tires, you receive the fourth tire free. What is the cost per tire if you decide to purchase 4 tires?

F. $500
G. $375.13
H. $125.25
J. $95.75
K. $93.75

11. For all x, $(2x + 1)^3 = ?$

    A. $6x + 3$
    B. $9x^2 + 3x + 3$
    C. $8x^3 + 12x^2 + x + 3$
    D. $8x^3 + 12x^2 + 6x + 1$
    E. $8x^3 + 12x^2 + 6x$

Step 6
Practice a
full-length
ACT exam

268

12. Olivia and her sister Gabby own a clothing shop that sells women's outfits. A single outfit consists of 1 blouse, 1 skirt, and 1 pair of shoes. If their clothing shop stocks 10 types of blouses, 5 types of skirts, and 3 types of shoes, how many unique outfits can Olivia and Gabby's shop sell?

    F. 10
    G. 15
    H. 50
    J. 150
    K. 450

13. If $c^2 = 64$ and $d^2 = 81$, which of the following CANNOT be a value of $c - d$?

    A. -1
    B. 1
    C. 17
    D. -17
    E. 155

14. On the real number line, what is the midpoint between -10 and 22?

    F. -6
    G. 6
    H. -12
    J. 12
    K. 16

15. If $2\dfrac{1}{3} = x^2 + \left(-x + \dfrac{1}{3}\right)$, then $x = ?$

    A. $-\dfrac{2}{3}$

    B. $\dfrac{2}{3}$

    C. -2

    D. 2

    E. $\dfrac{1}{3}$

16. A system of linear equations includes the following:

$y = 3x + 4$
$y = 3x - 4$

Which of the following accurately describes the graph of this system of equations on the standard (x, y) coordinate plane?

F. Two intersecting lines
G. Two parallel lines with a positive slope
H. Two parallel lines with a negative slope
J. A single line with a positive slope
K. A single line with a negative slope

17. What real number can be substituted for x to solve the equation $(3^x)(3) = x^4$?

A. 2
B. 3
C. 4
D. 5
E. -3

18. The following graph shows a line plotted on the standard (x, y) coordinate plane. If the points plotted were rotated $180°$ about the origin, what 2 quadrants would the line now pass through?

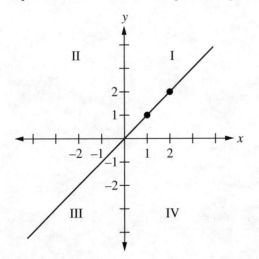

F. I and II
G. II and III
H. III and IV
J. I and IV
K. I and III

19. On the real number line, with coordinates set as labeled on the diagram below, a certain object moves as follows: starting at *B*, the object moves to the right to *D*, then to the left to *C*, then to the left to *B*, and finally returning to the right to *D*.

$$\begin{array}{cccc} A & B & C & D \\ \end{array}$$

$$\begin{array}{ccccccc} -6 & -4 & -2 & 0 & 2 & 4 & 6 \end{array}$$

Which of the following most closely estimates how far the object moves, in coordinate units, on the number line?

A. 8
B. 12
C. 16
D. 24
E. 32

20. If, by definition, the determinant of $\begin{bmatrix} e & f \\ g & h \end{bmatrix}$ equals $eh - fg$, then what is the value of the determinant of $\begin{bmatrix} 3x & 4y \\ 5x & 3y \end{bmatrix}$ if $x = 2$ and $y = -3$?

F. -33
G. -66
H. 33
J. 66
K. -174

21. Scruffy was refilling his bottles of cleaning solution. The smaller of the two bottles was $\frac{3}{4}$ full, but was only $\frac{1}{2}$ as large as the larger bottle. The larger bottle was only $\frac{1}{4}$ full. Scruffy decided to pour the contents of the smaller bottle into the larger bottle. How full was the larger bottle after Scruffy finished pouring?

A. $\frac{1}{2}$ full

B. $\frac{3}{4}$ full

C. $\frac{5}{8}$ full

D. Completely full

E. Overflowing

22. Before Emma goes out on a date, she spends 20 minutes choosing her outfit. The equation $d = m + 20$ represents the time, in minutes, that Emma has set aside for a date of m minutes, including the time she needs to choose her outfit. Which of the following statements is necessarily true, according to Emma's model?

F. She sets aside 20 minutes per date.
G. She sets aside 30 minutes per date.
H. She sets aside 90 minutes per date, 20 of which is spent choosing a restaurant.
J. She sets aside 80 minutes for a 60-minute date.
K. She sets aside 60 minutes per date, and figures in 30 minutes of travel time.

23. Fry flew 100,000 miles in 4 hours of actual flight time. If he had broken the intergalactic speed limit and had flown 25,000 miles per hour faster, how much travel time would he have saved, in hours?

A. 4
B. 2
C. 1
D. $\dfrac{1}{2}$
E. $\dfrac{1}{4}$

24. Assuming that the inequality $|c| > |d|$ is true, which of the following MUST be true?

F. $c = d$
G. $c < d$
H. $c > d$
J. $c = 0$
K. $c \neq d$

25. What is the slope of a line given by the equation $10x - 8y + 11 = 0$?

A. $\dfrac{4}{5}$
B. $-\dfrac{4}{5}$
C. $\dfrac{10}{8}$
D. $-\dfrac{10}{8}$
E. 10

26. Which of the following satisfies a value of x in the equation $\log_x 16 = 2$?

F. 2
G. 3
H. 4
J. 5
K. 8

Step 6

Practice a full-length ACT exam

272

27. In triangle CDE, G, H, and F are points on lines CD, DE, and EC, respectively. Lines FH and GH are congruent. What is the sum of the angles marked x and y?

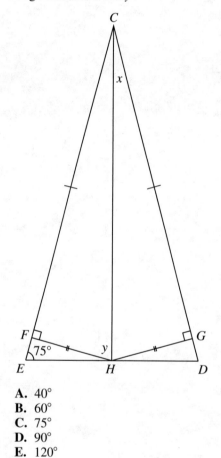

A. 40°
B. 60°
C. 75°
D. 90°
E. 120°

28. Which of the following expressions is equivalent to $(-3x^3y^3)^4$?

F. $9x^4y^4$

G. $-9x^4y^4$

H. $81x^{12}y^{12}$

J. $-81x^{12}y^{12}$

K. $162x^{24}y^{24}$

29. A line contains the points C, D, E, and F. Point D is between points C and F, and point E is between C and D. Which of the following equations MUST be true about the lengths of these segments?

A. $CF < DF$

B. $CF > DF$

C. $CE < CF$

D. $CD < CF$

E. $ED = CF$

30. Which of the following inequalities correctly defines the solution set for the inequality $8 - 3x \le 4$?

F. $x \ge \dfrac{4}{3}$

G. $x \ge \dfrac{3}{4}$

H. $x \ge -\left(\dfrac{3}{4}\right)$

J. $x \ge -\left(\dfrac{4}{3}\right)$

K. $x \ge -4$

31. The electrical resistance, r ohms, of 100 feet of sterling silver wire at 70°F can be approximately figured by the model $r = \left[\dfrac{5690}{d^2}\right] - 0.37$ for any wire diameter, d mils (1 mil = 0.001 inch), such that $1 \le d \le 75$. What is the approximate resistance, in ohms, for 100 feet of sterling silver wire with a diameter of 45 mils?

A. -1.74

B. 2.44

C. 4.44

D. 12.62

E. 126.30

32. The solution set of $\sqrt{(x-1)} > 4$ is a set of all real numbers x such that:

F. $x > 5$.
G. $x > 6$.
H. $x > 12$.
J. $x > 16$.
K. $x > 17$.

33. Suppose that the measure of each interior angle of a regular polygon with n sides is $\left[\dfrac{(n-1)180}{n}\right]$ degrees. What is the measure of each interior angle of a regular polygon with n sides, in *radians*?

A. $\left[\dfrac{(n-1)\pi}{n}\right]$

B. $\left[\dfrac{(n-1)\pi^2}{n}\right]$

C. $\left[\dfrac{(n-1)\pi}{n}\right]^2$

D. $\left[\dfrac{\pi}{n-1}\right]$

E. $\left[\dfrac{\pi}{n-1}\right]^2$

34. What is the distance, in coordinate units, between the points $(-2,4)$ and $(4,-2)$ on the standard (x,y) coordinate plane?

F. 12
G. $2\sqrt{3}$
H. 72
J. $6\sqrt{2}$
K. -12

35. The diagram below is a top-down view of a barrel of hydrochloric acid with 2 rectangular supports attached to its bottom for stability. The interior radius of the barrel, as shown, is 8 feet. The interior length of the barrel is 50 feet.

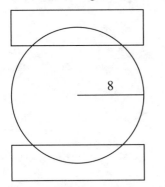

Which of the following is closest to the barrel's volume, in cubic feet?

A. 2,500
B. 5,000
C. 10,000
D. 20,000
E. 24,000

36. The barrel currently holds 12,000 gallons of acid. If a gallon of hydrochloric acid weighs 7 pounds, which of the following most closely approximates the weight of the acid, in pounds?

F. 8,400
G. 12,800
H. 64,000
J. 84,000
K. 124,000

37. The barrel is insulated so that the acid doesn't leak out. Which of the following expressions gives the volume of the metal used in the barrel (assume the circular ends and curved walls all have the same thickness) if the external dimensions are a radius of R feet and a length of L feet and the interior dimensions are a radius of 8 feet and a length of 50 feet.

A. $\pi R^2 L - 3,200\pi$
B. $\pi R L - 1,600\pi$
C. $\pi R^3 - 3,200\pi$
D. $\pi R^3 L - 3,200\pi$
E. $\pi R^2 L - 400\pi$

38. Canvas Unlimited is manufacturing a new style of bottomless canvas tent. The following diagram shows the height, length, and diagonal measurements, in feet, of the prototype of the tent. Based on these measurements, how many square feet of canvas would it take to completely cover the bottom of the tent, should the company decide to include an optional tent floor?

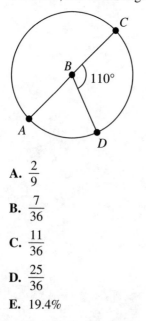

    F. 67
    G. 84
    H. 166
    J. 384
    K. 484

39. Points A and C are endpoints of the diameter of a circle with its center marked as B, as shown in the following diagram. Point D lies on the circle, and angle CBD has a measurement of $110°$. What percentage of the circle's area, written as a fraction, lies within angle ABD?

    A. $\dfrac{2}{9}$

    B. $\dfrac{7}{36}$

    C. $\dfrac{11}{36}$

    D. $\dfrac{25}{36}$

    E. 19.4%

40. Scott is going to cover a valuable painting with a sheet before painting the walls of his house. Assuming the length and width of the painting are 3 feet and its depth is 6 inches, what is the area of the smallest possible amount of fabric needed to completely cover the front and 4 sides of the painting?

   F. 15 square feet
   G. 16 square feet
   H. 21 square feet
   J. 24 square feet
   K. 36 square feet

41. For the right triangle shown below, which expression is equivalent to $(\tan B)(\sin A)$?

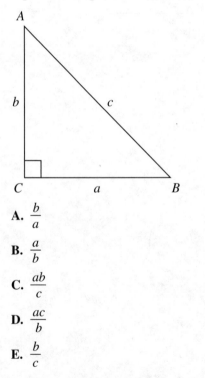

   A. $\dfrac{b}{a}$

   B. $\dfrac{a}{b}$

   C. $\dfrac{ab}{c}$

   D. $\dfrac{ac}{b}$

   E. $\dfrac{b}{c}$

Step 6
Practice a
full-length
ACT exam
....
278

42. A swimming pool is being filled with water by means of a garden hose, the end of which lies at the bottom of the pool. The following diagram shows the rate that water fills the pool as a function of depth over time.

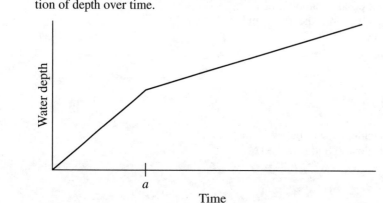

An event, marked *a,* occurred that indicated a drop in the rate of increase in the depth of the water. Which of the following could account for this event?

I. The flow of water coming from the hose increased.
II. The flow of water coming from the hose decreased.
III. The drain at the bottom of the pool was opened.

F. I only
G. II only
H. I and II only
J. II and III only
K. III only

43. Which of the following statements is/are true for the equation $y = 4x + 1$, assuming that $0 \le x \le 10$ and that the equation is plotted on the standard (x, y) coordinate plane?

I. The line plotted has a positive slope.
II. The line plotted has a negative slope.
III. The line plotted is parallel to the x-axis.

A. I only
B. II only
C. III only
D. I and III only
E. None of these statements is true.

44. Two parabolas plotted on the standard (x,y) coordinate plane both have vertices at point $(0,0)$ and intersect one another only at their vertices. Which of the following statements accurately describe(s) these parabolas?

   I. Each parabola must be described with an identical function.

   II. Each parabola must be described with a different function.

   III. A line that intersects one of the parabolas must intersect both parabolas.

  F. I only

  G. II only

  H. III only

  J. I and III only

  K. None of these statements is accurate.

45. Nortonic Industries has developed a cold-weather power cable with a radius of 4 inches, of which 3 inches are the internal copper wire and 1 inch is a weatherproof insulation, as shown in the diagram below. Which of the following most closely approximates the percentage of the cable composed of copper wire?

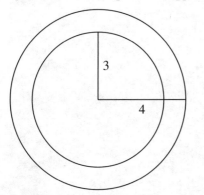

  A. 22%

  B. 24%

  C. 55%

  D. 56%

  E. 79%

46. If the ratio of a to b is 4 to 5, and the ratio of b to c is 8 to 10, what is the ratio of a to c?

  F. 1 to 4

  G. 2 to 3

  H. 4 to 5

  J. 8 to 10

  K. 16 to 25

47. Which of the following accurately represents the inequality shown on the following real number line?

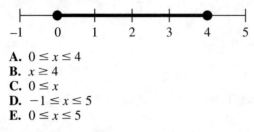

A. $0 \leq x \leq 4$

Step 6
Practice a
full-length
ACT exam

B. $x \geq 4$
C. $0 \leq x$
D. $-1 \leq x \leq 5$
E. $0 \leq x \leq 5$

48. If $(x - 6)$ is a factor of $x^2 + x + k$, what is the value of k?

F. -14
G. -48
H. 42
J. 7
K. The correct answer is not given.

49. Assume that $b = 10a + 2c + 10$. What will happen to the value of b if the value of a is increased by 2 and the value of c is decreased by 1?

A. It will increase by 22.
B. It will increase by 18.
C. It will decrease by 22.
D. It will decrease by 18.
E. It will stay the same.

50. A massive cube has edges that are 10 times as long as those of a small cube. How many times greater is the volume of the massive cube than the small cube?

F. 10
G. 100
H. 1,000
J. 10,000
K. 125,000

51. A circle has a diameter of 10 feet. Imagine that the circle is bisected (divided into 2 equal parts) and one of the parts is removed. What is the area, in square feet, of the remaining part?

A. 39
B. 79
C. 157
D. 314
E. The correct answer is not given.

52. In a city of 10,000 people, there are 2,000 men with an average age of 45 and 8,000 women with an average age of 25. What is the average age of the city's population, to the nearest year?

F. 27
G. 29
H. 31
J. 32
K. 33

53. On January 1, the price of a given cummerbund was $150. On March 1, the price was reduced by 10%. On July 1, the price was reduced by an additional 15%. On December 1, the price was reduced by an additional 25%. Assuming that the price wasn't changed after December 1, what is the price of the cummerbund at the end of the year?

A. $86.06
B. $114.75
C. $135
D. $147.75
E. The correct price is not given.

54. $4x^2 * 3x^3y^2 * 3x^3y^2$ is equivalent to which of the following?

F. $36x^5y^2$
G. $36x^8y^4$
H. $32x^6y^2$
J. $32x^8y^4$
K. $10x^8y^4$

55. Professor Fry teaches 204 days of the year, and his annual salary is $10,770. At Professor Fry's university, substitute teachers are paid $104 per day. If Professor Fry takes 36 days off with no pay and a substitute teacher is paid to teach his classes, how much more will the university have paid by using a substitute on those 36 days?

A. $180.41
B. $220.43
C. $1,843.56
D. $2,083.66
E. $2,204.30

56. The carbon dioxide (CO_2) level of a lake is found by dividing the amount of dissolved CO_2 in one liter of the lake's water by the dissolved CO_2 capacity per liter of the water and expressing the outcome as a percentage. If Finglonger Lake contains 4.7 milligrams of dissolved CO_2 per liter of water and the dissolved CO_2 capacity of the lake's water is 6.7 milligrams per liter, what is the CO_2 level of Finglonger Lake, to the nearest percentage point?

    F. 47%
    G. 94%
    H. 58%
    J. 61%
    K. 70%

57. A farm plot, in the shape of an equilateral triangle whose sides are 220 feet long, is completely fenced in. Which of the following most closely approximates the area, in square feet, of the farm plot?

    A. 660
    B. 21,000
    C. 24,000
    D. 12,000
    E. 42,000

58. If y is a real number such that $y^3 = 216$, then $y^2 + \sqrt{y} = ?$

    F. 8
    G. 8.45
    H. 180
    J. 19.45
    K. 38.45

59. If 1 candy is randomly picked from a box that contains 8 red candies, 10 blue candies, and 4 white candies, what is the probability that it will be a white candy?

    A. $\dfrac{1}{11}$

    B. $\dfrac{2}{11}$

    C. $\dfrac{4}{22}$

    D. $\dfrac{8}{22}$

    E. The correct answer is not given.

60. The number of packages delivered by a certain delivery company over the course of 1 year is sorted by destination, as shown in the following matrix:

$$\begin{bmatrix} \text{New York} & \text{Boston} & \text{Chicago} & \text{Portland} \\ 70 & 50 & 25 & 125 \end{bmatrix}$$

The head delivery boy estimates the percentage of packages that will actually be paid for by the end of the year as follows:

New York   .50
Boston   .50
Chicago   .28
Portland   .56

What is the total number of packages the head delivery boy expects to receive payment for by the end of the year?

F. 37
G. 74
H. 124
J. 135
K. 137

STOP!
END OF THE MATHEMATICS TEST

If you have time left over,
you may check your work on this section only.

SECTION 3
READING

35 minutes — 40 questions

DIRECTIONS: This test includes four passages, each followed by ten questions. Read the passages and choose the best answer to each question. After you have selected your answer, fill in the corresponding bubble on your answer sheet. You should refer to the passages as often as necessary when answering the questions.

Passage I

PROSE FICTION: This passage is adapted from the book *Oil* by Upton Sinclair (1927).

The number of the house was 5746 Los Robles Boulevard, and you would have had to know this land of hope in order to realize that it stood in a cabbage field. Los Robles means "the oaks"; and two or three
5 miles away, where this boulevard started in the heart of Beach City, there were four live oak trees. But out here there was just a bare slope of hill, plowed and trenched and covered with cabbages, with sugar beets down on the flat.

10 Two years ago the "subdividers" had been here; there had been full-page advertisements in the newspapers, and free auto rides from Beach City, and a free lunch, consisting of "hot dog" sandwiches, a slice of apple pie, and a cup of coffee. At that time the
15 fields had been cleared of cabbages, and graded, and the lots had blossomed with little signs: "Sold." This was supposed to refer to the lot, but in time it came to refer to the purchaser. The company had undertaken to put in curbs and sidewalks, water and gas and sew-
20 ers; but somebody made off with the money, and the enterprise went into bankruptcy.

But three or four months ago something unexpected had happened. A man who owned an acre or two of land on the top of the hill had set up an oil
25 derrick. Speculators began to look up the names and addresses of owners, and offers were made—there were rumors that some had got as high as a thousand dollars, nearly twice the original price of the lots.

The house numbered 5746 Los Robles Boule-
30 vard belonged to Joe Groarty, night watchman for the Altmann Lumber Company of Beach City. Mrs. Groarty had "taken in" washing to help support her seven children; now that they were grown up and scattered, she kept rabbits and chickens. Joe usually

35 left for his job at six p.m.; but on the third day after
    the "oil strike" at the top of the hill he had got up the
    nerve to give up his job, and now he was on his front-
    porch, a mild, grey-haired old fellow, wearing a black
    suit. Mrs. Groarty had had no clothing suitable for
40 this present occasion, so she had been driven down-
    town and spent some of her oil expectations for an
    evening gown of yellow satin. Now she felt embar-
    rassed because there was not enough of it, either at
    the top where her arms and bosom came out, or
45 below, where her fat calves were encased in embroi-
    dered silk stockings, so thin as to seem almost noth-
    ing. It was what "they" were wearing, the sales-
    woman had assured her; and Mrs. Groarty was grimly
    set upon being one of "them."

50   The house was in the conventional "bungalow
    style," and had been built by a wealthier family, in the
    days of the real estate boom. It had been offered at
    a sacrifice, and Mrs. Groarty had fastened upon it
    because of the wonderful living-room. When you
55 passed the threshold of the house, the first thing you
    saw was shine; the most marvelous gloss ever seen on
    woodwork. The fireplace was of many colored stones,
    highly polished and gleaming like jewels. In the back
    of the room, most striking feature of all, was a
60 wooden staircase, with a balustrade, also shiny; this
    staircase went up, and made a turn, and there was a
    platform with a palm-tree in a pot. You would take it
    for granted that it was a staircase like all other stair-
    cases, intended to take you to the second story. You
65 might go into the Groarty home a hundred times, and
    see it both day and night, before it would occur to you
    there was anything wrong; but suddenly—standing
    outside on some idle day—it would flash over you
    that the Groarty home had a flat roof over its entire
70 extent, and at no part was there any second story.

        Mrs. Groarty stood by the centre-table of her
    living-room, awaiting the arrival of the expected
    company. There was a bowl of roses in a vase on
    this table, and immediately in front of it, conspicuous
75 under the electric lamp, was a handsome volume
    bound in blue cloth and stamped with gold letters:
    "The Ladies' Guide: A Practical Handbook of Gen-
    tility." It was the only book in the Groarty home, and
    it had been there only two days; an intelligent clerk
80 in the department store, after selling the satin robe,
    had mentioned to the future "oil-queen" the existence
    of this bargain in the literature department. Mrs.
    Groarty had been studying the volume at spare mo-
    ments, and now had it set out as an exhibit of culture.

1. What can you reasonably infer from the second paragraph (lines 10–21) about how the author views the "subdividers"?

   A. He thinks they were honest salesmen trying to revitalize a shabby part of town.
   B. He admires their initiative in developing such a complete strategy to sell the lots.
   C. He feels they were dishonest men who tricked the purchasers into buying lots that seemed better than they actually were.
   D. He regards their idea as clever and wishes that he had thought of it himself.

2. Which of the following is NOT one of the methods employed by the "subdividers" to entice people to buy their lots?

   F. They put in curbs, sidewalks, water, and gas.
   G. They offered free auto rides to the lots from Beach City.
   H. They gave potential buyers a free lunch.
   J. They took out full-page advertisements in the local newspapers.

3. The phrase "taken in" in line 32 most nearly means:

   A. sheltered in her own home.
   B. brought in and washed in exchange for payment.
   C. offered a place to stay.
   D. tailored to fit.

4. What prompted Mrs. Groarty to buy the ill-fitting evening gown?

   F. She had extra money from all the oil she had sold, so she could afford to buy the new dress.
   G. Her other dresses no longer fit.
   H. Mr. Groarty bought a suit, so she needed to buy a dress to coordinate her clothing with his.
   J. She anticipated having many visitors in the near future and wanted to look like a member of high society.

5. How are the descriptions of Mrs. Groarty in her evening gown and the house similar?

   A. Both are described as being quite beautiful and ornate.
   B. Both are made of very expensive materials and cost a lot for the Groarty family to obtain.
   C. Both have a façade of luxury that suggests more grandeur than exists in reality.
   D. Both are relatively new acquisitions for the Groarty family.

6. What is one unexpected detail of the Groarty house?

   F. The woodwork is unexpectedly glossy.
   G. There is a staircase but no second floor.
   H. There is an indoor palm tree on the platform at the top of the stairs.
   J. The fireplace is made entirely of highly polished jewels.

7. Which of the following correctly identifies the order in which these four events occurred?

   I. Mrs. Groarty buys "The Ladies' Guide: A Practical Handbook of Gentility."
   II. Mrs. Groarty buys her satin dress.
   III. Mrs. Groarty took in washing to support her children.
   IV. The "oil strike" at the top of the hill took place.

   A. I, IV, III, II
   B. III, IV, I, II
   C. IV, III, I, II
   D. III, IV, II, I

8. Which description offers the most accurate representation of the character of Mrs. Groarty?

   F. A confident, hardworking woman who is not letting the discovery of oil go to her head
   G. A shrewd woman who is suspicious of the promise of wealth that the oil brings and is hesitant to buy into the whole movement
   H. A working woman who has been caught up thoroughly in the oil strike and eagerly embraces, if somewhat clumsily, the chance to be a part of the upper class
   J. A depressed, hopeless woman who views the oil strike as the only way to get away from her husband and their house

9. Which of the following best describes Upton Sinclair's tone as he describes the oil boom, and particularly Mr. and Mrs. Groarty?

   A. Dismissive
   B. Admiring
   C. Critical
   D. Sympathetic

10. Which of the following statements provides the most accurate summary of the passage?

F. A big oil company convinces families to buy lots on Los Robles Boulevard, enticing them with free lunch and automobile rides, only to steal their oil and leave the neighborhood stripped.

G. Oil is discovered in the once-quiet neighborhood of Los Robles Boulevard, leading to an oil boom that transforms the lives of the residents, including the Groartys, who prepare to enter the upper class.

H. A couple, the Groartys, uses money from the oil boom to buy expensive luxury items, such as an evening gown and an etiquette book.

J. The "subdividers" conned many families into buying lots on Los Robles Boulevard, although they didn't provide the curbs, sidewalks, water, or gas that was promised and the neighborhood fell into ruin.

Passage II

SOCIAL SCIENCE: This passage is adapted from chapter 4 of the book *An Inquiry into the Nature and Causes of the Wealth of Nations* by Adam Smith (1776).

When the division of labour has been once thoroughly established, it is but a very small part of a man's wants which the produce of his own labour can supply. He supplies the far greater part of them by
5 exchanging that surplus part of the produce of his own labour, which is over and above his own consumption, for such parts of the produce of other men's labour as he has occasion for. Every man thus lives by exchanging, or becomes in some measure a
10 merchant, and the society itself grows to be what is properly a commercial society.

But when the division of labour first began to take place, this power of exchanging must frequently have been very much clogged and embarrassed in its
15 operations. One man, we shall suppose, has more of a certain commodity than he himself has occasion for, while another has less. The former consequently would be glad to dispose of, and the latter to purchase, a part of this superfluity. But if this latter
20 should chance to have nothing that the former stands in need of, no exchange can be made between them.

In order to avoid the inconveniency of such situations, every prudent man must naturally have endeavoured to manage his affairs in such a manner
25 as to have at all times by him, besides the peculiar produce of his own industry, a certain quantity of some one commodity or other, such as he imagined few people would be likely to refuse in exchange for the produce of their industry.

30 Many different commodities, it is probable, were successively both thought of and employed for this purpose. In the rude ages of society, cattle are said to have been the common instrument of commerce. Salt is said to be the common instrument of commerce
35 and exchanges in Abyssinia; a species of shells in some parts of the coast of India; dried cod at New-foundland; tobacco in Virginia; sugar in some of our West India colonies; hides or dressed leather in some other countries; and there is at this day a village in
40 Scotland where it is not uncommon, I am told, for a workman to carry nails instead of money to the baker's shop or the alehouse.

Step 6
Practice a
full-length
ACT exam
....
290

In all countries, however, men seem at last to have been determined by irresistible reasons to give
45 the preference, for this employment, to metals above every other commodity. Metals can not only be kept with as little loss as any other commodity, scarce anything being less perishable than they are, but they can likewise, without any loss, be divided into any
50 number of parts, as by fusion those parts can easily be reunited again; a quality which no other equally durable commodities possess, and which more than any other quality renders them fit to be the instruments of commerce and circulation.

55 Different metals have been made use of by different nations for this purpose. Iron was the common instrument of commerce among the ancient Spartans; copper among the ancient Romans; and gold and silver among all rich and commercial nations.

60 Those metals seem originally to have been made use of for this purpose in rude bars, without any stamp or coinage. The use of metals in this state was attended with two very considerable inconveniencies; first, with the trouble of weighing; and, sec-
65 ondly, with that of assaying them. In the precious metals, where a small difference in the quantity makes a great difference in the value, even the business of weighing, with proper exactness, requires at least very accurate weights and scales. The operation
70 of assaying is still more difficult, still more tedious, and, unless a part of the metal is fairly melted in the crucible, with proper dissolvents, any conclusion that can be drawn from it, is extremely uncertain. Before the institution of coined money, however, unless they
75 went through this tedious and difficult operation, people must always have been liable to the grossest frauds and impositions, and instead of a pound weight of pure silver, or pure copper, might receive in exchange for their goods an adulterated composition
80 of the coarsest and cheapest materials, which had, however, in their outward appearance, been made to resemble those metals. To prevent such abuses, to facilitate exchanges, and thereby to encourage all sorts of industry and commerce, it has been found
85 necessary, in all countries that have made any considerable advances towards improvement, to affix a public stamp upon certain quantities of such particular metals as were in those countries commonly made use of to purchase goods. Hence the origin of coined
90 money, and of those public offices called mints.

11. What sentence best summarizes the main idea of the first paragraph (lines 1–11)?

   A. When there's enough land for everyone, people trade what's on their land for what's on other people's land so that people can have more than just what's growing on their land.

   B. In a commercial society, everyone is a merchant, traveling to different lands and buying and selling goods.

   C. As the division of labor becomes more established, men physically produce only a small part of the products they use, and obtain the rest by trading the excess of what they do produce for the products that others produce, resulting in a commercial society.

   D. Division of labor results in a commercial society of merchants.

12. The meaning of the word "consumption" in lines 6–7 is closest to which of the following?

   F. A severe respiratory infection
   G. Ingestion
   H. Output
   J. Use

13. According to Smith, why was the power of exchange at first "clogged and embarrassed" (line 14)?

   A. In order to trade, each person needed both to have the commodity that the other wanted, and want the commodity that the other had, which did not always happen.

   B. Individuals who were trading could not always decide on how much of one commodity to exchange for the other, since the two commodities were different and thus a standard metric could not be used.

   C. People weren't used to having a surplus of any given commodity, so everyone was reluctant at first to trade away their excess in case they found that they needed it in the future.

   D. An exchange could only take place if both individuals had an excess of some commodity, but when the division of labor first began to take place, only a few people had an excess of any one commodity.

14. In the third paragraph (lines 22–29), what does Smith suggest that "every prudent man" have with him at all times?

   F. A commodity that he is willing to part with
   G. A commodity that some people would agree to trade for
   H. A commodity that almost everyone would agree to trade for
   J. Smith doesn't mention what the man should keep with him.

15. Which of the following is NOT listed in the fourth paragraph (lines 30–42) as an example of an instrument of commerce used in some part of the world?

   A. Cattle
   B. Coins
   C. Salt
   D. Nails

16. It could be reasonably inferred from the author's discussion of the use of metals as a common instrument of commerce that:

   F. Smith is surprised at the use of metals, considering their disadvantages when compared to other options.
   G. Smith understands why the use of metals was so common, considering the advantages he mentions in the text.
   H. Smith knows the advantages of using metals as a medium of commerce, but has a sentimental attachment to the alternative instruments that he mentions (such as cattle and shells).
   J. Although initially appreciative of the advantages of metals as a medium of commerce, Smith realizes that the issues of weighing and assaying bars of metal make it a less attractive alternative than the other options he mentions earlier in the passage.

17. Which of the following statements most accurately summarizes the relationship between Smith's description of the different instruments of commerce used (in the fourth paragraph (lines 30–42)) and the different metals used (in the sixth paragraph (lines 55–59))?

A. The two descriptions are similar, as Smith describes which materials were used in which regions, but doesn't offer an explanation of why each was used in that place.

B. The two descriptions are different; in the fourth paragraph, Smith explains why different instruments of commerce were used in different places, while in describing metals in the sixth paragraph, he simply lists where each type of metal was used.

C. The two descriptions are similar, as Smith develops a list of where each medium was used as well as why that medium was used in a particular location.

D. The two descriptions are different; in the fourth paragraph, Smith discusses the different types of media used by a single culture over a variety of time periods, while the metals listed in the sixth paragraph belong to different cultures.

18. Which of the following best describes the point of view of the author?

F. A firsthand witness to the economic revolution described, sharing his story of how the transformation progressed

G. A philosopher, speculating as to why modern commerce evolved in the way that it did

H. A psychologist, using principles of modern science to understand the motivation behind the individuals who sparked the transformation to a modern, commerce-based economy

J. An economist, explaining the historical events that eventually led to the use of money and a commerce-based economy

19. Which of the following correctly orders these four items as they appear in the passage?

    I. A description of the driving force behind a commerce-based economy

   II. A discussion of the advantages of metal

  III. A review of the reasons behind the use of coins

  IV. A list of interesting instruments of commerce that have been used around the world.

A. I, IV, II, III

B. I, II, III, IV

C. I, III, IV, II

D. IV, I, III, II

20. Which of the following is an accurate summary of the main idea of the passage as a whole?

F. To convey the everyday life of an individual involved in the commercial revolution

G. To show how regional differences accounted for different media of commerce in different parts of the world

H. To explore the origin of the modern commercial economy, from the division of labor to the adoption of coinage

J. To provide a comprehensive report on the use of money and how it evolved throughout time

Passage III

HUMANITIES: This passage is adapted from the book *Rural Architecture: Being a Complete Description of Farm Houses, Cottages, and Out Buildings* by Lewis Falley Allen (1852).

It is an opinion far too prevalent among those engaged in the more active occupations of our people,—fortified indeed in such opinion, by the too fre-quent example of the farmer himself—that every-
5 thing connected with agriculture and agricultural life is of a rustic and uncouth character; that it is a profes-sion in which ignorance, as they understand the term, is entirely consistent, and one with which no aspira-tions of a high or an elevated character should, or at
10 least need be connected.

We hold, that although many of the practical operations of the farm may be rough, laborious, and untidy, yet they are not, and need not be inconsistent with the knowledge and practice of neatness, order,
15 and even elegance and refinement within doors. As the man himself—no matter what his occupation— be lodged and fed, so influenced, in a degree, will be his practice in the daily duties of his life.

As a question of economy, both in saving and
20 accumulating, good and sufficient buildings are of the first consequence, in a pecuniary light, and when to this are added other considerations touching our social enjoyment, our position and influence in life, and, not least, the decided item of national good taste
25 which the introduction of good buildings throughout our extended agricultural country will give, we find abundant cause for effort in improvement.

The farmer and his family are plain people, although none the less worthy, useful, or exalted, on
30 that account. A farmer has quite as much business in the field, or about his ordinary occupations, with ragged garments, out at elbows, and a crownless hat, as he has to occupy a leaky, wind-broken, and dilapi-dated house. Neither is he any nearer the mark, with
35 a ruffled shirt, a fancy dress, or gloved hands, when following his plough behind a pair of fancy horses, than in living in a finical, pretending house, such as we see stuck up in conspicuous places in many parts of the country.

40 It may be asked, of what consequence is it that the farmer should conform to given rules, or mode, in the style and arrangement of his dwelling, or out buildings, so that they be reasonably convenient, and

answer his purposes? For the same reason that he
45 requires symmetry, excellence of form or style, in
his cattle, or other farm stock, household furniture,
or personal dress. It is an arrangement of artificial
objects, in harmony with natural objects; that costs
little or nothing in the attainment, and, when attained,
50 is a source of gratification through life. Every human
being is bound, under ordinary circumstances, to
leave the world somewhat better, so far as his own
acts or exertions are concerned, than he found it, in
the exercise of such faculties as have been given him.
55 Such duty, among thinking men, is conceded, so far
as the moral world is concerned; and why not in the
artificial?

There are found in the older states many farm
and country houses that are almost models, in their
60 way, for convenience in the main purposes required
of structures of their kind, and such as can hardly be
altered for the better. Such, however, form the exception, not the rule; yet instead of standing as objects
for imitation, they have been ruled out as antiquated,
65 and unfit for modern builders to consult, who have in
the introduction of some real improvements, also left
out, or discarded much that is valuable.

A man, finding himself prosperous in life, sets
about the business of building a house for his own
70 accommodation. Looking back to the days of his
boyhood, in a severe climate, he remembers the not
very highly-finished tenement of his father, and the
wide, open fireplace which, with its well piled logs,
was scarcely able to warm the large living-room,
75 where the family were wont to huddle in winter. He
possibly remembers, with shivering sympathy, the
sprinkling of snow which he was accustomed to find
upon his bed as he awaked in the morning, that had
found its way through the frail casing of his chamber
80 window—but in the midst of all which he grew up
with a vigorous constitution, a strong arm, and a
determined spirit. He is resolved that his children
shall encounter no such hardships, and that himself
and his excellent helpmate shall suffer no such incon-
85 venience as his own parents had done, who now perhaps, are enjoying a strong and serene old age, in
their old-fashioned, yet to them not uncomfortable
tenement. He therefore determines to have a snug,
close house, where the cold cannot penetrate. He
90 employs all his ingenuity to make every joint an air-
tight fit; and to perfect the catalogue of his comforts,
an air-tight stove is introduced into every occupied
room which, perchance, if he can afford it, are further

warmed and poisoned by the heated flues of an air-
95 tight furnace in his air-tight cellar. His family breathe
an air-tight atmosphere; they eat their food cooked in
an "air-tight kitchen witch," of the latest "premium
pattern"; and thus they start, father, mother, children,
all on the high road—if persisted in—to a galloping
100 consumption, which sooner or later conducts them to
an air-tight dwelling, not soon to be changed.

21. Which of the following would the author of the passage NOT be likely to agree with, based on the first
paragraph (lines 1–10)?

   A. The opinion that everything connected with agriculture is rough and uncouth is far too common
   among nonfarmers.
   B. Many farmers encourage the negative stereotype associated with agriculture by behaving in
   uncouth or ignorant ways.
   C. Some nonfarmers think that those associated
   with agriculture have no aspirations for high
   character.
   D. Farmers are, as a whole, a rustic and ignorant lot.

22. Which of the following best summarizes the main
idea of the second paragraph (lines 11–18)?

   F. Much of the work to be done on the farm is
   messy, which makes it difficult for farmers to
   have the same neatness and refinement in their
   households as members of other occupations.
   G. Although farmwork can be dirty and rough, this
   does not mean that a farmer's home is the same
   way—his household can have the same neatness
   and order as anyone else's.
   H. How a man is raised determines how he will
   comport himself in the daily duties of his life—
   whether this be in elegance or roughness.
   J. It is possible for a farmer to achieve neatness and
   elegance in his household, despite his lazy and
   uncouth nature.

23. The word "finical," in the context of line 37, most
nearly means:

   A. fastidious.
   B. fickle.
   C. furnished.
   D. fancy.

Step 6
Practice a
full-length
ACT exam
....
298

24. What literary device does the author use in the fourth paragraph (lines 28–39) to express his thoughts on the style of agricultural housing?

    F. Metaphor
    G. Personification
    H. Simile
    J. Hyperbole

25. What is the strongest reason that the author provides in the fifth paragraph (lines 40–57) that farmers should build their properties as to be convenient to their purposes?

    A. So that they will look similar to the houses of townspeople
    B. Because it costs nothing to arrange them in this way and yet it provides the farmer with great gratification through life
    C. Because the farmer is morally obligated to do so, so that he leaves the world somewhat better than he found it
    D. So that future generations of his family will live in the same way that he has, and so there will be continuity

26. Why are the older farmsteads, which can "hardly be altered for the better," not used as models when constructing new farms?

    F. There are new technologies that make the old designs impractical.
    G. The old designs contained unanticipated hazards that should be avoided if possible.
    H. The older farmsteads are from one particular region, whose architecture and style cannot naturally be applied to other parts of the country.
    J. The older farmsteads have been dismissed as being "antiquated."

27. What is the purpose of the final paragraph (lines 68–101)?

    A. To provide a particular hypothetical example of how a well-meaning farmer can end up doing harm by trying to improve on the old ways
    B. To explain why many farming families are stricken with consumption
    C. To share a memorable story about a farmer that he knew personally and his ill-fated attempts to better the lives of his children
    D. To provide an example of an occasion in which a farmer reinforces the stereotype of agricultural ignorance

28. Which of the following statements about farmers would the author of the passage be MOST likely to agree with?

   F. They're a well-meaning—but generally dumb and uneducated—bunch who try to imitate the townspeople but don't really succeed.

   G. They are constantly trying to develop new ways of doing agriculture when they should really stick to the age-old methods to avoid confusing themselves and other farmers.

   H. They are not so different from the rest of us, and are simply trying to improve their lives and the lives of their children, but occasionally in misguided ways.

   J. They were left behind in the wave of modernization that swept over the world, and will always be one step behind whatever new trends are currently in fashion.

29. Which of the following correctly orders the events of the final paragraph chronologically?

   I. A farmer finds himself prosperous in life and decides to build a house.

   II. The farmer's youth was riddled with cold, as snow often came in through drafty windows.

   III. The farmer's family is riddled with consumption.

   IV. The farmer builds his new house to be entirely airtight and extremely warm.

   A. II, III, I, IV
   B. I, II, III, IV
   C. I, II, IV, III
   D. II, I, IV, III

30. What is Allen's tone as he discusses the lives and architecture of farmers?

   F. Mocking
   G. Paternal
   H. Condescending
   J. Reverent

Passage IV

NATURAL SCIENCE: This passage is adapted from chapter 1 of the book *Studies of Trees* by Jacob Joshua Levison (1914).

There are many ways in which the problem of identifying trees may be approached. The majority attempt to recognize trees by their leaf characters. Leaf characters, however, do not differentiate the
5 trees during the other half of the year when they are bare. In almost every tree there is some one trait that marks its individuality and separates it, at a glance, from all other trees. It may be the general form of the tree, its mode of branching, bark, bud or fruit. It may
10 be some variation in color, or, in case of the evergreen trees, it may be the number and position of the needles or leaves.

The pines belong to the coniferous class of trees; that is, trees which bear cones. The pines may be told
15 from the other coniferous trees by their leaves, which are in the form of needles two inches or more in length. These needles keep green throughout the entire year. This is characteristic of all coniferous trees, except the larch and cypress, which shed their
20 leaves in winter.

The pines include about 80 distinct species with over 600 varieties. Each species has a certain characteristic number of needles to the cluster and this fact generally provides the simplest and most direct way
25 of distinguishing the different pines. In the white pine there are five needles to each cluster, in the pitch pine three, and in the Scotch pine two. The Austrian pine also has two needles to the cluster, but the difference in size and character of the needles will distin-
30 guish this species from the Scotch pine.

The spruce and hemlock belong to the evergreen class and may be told from the other trees by their leaves. The leaves of the hemlock are much shorter than the needles of the pines but are longer than the
35 leaves of the red cedar or arbor vitae. They are neither arranged in clusters like those of the larch, nor in feathery layers like those of the cypress. There are eighteen recognized species of spruce. The hemlock is represented by seven species.

40 The larch and the cypress are both coniferous trees and, unlike the other Conifers, are both deciduous. In winter they can be distinguished by their characteristic forms. The larch is a broader tree as

compared with the cypress and its form is more con-
45 ical. The cypress is more slender and it is taller. There
are nine recognized species of larch and two of bald
cypress.

The horsechestnut, ash, and maple have their
branches and buds arranged on their stems opposite
50 each other. In other trees, this arrangement is alternate. The white ash is apt to be confused with the
black ash, but differs from the latter in having a
lighter-colored bud. The bark of the white ash is
darker in color than the black ash.

55 Trees told by their form include the elm, poplar,
gingko and willow. The Carolina poplar, or Cotton-
wood, is commonly planted in cities because it grows
rapidly and is able to withstand the smoke and drouth
conditions of the city. Its very fast growth is really a
60 point against the tree, because it grows so fast that it
becomes too tall for surrounding property, and its
wood being extremely soft and brittle, the tree frequently breaks in windstorms. In many cases it is
entirely uprooted, because it is not a deep-rooted tree.
65 Its larger roots, which spread near the surface, upset
the sidewalk or prevent the growth of other vegeta-
tion on the lawn, while its finer rootlets, in their eager
search for moisture, penetrate and clog the joints of
neighboring water and sewer pipes. The female form
70 of this tree is even more objectionable than the male,
because in the early spring the former produces an
abundance of cotton from its seeds which litters the
ground and often makes walking dangerous.

Trees told by their bark or trunk include the
75 sycamore, birch, beech, ironwood and hackberry.
The bark of the white birch is marked by small raised
horizontal lines which are the lenticels or breathing
pores. These lenticels are characteristic of all birch
and cherry trees. The oaks are rather difficult to iden-
80 tify and, in studying them it will often be necessary
to look for more than one distinguishing character.
The oaks differ from other trees in bearing acorns.
There are two groups of oaks, the white oak and the
black oak. The white oak is the type of the white oak
85 group and the black, red and pin oaks are types of the
other.

Step 6
Practice a
full-length
ACT exam
....
302

31. Which sentence from the first paragraph (lines 1–12) best represents the main idea of the paragraph?

    A. "In almost every tree there is some one trait that marks its individuality and separates it, at a glance, from all other trees."

    B. "It may be some variation in color, or, in case of the evergreen trees, it may be the number and position of the needles or leaves."

    C. "There are many ways in which the problem of identifying trees may be approached."

    D. "The majority attempt to recognize trees by their leaf characters."

32. Which of the following is an identifying characteristic of trees that the author of this passage would NOT likely use when differentiating one tree from another, based on the content of the first paragraph (lines 1–12)?

    F. Leaf shape

    G. Bark

    H. Mode of branching

    J. Variations in color

33. Which of the following is an interesting contradiction between the first and second paragraphs of the passage?

    A. In the first paragraph, the author talks about trees that lose their leaves for part of the year, but he spends the second paragraph discussing pines, which don't lose their leaves in the winter.

    B. In the second paragraph, the author discusses how to tell pines from other kinds of conifers, but not how to tell one pine from another.

    C. The first paragraph has a topic sentence, while the second paragraph begins with a definition.

    D. In the first paragraph, the author cautions against using leaves to distinguish one type of tree from another, yet he spends the second paragraph explaining how to do just that.

34. According to the third paragraph (lines 21–30), which of the following details of pine identification is incorrect?

    F. The Austrian pine and the Scotch pine can be told apart by differences in the size and character of their needles.

    G. The Austrian pine and Scotch pine have the same number of needles.

    H. The white pine has five needles per cluster, while the pitch pine has three.

    J. There are over 600 species of pine.

35. What word is closest in meaning to "character" in the context of line 29?

   A. Personality
   B. Characteristics
   C. Shape
   D. Length

36. Which of the following statements is supported by evidence from the sixth paragraph (lines 48–54)?

   F. Horsechestnut, ash, and maple all display alternate arrangement of leaves.
   G. The white ash has a darker-colored bud than the black ash.
   H. The white ash has darker-colored bark than the black ash.
   J. The white ash has lighter bark than the black ash.

37. Which of the following is NOT a reason given for the Carolina poplar breaking or falling down during windstorms?

   A. The extremely fast growth of the tree
   B. The large size of the tree's roots
   C. The soft and brittle nature of the tree's wood
   D. The shallowness of its roots

38. Which of the following best conveys the purpose of the passage?

   F. To explain why identifying trees can be so difficult and caution amateurs against relying on differences in trees' leaves to tell them apart
   G. To provide an introduction to a variety of different species of trees, indicating their size, shape, favored biome, and geographical range
   H. To act as an easy-access, quick-reference field guide for foresters interested in rapid tree identification
   J. To introduce various solutions to the problem of how to identify trees, with examples provided from a variety of different tree families and species

39. Which of the following is the most likely identity of the author of the passage?

   A. A student who has been assigned a report on tree identification with no prior knowledge of forestry
   B. A professor or other academic with a vast knowledge of forestry
   C. A member of a conservation group who is desperate to reduce logging in local forests
   D. A wilderness explorer recounting the various trees encountered on his travels

40. What word best describes the tone of the passage?

   F. Angry

   G. Passionate

   H. Cautious

   J. Academic

STOP!
END OF THE READING TEST

If you have time left over,
you may check your work on this section only.

SECTION 4
SCIENCE
35 minutes — 40 questions

> **DIRECTIONS:** This test includes seven passages, each followed by several questions. Read the passage and choose the best answer to each question. After you have selected your answer, fill in the corresponding bubble on your answer sheet. You should refer to the passages as often as necessary when answering the questions. You may NOT use a calculator on this test.

Passage I

Three students were asked to read from an optometrist's eye chart and describe the symbols they saw from a distance of 25 feet. Various results of the exercise are given.

Activity I

Table 1 depicts the eye chart used to test each student in the right column. Note the decrease in size of the symbols from top to bottom.

Table 1
Eye chart

Row 1	A E
Row 2	B 8 Q
Row 3	I L M N
Row 4	M Z 3 Q
Row 5	P Z X P

Experiment 1

Table 2 shows the results of each student's being asked to identify the symbols in the eye chart in Experiment 1. The correct answers are shown as fractions of the number of symbols possible (for example, Row 1 has 2 symbols, "A E"; correctly identifying 1 symbol would result in a score of "1/2," while correctly identifying both would result in a score of "2/2."

Table 2			
Correct identification of symbols / symbols possible—Attempt 1			
Row	Student 1	Student 2	Student 3
1	2/2	2/2	2/2
2	3/3	2/3	3/3
3	4/4	2/4	3/4
4	3/4	1/4	1/4
5	2/4	1/4	0/4

Experiment 2

Immediately after the completion of Experiment 1, all 3 students were shown the eye chart close up and allowed to examine it along with a copy of their answers in Experiment 1 for 60 seconds. Experiment 2 was conducted with the same parameters; the results are shown in Table 3.

Table 3			
Correct identification of symbols / symbols possible—Attempt 2			
Row	Student 1	Student 2	Student 3
1	2/2	2/2	2/2
2	3/3	3/3	3/3
3	4/4	3/4	4/4
4	4/4	2/4	2/4
5	4/4	1/4	2/4

1. Which student(s) correctly identified the most symbols in the first experiment?

   A. Students 1 and 2
   B. Student 1
   C. Student 2
   D. Student 3

2. Compare the results of Experiments 1 and 2. Which of the following statements is NOT true, based on the information available in Tables 2 and 3?

   F. All students accurately identified more symbols in Experiment 2 than Experiment 1.
   G. No student accurately identified fewer symbols in Experiment 2 than Experiment 1.
   H. All students accurately identified fewer symbols in Experiment 2 than Experiment 1.
   J. No student accurately identified more symbols in Experiment 1 than Experiment 2.

3. The eye chart in Table 1 is made up exclusively of:

    A. vowels.
    B. numbers.
    C. letters.
    D. symbols.

4. What is the percentage of correctly identified symbols from Row 5, Experiment 2, averaged by all 3 students' scores?

    F. 100%
    G. 78%
    H. 58%
    J. 25%

5. Which of the following is a plausible reason that the scores of all 3 students increased from Experiment 1 to Experiment 2?

    A. The students could see the correct symbols up close before trying to guess them a second time, so they knew what their errors were.
    B. The students had practice reading symbols on eye charts.
    C. The students were allowed to simply read off the symbols up close instead of having to stand at a distance as in Experiment 1.
    D. The students were provided with an extra incentive to identify the symbols correctly, so they tried harder and thus did better.

6. Would you expect the results of Experiment 2 to be different if another set of subjects was used (not the subjects in Experiment 1)?

    F. No; because the experiment is unchanged, the results should be similar.
    G. Yes; having the incorrect guesses of a previous student to compare to the correct eye chart is unlikely to be as helpful as having performed the test yourself and looking at your own mistakes, so the scores for Experiment 2 may be lower.
    H. No; the new subjects are likely to have the same eyesight abilities as the 3 original subjects.
    J. Yes; due to random chance, it's unlikely that the results will be the same.

Passage II

According to Boyle's law, the absolute pressure and volume of a given mass of gas inside a closed system are inversely proportional, provided that the temperature remains unchanged. This means that, assuming the temperature does not change, an increase in pressure will result in a decrease in volume (and vice versa: an increase in volume will lead to a decrease in pressure). A barbell-shaped gas chamber is shown, connected in the center by a closed valve. If the valve is closed, the gas on each side is sealed and separate from the gas on the other side; once the valve is opened, however, gases from both sides of the chamber can mix freely.

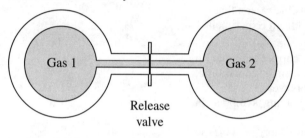

Release
valve

The following questions propose experiments using the apparatus shown in the diagram, based on the behavior of an ideal gas in a closed system.

7. Assume that both Gas 1 and Gas 2, as labeled, are composed of the same ideal gas at the same temperature, pressure, and volume. What will happen when the valve is opened?

   A. The gases will swap sides in the chamber.

   B. The gases will increase in temperature as the volume increases.

   C. The gases will decrease in temperature as the volume increases.

   D. Nothing: the gases are in equilibrium.

8. Assume that Gas 1, as labeled, is heated to a temperature considerably higher than that of Gas 2. What will happen when the valve is opened?

   F. Gas 1 will rush to expand into Gas 2's side of the chamber.

   G. Gas 2 will rush to expand into Gas 1's side of the chamber.

   H. Nothing: the gases are in equilibrium.

   J. The gases will swap sides in the chamber, but not mix.

9. If increasing the temperature of an ideal gas causes it to expand in volume, what will happen to the pressure of this heated gas if there is no room for its volume to increase (because it is inside a closed system)?

   A. The pressure will decrease.
   B. The pressure will remain the same.
   C. The pressure will increase.
   D. It is not possible to know.

10. Assume that Gas 1, as labeled, is cooled a considerable amount, compared to Gas 2. What will happen when the valve is opened?

   F. Gas 2 will rush to expand into Gas 1's side of the chamber.
   G. Gas 1 will rush to expand into Gas 2's side of the chamber.
   H. The two gases will mix equally.
   J. Nothing will happen—the cool temperature decreases the activity of the gases.

11. Assume that the volume of the side of the chamber that Gas 1 fills is doubled, and the volume of gas is doubled as well. What is the relationship between Gas 1 and Gas 2, as labeled, in this circumstance?

   A. The temperature of Gas 1 will be greater than that of Gas 2.
   B. The temperature of Gas 1 will be less than that of Gas 2.
   C. The pressure of Gas 1 will be double that of Gas 2.
   D. Both gases will be at equilibrium.

12. To make use of Boyle's law, what variable must be constant?

   F. Temperature
   G. Volume
   H. Pressure
   J. Gas

Passage III

Viscosity is a measurement of the resistance of a fluid to deformation by stress or force. The higher the viscosity of a given liquid, the more it will resist being deformed and the less easily it will move.

Step 6
Practice a
full-length
ACT exam
....
310

Three liquids of varying viscosities are used in an experiment: molasses, cold water (40°F), and hot water (100°F). Each liquid is placed in a wave pool, and a wave is forced through it by mechanical means. The size of the wave produced is represented on the following graph at regular intervals of 0.1 seconds.

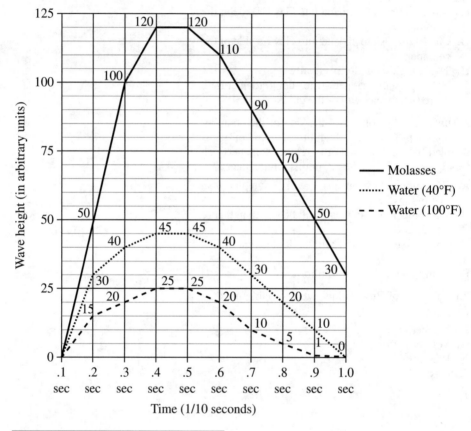

Table 1		
Viscosity of liquids used (viscosity units)		
Molasses (room temperature)		8,000
Water (40°F)		10
Water (100°F)		8

13. According to the introduction and Table 1, which liquid should resist deformation the most?

   A. Molasses
   B. Water (40°F)
   C. Water (100°F)
   D. Water at either temperature

14. What relationship does viscosity have with wave height, based on the information in the graph and in Table 1?

   F. There is no relationship between viscosity and wave height.
   G. The more viscous the liquid, the larger the wave height.
   H. The less viscous the liquid, the larger the wave height.
   J. Viscosity increases wave height in a 1:1 ratio (1% increase in viscosity = 1% increase in height).

15. Based on information in the graph, what would happen if the temperature of the molasses were increased, assuming that it behaves in a manner similar to water?

   A. The molasses's viscosity would increase.
   B. The molasses's viscosity would decrease.
   C. The molasses would turn into water.
   D. There would be no detectable change in the molasses.

16. When did the height of the waves peak for each of the 3 liquids tested?

   F. 0.2 seconds
   G. 0.4 seconds
   H. 0.04 seconds
   J. 120 seconds

17. At what point do all 3 liquids return to a wave height of 0, after 0.1 seconds?

   A. 0.4 seconds
   B. 1.0 seconds
   C. 1.2 seconds
   D. There is not enough data to answer this question.

Passage IV

Heat often needs to be dispersed after it is created, either to heat an area by introducing more heat or to cool an area by absorbing excess heat and transporting it elsewhere. Both heating and cooling processes in daily life often use a series of meandering pipes, called a radiator because it distributes heat via radiation, to introduce more heat or draw it away. The following diagram shows a radiator that brings heat into an area by piping hot water or gas in and allowing it to radiate heat before the cooled medium (water or gas) is drawn away.

Heat is radiated off and
the water/air cools

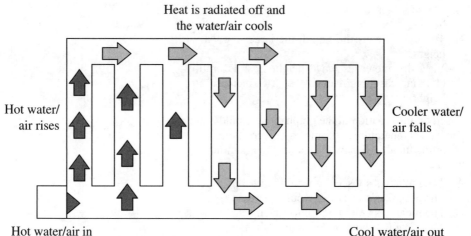

Hot water/
air rises

Cooler water/
air falls

Hot water/air in

Cool water/air out

Study 1

Thermal conductivity is a measure of the amount of heat a particular material or substance can carry at a particular time. It is a measurement of heat flowing through the length of the substance and *not* how much total heat it can hold at one time. Tables 1 and 2 list the conductivity levels of a variety of liquids, gases, and solids.

Table 1			
Thermal conductivity of various liquids and gases			
Liquid	Conductivity	Gas	Conductivity
Mercury	8.3	Hydrogen	0.18
Water	0.67	Helium	0.15
Methanol	0.25	Air	0.026
Glycol (antifreeze)	0.025	Nitrogen	0.025

Table 2	
Thermal conductivity of various solids	
Diamond	1,000–2,500
Silver	429
Copper	401
Gold	318
Ice (at 5°C)	1.6
Wood	0.12–0.04

18. What gases are almost identical in thermal conductivity to glycol?

    F. Nitrogen and air
    G. Nitrogen and hydrogen
    H. Nitrogen and helium
    J. Air and helium

19. How much more conductive is mercury than water?

    A. More than 10 times
    B. More than 20 times
    C. More than 50 times
    D. More than 100 times

20. What is the most conductive material listed in Tables 1 and 2?

    F. Copper
    G. Wood
    H. Mercury
    J. Diamond

21. If you were creating an insulating box that needed to be able to carry a large amount of heat in a given time, which material would you probably NOT want to use?

    A. Diamond
    B. Gold
    C. Ice
    D. Silver

Passage V

The following study analyzes salmon runs (the return of salmon to their native breeding grounds to spawn) in the Pacific Northwest since 1925. The first graph details the size of salmon runs from 1925 to 2015 (projected) in millions of fish per year. The second graph adds data showing the number of fish harvested as well as the total number of fish in the runs (in millions of fish).

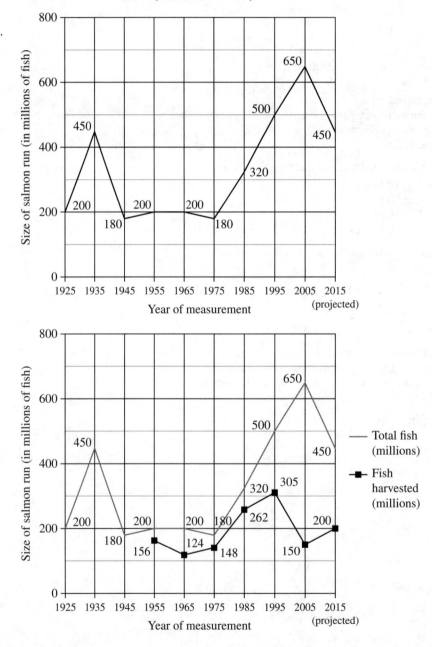

Using the data provided in the graphs, answer the questions about how salmon runs have changed over time.

22. According to the graphs, in what year was the salmon run the largest?

    F. 1935
    G. 1995
    H. 2015
    J. 2005

23. According to the second graph, in what year was the highest proportion of salmon harvested?

    A. 1955
    B. 2005
    C. 1975
    D. 1965

24. An environmental group hopes to convince fishermen to reduce harvesting by arguing that increased harvesting leads to smaller salmon runs in the coming years. Should the group include the graphs in its presentation?

    F. Yes, because they show that as the number of salmon harvested increases, the size of the salmon run in the following years decreases.
    G. Yes, because they show a positive correlation between the number of salmon harvested and the size of the salmon run.
    H. No, because they show that as the number of salmon harvested increases, the size of the salmon run in the following years increases—which contradicts the group's argument.
    J. No, because they show that the number of salmon harvested and the size of the salmon run in the following years are not related.

25. What proportion of salmon was harvested in 1945?

    A. 156/200 million tons
    B. 135/200 million tons
    C. 124/200 million tons
    D. There is not enough data to answer this question.

26. Why might the data presented in the second graph be unexpected?

F. Because the size of the salmon runs should be decreasing steadily over time, not rising and falling as it does in the graph

G. Because the amount of salmon harvested hasn't remained constant, as expected

H. Because as the number of salmon harvested increases, the size of the salmon runs decreases—which is unexpected, because one would assume that more harvesting would result in a higher population of salmon

J. Because as the number of salmon harvested increases, the size of the salmon runs increases, and when harvesting decreases, there is a decrease in the size of the run in the following years—which is unexpected, because one would assume that as the number of salmon harvested increases, the run size should decrease

Passage VI

A team of high school students performed 2 studies to investigate the factors that influence the success rate of germination of bean sprouts.

Study 1

Bean sprout seeds were separated into 12 groups of 30 seeds each. Each of 9 groups of seeds was placed in a sealed plastic baggie, which was stored at 10°C for 2, 4, or 6 weeks (3 groups per storage period).

After each designated storage period was complete, 3 pots were prepared with damp starter soil and each set of 30 seeds was placed in its own pot. The 12 pots were maintained at 1 of 3 temperatures for 30 days, and the number of seeds that successfully sprouted in each pot was recorded. Table 1 shows the number of seeds that sprouted per pot.

Table 1			
Storage period (weeks)	Successful sprouts (15°C)	Successful sprouts (20°C)	Successful sprouts (25°C)
0	0	0	0
2	1	3	0
4	5	10	2
6	9	17	3

Study 2

Bean sprout seeds were separated into 12 groups of 30 seeds each. Each group of seeds was stored in a plastic baggie at 1 of 4 different temperatures for a period of 6 weeks.

After 6 weeks, 12 pots were prepared and each set of 30 seeds was planted in its own pot. The pots were maintained at 1 of 3 temperatures for 30 days, after which the number of successful sprouts in each pot was recorded. Table 2 shows the results of this study.

Table 2			
Storage temperature (°C)	Successful sprouts (15°C)	Successful sprouts (20°C)	Successful sprouts (25°C)
0	18	26	24
5	22	24	20
10	0	8	5
15	0	0	0

Step 6
Practice a
full-length
ACT exam
....
318

27. For the beans in Study 1 that were stored for 4 weeks, as temperature increased from 15°C to 25°C, the number of seeds that successfully sprouted:

    A. increased only.
    B. decreased only.
    C. increased, then decreased.
    D. decreased, then increased.

28. In general, the results of Study 2 suggest that bean sprout seeds are most likely to sprout when stored at which temperature?

    F. 5°C
    G. 10°C
    H. 15°C
    J. 20°C

29. The experimental design of Study 1 and Study 2 differed in that for Study 1:

    A. storage time was varied.
    B. storage temperature was varied.
    C. germination time was varied.
    D. storage time was held constant.

30. Based on the results of Study 1 and Study 2, which of the following combinations of storage time and storage temperature would most likely result in the fewest successful sprouts?

    F. Stored at 0°C for 2 weeks
    G. Stored at 10°C for 4 weeks
    H. Stored at 5°C for 6 weeks
    J. Stored at 15°C for 0 weeks

31. Another team from the same classroom had performed the same experiment, but forgot to label their pots in Study 1. If their results were as follows, which temperature were the pots most likely kept at?

Storage period (weeks)	Number of seeds that sprouted
0	0
2	1
4	0
6	2

    A. 15°C
    B. 20°C
    C. 25°C
    D. There is not enough information to draw a conclusion.

32. Which of the following is NOT a variable that should be kept constant in both Study 1 and Study 2?

    F. The amount of water applied to seeds over the 30-day period

    G. The person watering the seeds

    H. The hours of light that seeds are exposed to

    J. The depth at which the seeds are planted

33. Given the trend of the data in Study 1, would further investigation with longer storage times likely give additional information about the relationship between storage time and sprout success rate?

    A. No, because the number of successful sprouts had increased, then decreased, so longer storage times would result in fewer sprouts.

    B. No, because the number of successful sprouts increased as storage time increased, so it can be concluded that for any length of time (weeks, months, and so on), the longer the storage time, the greater the number of successful sprouts.

    C. Yes, because it is unclear at what point, if any, a longer storage time would no longer result in an increase in the number of successful sprouts.

    D. Yes, because more data is always better in scientific experiments, and the team should perform the extra trials regardless of the information they've already obtained.

Passage VII

Step 6

Practice a
full-length
ACT exam

. . . .

320

The Big Bang is the leading scientific model of the early development of the universe and attempts to explain the matter, energy, and all other aspects that make up the universe. The term "Big Bang" is used because the model theorizes that when the universe was first created, it was very small and very dense—all matter and energy were packed together randomly in an unimaginably small amount of space. This superdense pocket of space expanded in volume by 10^{78} in well under a billionth of a second and gave the Big Bang its name.

In the following two accounts, two scientists discuss the observational evidence for the Big Bang.

Scientist 1

Some of the best evidence we have for the existence of the Big Bang can be seen through distant galaxies' adherence to Hubble's law, which is $v = H_0 D$ (where v is the velocity of a distant galaxy, H_0 is the Hubble constant, and D is comoving distance). To put it simply, Hubble's law expects that cosmically distant objects are all moving away from the earth and all move at a speed that can be predicted based on how far from the earth they are now. Decades of research and measurements taken by thousands of astronomers confirm that not only are these distant galaxies moving away from us, but they are moving at the speed predicted by Hubble's law. This is excellent supporting evidence for the Big Bang theory, which postulates that the Big Bang began the universe expanding in all directions, though other evidence validates the theory just as thoroughly.

Scientist 2

The most compelling evidence for the Big Bang theory must be the existence of cosmic background radiation, which is a type of thermal radiation that can be found in uniform distribution everywhere in the universe. Since the Big Bang theory predicts that, at the beginning of the universe, energy was packed randomly and as it expanded explosively, it would be distributed nearly evenly throughout the universe. Experiments in the 20th century predicted that, if the Big Bang theory were true, a certain frequency of radiation would be nearly omnipresent in the universe. Within 25 years, further experiments confirmed that such radiation existed at both the frequency and distribution predicted. Other evidence further supports the theory, but cosmic background radiation is clearly the most compelling evidence to date.

34. According to the passage, the Big Bang theory is:

    F. nonscientific.
    G. unsupported by evidence.
    H. the leading scientific model of the universe's development.
    J. a misnomer.

35. The information in the passage indicates that the Big Bang was so named because:

    A. it describes the explosive beginnings of energy and matter in the universe.
    B. no one took it seriously.
    C. the universe has always been big and loud.
    D. no one had a better name for it.

36. In what way do the two scientists differ regarding how each views his own evidence for the Big Bang?

    F. Scientist 1 seems to think that the Big Bang is misnamed.
    G. Scientist 1 seems open to other evidence as being just as compelling, while Scientist 2 is convinced his evidence is best.
    H. Scientist 2 needs to see that the math works out properly before subscribing to a particular theory.
    J. Scientist 2 is convinced that his evidence is not all that convincing.

37. Why is cosmic background radiation evidence for the Big Bang, according to Scientist 2?

    A. Because the radiation predicted by the theory is observable at the expected frequency only
    B. Because the radiation predicted by the theory is observable at the expected distribution only
    C. Because the radiation predicted by the theory is observable with a telescope
    D. Because the radiation predicted by the theory is observable both at the expected frequency and distribution

38. According to Scientist 1, if a distant galaxy is farther from the earth than a closer galaxy, it should be moving away from the Earth:

    F. faster than the closer galaxy.
    G. at the same rate as the closer galaxy.
    H. slower than the closer galaxy.
    J. The relative speed cannot be determined from the information in the passage.

39. Why did the Big Bang occur, according to the passage?

    A. Because of the unstable nature of so much energy and matter being packed together

    B. Because of the repulsive forces that exist when matter is packed together too densely

    C. Because gravity had not been created yet

    D. The passage does not speculate as to why the Big Bang occurred.

40. What does D stand for, according to Scientist 1?

    F. Hubble's law

    G. Hubble's constant

    H. comoving distance

    J. distance

STOP!
END OF THE SCIENCE TEST

If you have time left over,
you may check your work on this section only.

SECTION 5
WRITING

30 minutes — 1 essay

> **DIRECTIONS:** This test is designed to assess your writing skills. You have thirty (30) minutes to plan and write an essay based on the stimulus provided. Be sure to take a position on the issue and support your position using logical reasoning and relevant examples. Organize your ideas in a focused and logical way, and use the English language to clearly and effectively express your position.

Budget cuts in high schools across the country have prompted administrators to consider abandoning the traditional 5-day week in favor of a 4-day week in which each day is 1 to 2 hours longer to make up for lost time on the last day. Administrators hope to save money in teacher salaries and in heating/cooling and electricity costs, making it easier to stay within budget. Some parents and students, however, are concerned that a 4-day week won't deliver the same education as the traditional 5-day model. The issue about switching to a 4-day week has recently surfaced at your high school, and a decision will be made at the next school board meeting about the length of the school week for the coming year.

In your essay, write a letter to the chair of the school board and either defend or attack the new 4-day plan. You may write about either one of the two points of view presented, or you may present a different point of view on this question. Use specific reasons and examples to support your position.

NOTE On the actual ACT exam, you will receive two or three sheets of scratch paper on which to develop your essay, and four pages of notebook paper on which to write your essay. The following page is similar to those provided by the ACT. Although the ACT allows you to write on the back of each page if you need more space, I recommend that you limit yourself to four pages when you write your practice essay.

Guidelines for scoring your essay are provided in the box "ACT Writing score sheet" at the beginning of Step 5.

Review the ACT practice exam

And here are the solutions! I've detailed my thinking process for solving each of the problems on the ACT practice exam in Step 6. Use the solutions to identify your mistakes and to determine how you should have employed the ACT 36 strategies to solve the problems you had trouble with. Be sure to enter these problems under "Problems to review" in the appropriate section of your 36 Review notebook.

1. **C.** Since the subject, "Minneapolis and St. Paul," is plural, the verb must be plural: "are." The article "a" must be used with the phrase "conjoined metropolis."

2. **J.** A comma is necessary, because the clause modifying "settlers" is not a complete sentence. "Who" is correct, because it is the subject of its clause.

3. **B.** Because the action of growing was completed by a certain time in the past ("within only a few decades"), the past perfect "had" is correct. Answer choice D is incorrect, because the subject, "the city," is singular.

4. **G.** Since more than two metropolitan areas are being compared, "largest" is correct. "In" is correct, because "the United States" is considered a single geographical entity.

5. **C.** The rest of the paragraph addresses the population size of the cities and area. Sentence 2 explains the origin of Minneapolis's name and is out of place here.

6. **F.** The second part of the sentence provides an example of the residents' passion for the outdoors. A semicolon would be used if the sentences were related but equal. A dash would be used to introduce a contrasting idea or exclamation. A period would ignore the relationship between the two sentences.

7. **D.** Because there are more than two cities, "among" is used instead of "between."

8. **G.** Parallel structure is the key; all of the phrases must match the infinitive "(to) visit an opera." All other answer choices contain at least one verb with an "-ing" ending.

9. **C.** This is a contraction of "it" and "is." Without an apostrophe, "its" is a possessive. "Its'" is ungrammatical. "It was almost" is past tense, which doesn't match the present tense earlier in the sentence.

10. **J.** Since the subject, "Minneapolis and St. Paul," is plural, the verb must be plural: "are." The author is obviously talking about the cities' current characteristics, so the present tense is correct, eliminating answer choices G and H.

11. **C.** Although "themselves" is commonly used to refer to "anyone" in every-day language, the pronoun must be singular: "himself or herself."

12. **J.** The "if" clause is a sentence fragment, so it must be joined to another clause or a sentence. A period, colon, or dash in this context would incorrectly indicate separation of complete sentences.

13. **D.** To achieve parallel structure, the verb must be omitted so that only nouns are the objects of the series of prepositions.

14. **G.** This is a contraction of "there" and "is." "Theres" and "they'res" are ungrammatical. "Theirs" is a pronoun.

15. **D.** The essay lists many positive features of the Twin Cities, but nowhere does the author try to convince the reader to live there.

16. **G.** "The fields" is the object of "brings together"; it would be incorrect to interrupt the predicate with a punctuation mark after "together." Because two "fields" are involved, "and" is correct.

17. **B.** Since the subject, "research," is singular, the verb must be singular: "hopes." The paragraph addresses the current situation, so a present-tense verb is required, eliminating answer choices C and D.

18. **J.** To achieve parallel structure, the infinitive "to digest" must be changed to the verb's "-ing" form to match "producing." A comma after "biofuels" is incorrect, because both "-ing" phrases are objects of "capable of."

19. **B.** "It's" is a contraction of "it" and "is" and makes no sense in this context. "Its" indicates possession, here referring to the subject of the sentence, "this exciting new field." Since the subject is singular, "their" is incorrect.

20. **H.** Since the clause "which was coined in the early 20th century" is unnecessary to the meaning of the sentence, "which" is used and the clause is set off by commas.

21. **A.** The punctuation mark links two complete and related sentences. A dash would incorrectly introduce a contrasting idea or exclamation. A period would ignore the relationship between the two sentences. It is incorrect to separate two complete sentences with a comma.

22. **G.** The modifier of "field" should be an adjective, which eliminates "conglomeration." While "conglomerated" is a past participle acting as an adjective, it makes no sense as a modifier of "field." "Conglomerater" is not a word.

23. **D.** Since the subject, "a scientist," is singular, references to it must be singular: "his or her." The homonyms of "their"—"they're" and "there"—make no sense in this context.

24. **H.** An adverb—not an adjective—modifies a verb, so "well" is used instead of "good." Since the subject of the main clause, "someone," is singular, the verb of the dependent "who" clause must also be singular; this eliminates answer choices G and J.

25. **B.** The transition word introduces a new paragraph that builds on the previous one, so a contrasting transition word, as offered in answer choices A, C, and D, would be inappropriate. "As such" in this context signals that an example will follow.

26. **G.** The comma sets off "when choosing their classes" as a clause that is unnecessary to the meaning of the sentence. "They're" is a contraction of "they" and "are" and makes no sense here; "their" is a possessive referring to "undergraduate students."

27. **A.** Since the subject, "they," is plural, the verb must be plural, eliminating answer choices B and C. There are more than two offerings, so "among" is correct.

Step 7

Review the
ACT practice
exam

. . . .

328

28. **G.** The second sentence, "there are . . . need answers," serves as an example of "challenges" in the first sentence. This relationship is best expressed by a colon, not by a period or semicolon. A dash would be used to introduce a contrasting idea or exclamation.

29. **C.** To avoid wordiness and to maximize clarity, the simple present-tense verb "demonstrates" is the best answer choice. "Have demonstrated" is incorrect, because its subject is "backlash," which is singular.

30. **G.** "Surrounds" makes the sentence ungrammatical. "Surrounding" conveys the notion that the suspicion continues in a way that "that surrounds" doesn't. "That will surround" makes no sense in this context.

31. **D.** A colon indicates that "a pony" is "the most asked-for present"; a comma doesn't necessarily signify this. A period would create a sentence fragment, and no punctuation at all would create a run-on sentence.

32. **G.** To compare more than two items, the suffix "-est" is used instead of "-er." "Most cutest" is repetitive and ungrammatical.

33. **D.** An adverb—not an adjective—modifies a verb, so "quickly" is used instead of "quick" to modify "abandoned." "Soon" could be used in this sentence, but only if it immediately preceded "abandoned."

34. **F.** "It's" is a contraction of "it" and "is"; "its'" is ungrammatical and "its" makes no sense here. Since the opinion is expressed from the viewpoint of the present, present-tense "it's" is correct, eliminating answer choice J.

35. **C.** "Fracturing" is correct, since it is the object of the preposition "aside from"; the other answer choices are active or passive verb forms. Reading the choices "aloud" in your mind quickly narrows the choice to C.

36. **H.** The phrase "never tiring . . . around" must be placed next to the noun that it modifies, eliminating answer choices F and J. Choice G is incorrect, because "I" should be "me" as the object of the preposition "by." Choice H, which converts the modifying phrase into a "who" clause, is correct; in addition, unlike choice G, choice H is written in the active voice.

37. **C.** To achieve parallel structure, "pretending" is correct, because it matches "riding" earlier in the sentence.

38. **J.** The object of "carry" refers to "picnics" and must therefore be plural. The verb "carried" is incompatible with "would pack."

39. **D.** To avoid wordiness, "without fail" should be deleted. The verb "would tolerate" doesn't match the other verbs in the paragraph; the past-tense verb "tolerated" expresses the idea simply and well.

40. **G.** "One student" avoids the wordiness of answer choices F and H. "Some student" would compromise specificity.

41. **C.** Since this pronoun refers to "one student," it must be singular: "himself or herself." "His or herself" is ungrammatical, and "theirselves" isn't a word.

42. **F.** This sentence introduces the topic of the paragraph; without it, the rest of the sentence wouldn't make sense.

43. **B.** This sentence contrasts with the preceding one—the author writes that the pony is "probably enjoying peace and quiet," but wonders if the pony misses "all the fun we had." A contrasting transition word is therefore required: "still."

44. **H.** "Standing quietly . . . to see her" lists examples of how Goldilocks was "there for me," so a colon is correct. A comma would not clearly express this relationship. A period would create a sentence fragment, as would a semicolon.

45. **B.** Before the last two paragraphs, the essay is written in chronological order. Placing this paragraph about middle school between the paragraph about elementary school and the paragraph about college would preserve chronological integrity.

46. **J.** "Your," a possessive, is correct; "you're" is a contraction of "you" and "are" and makes no sense. Since the subject, "eyes," is plural, the verb must be plural, eliminating answer choices F and G.

47. **B.** Since "BANG!" is an exclamation and completely interrupts the flow of the sentence, it should be set off by a pair of dashes. Answer choice C creates a sentence fragment. Since "BANG!" was not spoken, it should not be in quotation marks.

48. **J.** This paragraph generally uses the present tense. The simple present tense is correct here, as a transition from the present-perfect form "has slammed."

49. **B.** An adverb—not an adjective—modifies an adverb, so "alarmingly" is correct, not "alarming." Answer choice C is wordy.

50. **G.** "Than" is used in comparisons, not "then." Since "the recommended 8 hours" refers to a block of time, "less" is correct. If "the recommended 8 hours" were replaced by "8 hours," "fewer" would be correct, since "8 hours" by itself is countable (see No. 57 below).

51. **A.** The clause "that one . . . amount" is necessary to the meaning of the sentence, so it is not set off by commas or dashes.

52. **H.** To indicate the correct cause-and-effect relationship, the cause ("your sleep debt") must be placed before the effect ("physical and psychological impairments"). Answer choices G and J are sentence fragments.

53. **B.** "Include" is never followed by a colon when it introduces a list. Answer choice D would create a sentence fragment.

54. **H.** "Their" is possessive; "there" and "they're" make no sense here. Since the possessive refers to "athletes," which is plural, it must also be plural, eliminating answer choice J.

55. **D.** "Effects," a noun, is correct. "Due to," as opposed to "of," is wordy.

Step 7
Review the
ACT practice
exam
....
330

56. **H.** To achieve parallel structure, "reduced mental quickness" is correct, since it matches the two other noun phrases in the list (a past participle modifying a noun).

57. **C.** "Fewer" is correct, since "8 (hours)" is countable. Answer choice B is eliminated, because it uses the passive voice.

58. **G.** Because the subject, "studies," is plural, the verb must be plural: "have." The phrase "conducted . . . University" is necessary to the meaning of the sentence, so it is not set off by commas.

59. **B.** Since this is an "if/then" sentence, the "if" clause must be separated from the "then" clause by a comma. A comma after "ahead" is incorrect, because "plan ahead" and "sleep in" are parts of the same concept.

60. **J.** To achieve parallel structure, "maintaining" matches "succeeding." Answer choice J reads most smoothly, because it places the verb phrase with two objects ("a student and an athlete") at the end of the sentence, rather than in the middle, where the syntax might confuse the reader.

61. **C.** The clause "that ranged there" is critical to the meaning of the sentence, so "that" is used and the clause is not set off by commas.

62. **F.** The introductory phrase "in one tradition of the red men" must be set off from the rest of the sentence by a comma. There is no reason to capitalize the adjective "red." "These" explicitly identifies the hills being discussed; "the" is not specific.

63. **B.** The phrase "floundering toward the ocean to bathe" describes the monster that was turned into stone. It is important to note that the monster was floundering, not the stone. For this reason, the sentence reads most smoothly with the transition word "as" (answer choice B), which indicates when the Great Spirit turned the monster into stone. The other choices don't make this connection clear.

64. **H.** Since the subject, "the two lakes," is plural, the verb must be plural: "were." "It's" is a contraction of "it" and "is," which makes no sense here; "its" is a possessive modifying "eyes."

65. **C.** Answer choice A is not a complete sentence. There is no reason to capitalize "witch," so choice D is eliminated. It is unclear in choice B whether "adjusting" modifies "these peaks" or "an Indian witch." Choice C expresses the relationship between the witch, the peaks, and "adjusting" clearly and succinctly.

66. **H.** Answer choices F, G, and J are run-on sentences—reading them "aloud" would quickly indicate this. "Holding" (choice H) correctly expresses the relationship between the clause "it was she . . ." and the remainder of the sentence.

67. **C.** Don't be concerned about the streak of C and H answers. Such a sequence happens occasionally on the ACT exam, so don't start second-guessing yourself. "Into" is the correct preposition, not "in to." Answer choice D, because it inverts the relationship between "old moons" and "stars," makes no sense.

68. **J.** The transition word "for" is required to introduce the result of the residents' irreverence. Answer choice H, which has no comma before "for," creates a run-on sentence.

69. **D.** It is necessary to emphasize the timing of the actions in this sentence; the witch would vanish *when* the hunters overtook her, not *because* they overtook her or *so that* they'd think they had overtaken her.

70. **F.** Answer choice G creates an incomplete sentence before the comma. Choice H creates an incomplete sentence and makes no sense. The comma in choice J separates the verb "stopped" from "with a shudder," a prepositional phrase that modifies it. Reading choice F "aloud" shows that it flows well and makes sense.

71. **D.** Answer choices A and B use the passive voice, while choice D is in the active voice. Choice C incorrectly indicates that the Indians, not Garden Rock, were held in awe.

72. **G.** Reading answer choices F and J "aloud" shows that the past-tense verb "feared" creates an awkward, ungrammatical sentence. Since the hunter took a gourd, then turned to leave, a contradicting conjunction is required: "but."

73. **A.** The revenge belongs to a single witch, so "witches" and "witchs'" are incorrect. The comma in answer choice C incorrectly separates the subject of the sentence from its verb.

74. **G.** To achieve parallel structure, the past participle "dashed" is used to match "engulfed" and "swept." Series punctuated with commas use a comma after the second-to-last item, so a comma is placed after "Cove."

75. **C.** The second sentence tells the story that led to the creek's naming and so should be placed first.

Section 2 | Mathematics

1. **C.** Substitute 3 for x in the equation:

$$y = 3(3 + 4)^3 = 3(7)^3 = 3(343) = 1,029$$

Following *PEMDAS*, ^3 applies only to values in parentheses. A calculator will facilitate the computations.

2. **G.** To determine the price per pound of each of the coffees, divide the price by the number of pounds:

Beanblaster $\$39.99 \div 12 = \$3.33$ per pound
JavaJuice $\$54.99 \div 16 = \$3.44$ per pound

3. E. First, sketch a diagram:

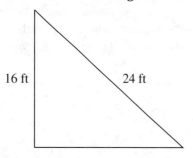

16 ft   24 ft

Because this is a right triangle, the Pythagorean identity can be used:

$a^2 + b^2 = c^2$

$16^2 + b^2 = 24^2$

$256 + b^2 = 576$

$b^2 = 320$

$b = \sqrt{320}$

4. J. The most efficient way to solve a logic problem is to scan the answer choices and eliminate those that contradict one of the statements or are not directly supported by one of the statements. Choice F is eliminated, because according to the first statement, all tall men play basketball. Choice G is eliminated, because no statement indicates whether Man A is tall or short. Choice H is eliminated, because according to the second statement, Man A does not play basketball. Choice K is eliminated, because the third statement says that Man B is tall. The only remaining choice is J.

5. A. Write an equation using the information given. Since the $20 charge is fixed without regard to the number of recycling pickups, $20 can be a constant in the equation. The number of recycling pickups varies, so a variable is multiplied by $10, the charge for one recycling pickup. These are added to yield $20 + $10x.

6. H. The value of x is determined as follows:

$x^2 + 3x = x$

$x^2 + 2x = 0$

$x(x + 2) = 0$

There are two solutions: $x = -2$ and $x = 0$.

7. D. Because alternate interior angles are equivalent, angle *FEI* is equivalent to angle *EIH*. Because the base angles of an isosceles triangle are equal, angle *EHI* = angle *EIH* = angle *FEI* = 40°. *GHE* + 40° = 180°, so *GHE* = 140°.

8. K. The least common denominator of 2, 4, 6, and 8 is the smallest number of which all four denominators are factors: 24.

9. **A.** To reduce this expression, $2x$ is distributed among the terms in parentheses:

$2x(x^2 + xy - 2xy)$
$2x(x^2) + 2x(xy) - 2x(2xy)$
$2x^3 + 2x^2y - 4x^2y$
$2x^3 - 2x^2y$

10. **K.** If you buy 4 tires, you are paying for only 3, so $3(\$125) = \$375$. Since you are buying 4 tires, however, divide $375 by 4 to determine the price per tire: $\$375 \div 4 = \$93.75$.

11. **D.** To solve this equation, expand the expression:

$(2x + 1)^3 = (2x + 1)(2x + 1)(2x + 1) = (4x^2 + 4x + 1)(2x + 1)$
$= 8x^3 + 4x^2 + 8x^2 + 4x + 2x + 1$
$= 8x^3 + 12x^2 + 6x + 1$

12. **J.** To find the total number of unique outfits, multiply the number of blouses (10) by the number of skirts (5) by the number of shoes (3):

$10 \times 5 \times 3 = 150$

13. **E.** If $c^2 = 64$, c can be either $+8$ or -8; similarly, d can be either $+9$ or -9. Thus, the possible values are as follows:

$8 + 9 = 17$
$8 - 9 = -1$
$9 - 8 = 1$
$-9 - 8 = -17$

14. **G.** The total distance between -10 and 22 is 32, so the midpoint can be found by adding the quotient of $32 \div 2$ (16) to the smaller number (-10) or subtracting 16 from the larger number (22). Either way, the result is $+6$.

15. **D.** To solve this equation, subtract the expression to the left of the equals sign from both sides:

$0 = x^2 - x - 2$
$0 = (x - 2)(x + 1)$

There are two solutions: $x = 2$ and $x = -1$.

16. **G.** Both $3x + 4$ and $3x - 4$ have a positive slope of 3, so they are parallel. Only answer choice G fulfills both conditions.

17. **B.** To solve this equation, multiply the terms in parentheses:

$(3^x)(3) = x^4$
$(3^{x+1}) = x^4$

The only answer choice that works is $x = 3$, as $(3^4) = 3^4$.

18. **K.** Rotating about the origin would place the line exactly where it is now, so it would still pass through quadrants I and III.

19. **D.** The move from B to D is 8 units, from D to C is 4 units, and from C to B is 4 units, and from B to D is 8 units: $8 + 4 + 4 + 8 = 24$.

20. **J.** For the matrix, the determinant is $(3x)(3y) - (4y)(5x) = 9xy - 20xy = -11xy$. Entering the values for x and y yields $(-11xy) = (-11)(2)(-3) = (33)(2) = 66$.

21. **C.** Assume that the larger bottle has a capacity of 1,000 mL and the smaller bottle has a capacity of 500 mL:

$$250 \text{ mL} + 375 \text{ mL} = 625 \text{mL}$$

$$625 \text{ mL} \div 1,000 \text{ mL} = \frac{5}{8}$$

Step 7
Review the
ACT practice
exam

334

22. **J.** Neither answer choice F nor G is correct, since the number of minutes Amy sets aside for a date depends on how long the date will last, plus the time it takes her to choose an outfit. Choices H and K are also incorrect, since time spent choosing a restaurant and travel time are not included in the equation. Only choice J fits the equation.

23. **B.** To fly 100,000 miles in 4 hours, Fry would have to be flying $100,000 \div 4 = 25,000$ mph. Going 25,000 mph faster would have him traveling 50,000 mph, so it would have taken him only 2 hours to travel 100,000 miles. Thus, he would save 2 hours ($4 - 2 = 2$).

24. **K.** Answer choice F cannot be true, since the $>$ sign doesn't allow c and d to be equal. Depending on whether c and d are positive or negative (or equal to zero), choices G, H, and J *could* be true, but are not necessarily true. Choice K remains, which makes sense, since the $>$ sign doesn't allow c and d to be equal.

25. **C.** To obtain the slope, solve the equation for y to determine the coefficient of x:

$$10x - 8y + 11 = 0$$
$$10x + 11 = 8y$$
$$\frac{10}{8}x + \frac{11}{8} = y$$

The slope is $\frac{10}{8}$.

26. **H.** In exponential form, $2^x = 16$. Since $2 \times 2 \times 2 \times 2 = 16$, $x = 4$.

27. **D.** Because triangles CFH and CGH share three side lengths, they are similar by the side-side-side theorem of triangle similarity. Because the triangles are similar, the smaller angle in triangle CFH is congruent to angle x, so $x + y + 90° = 180°$, and $x + y = 90°$.

28. **H.** To solve this problem, distribute the ^4 power:

$$(-3x^3y^3)^4 = (-3)^4 (x^3)^4 (y^3)^4 = 81x^{12}y^{12}$$

29. **B.** First, sketch a diagram:

The only inequality consistent with our sketch is $CF > DF$.

30. **F.** To solve this equation, remember to flip the inequality when multiplying by -1:

$$8 - 3x \leq 4$$
$$-3x \leq -4$$
$$x \geq \frac{4}{3}$$

31. **B.** Enter 45 for d. Using a calculator, $r = 2.44$.

32. **K.** Square both sides:

$$x - 1 > 4^2$$
$$x > 4^2 + 1$$
$$x > 16 + 1$$
$$x > 17$$

33. **A.** To convert degrees to radians, divide by 180 and multiply by π.

34. **J.** Use the distance formula:

$$\sqrt{(4 - (-2))^2 + (-2 - 4)^2} = \sqrt{6^2 + 6^2} = \sqrt{36 + 36} = \sqrt{72} = 6\sqrt{3}$$

35. **C.** Use the formula for the volume of a cylinder:

$$\pi r^2 h = \pi(8)^2(50) = 3{,}200\pi \approx 10{,}048$$

This is closest to answer choice C.

36. **J.** To find the weight, multiply the number of gallons by the weight per gallon: $(12{,}000)(7) = 84{,}000$ pounds.

37. **A.** Calculate the volume of the cylinder using the external dimensions, then subtract the volume using the internal dimensions:

$$\pi R^2 L - \pi(8)^2(50) = \pi R^2 L - 3{,}200\pi$$

38. **H.** To find the dimensions of the tent bottom, calculate the base of the right triangle with a height of 4 feet and a hypotenuse of 8 feet, using the Pythagorean identity:

$$a^2 + b^2 = c^2$$
$$4^2 + b^2 = 8^2$$
$$b^2 = 64 - 16$$
$$b^2 = 48$$
$$b = \sqrt{48}$$

Thus, the width of the tent floor is $2\sqrt{48}$ feet. Since the length is given as 12 feet, the tent bottom is $24\sqrt{48}$ square feet, or about 166 square feet.

39. **B.** Because AC is the diameter of the circle, we know that the sum of angle ABD and angle CBD is 180°. Given that angle CBD is 110°:

$$ABD + 110° = 180°$$
$$ABD = 70°$$

Since the total angle measure of the circle is 360°, the percentage of the circle's area that lies within angle ABD can be calculated by dividing the angle measure of ABD by the angle measure of the circle:

$$\frac{70}{360} = \frac{7}{36}$$

40. **F.** To find the total area of the sheet needed to cover the painting, take into account not only the two-dimensional surface of the painting, but also its depth. Imagine the painting as a rectangular prism. The front of the prism is 3 feet by 3 feet (9 square feet), while each of the prism's four sides is 6 inches by 3 ft (1.5 square feet). Add the front and four sides:

$$(9 + 4(1.5)) = (9 + 6) = 15 \text{ square feet}$$

41. **E.** To solve this problem, it's necessary to use the SOHCAHTOA identity. Replace $(\tan B)(\sin A)$ as follows:

$$\left(\frac{b}{a}\right)\left(\frac{a}{c}\right) = \left(\frac{ba}{ac}\right) = \left(\frac{b}{c}\right)\left(\frac{a}{a}\right) = \left(\frac{b}{c}\right)(1) = \left(\frac{b}{c}\right)$$

42. **J.** The best approach to this type of problem (in which a set of statements is given and each of the answer choices offers some combination of those statements) is to independently assess each of the statements and determine whether it is true.

Statement I: If the water coming from the hose increases, the rate at which the pool is filling should increase; therefore, an increase in slope would be expected after event a rather than the line shown.

Statement II: If the water coming from the hose decreases, the rate at which the pool is filling should decrease; therefore, a decrease in slope, as shown, would be expected after event a.

Statement III: If the drain at the bottom of the pool were opened, the rate at which the pool is filling should decrease; therefore, a decrease in slope, as shown, would be expected after event a.

Based on the slope of the line in the diagram, only statements II and III could be true.

43. **A.** The best approach is to assess each statement separately before selecting an answer choice. The line $4x + 1$ is a straight line with a slope of 4 and a y-intercept of 1. Since the line has a positive slope, Statement I is true. Since the line doesn't have a negative slope, Statement II is false. Since a line parallel to the x-axis would have a slope of 0, Statement III is false. Thus, only Statement I is true.

44. G. Statement I is clearly false: if the parabolas had identical functions, they would overlap at every point, not just at their vertices. Statement II is true, since the parabolas need to be described with different functions if they are to overlap at one point instead of at all points. Statement III is false, since a horizontal line (for example, $y = 3$) could easily intersect a parabola that opens upward (for example, x^2) without touching another parabola that opens downward (for example, $-x^2$). Thus, only Statement II is accurate.

45. D. To calculate the percentage of cable composed of copper wire vs. the weatherproof insulation, calculate and compare the cross-sectional area of the copper to the cross-sectional area of the cable.

Area of the copper $= \pi r^2 = 9\pi$
Area of the cable $= \pi r^2 = 16\pi$

$$\frac{9\pi}{16\pi} = .5625 \approx 56\%$$

46. K. If the ratio of a to b is $4:5$, then $5a = 4b$. The ratio of b to c is $8:10$, which is the same as $4:5$, so the ratio of a to c is $4^2:5^2$, or $16:25$.

47. A. Because the two endpoints are solid, the inequality must be represented by $\leq$ or $\geq$ signs. Since the two endpoints are at 0 and 4, the correct answer is A.

48. K. If $(x - 6)$ is a factor, the other factor must be $(x + 7)$, since $(-6 + 7) = 1$ for the coefficient of x. Thus, k would be $(-6)(7) = -42$, which is not among the answer choices.

49. B. If the value of a is increased by 2, then b increases by $10(2) = 20$, due to the coefficient of a. If c decreases by 1, then b decreases by $2(1) = 2$. An increase of 20 and a decrease of 2 results in a net increase of 18 for b.

50. H. Since cubes have three dimensions, a tenfold increase in each dimension results in a volume increase of 10^3, or 1,000.

51. A. To determine the area of the remaining half of the circle, calculate the area of the entire circle and divide by 2. Be sure to avoid entering 10 for the radius—the diameter is 10, so the radius is 5.

Area $= \pi r^2 = \pi(5)^2 = 25\pi$

Half of the area is $25\pi \div 2 = 12.5\pi \approx 39$ square feet

52. G. To compute the average of averages, perform a weighted average by multiplying the average age of men by the number of men, multiplying the average age of women by the number of women, adding the two products, then dividing by the total number of people.

$$\frac{(2,000)(45) + (8,000)(25)}{(2,000 + 8,000)} = \frac{90,000 + 200,000}{10,000} = \frac{290,000}{10,000} = 29$$

53. **A.** Each successive discount affects the previous discounted price, so the total discount cannot be calculated simply by adding up the percentages of all discounts and subtracting the total discount from the original price. The discounts must be applied one at a time:

First discount	($150)(1 − .10) = ($150)(.9) = $135
Second discount	($135)(1 − .15) = ($135)(.85) = $114.75
Third discount	($114.75)(1 − .25) = ($114.75)(.75) = $86.06

This problem can be quickly solved using a calculator.

54. **G.** To solve this problem, multiply the coefficients ($4 \times 3 \times 3 = 36$) and add the exponents of the x and y terms ($x^{2+3+3} = x^8$ and $y^{2+2} = y^4$). The product is $36x^8y^4$.

55. **C.** To solve this problem, two pieces of information must be compared: (1) how much the university saves by not paying Professor Fry for 36 days and (2) how much the university pays a substitute teacher for 36 days. The university is paying Professor Fry $10,770 ÷ 204 days = $52.79 per day. If he takes 36 days off with no pay, the university saves $52.79 × 36 days = $1,900.44. The university pays $104 per day for a substitute teacher: $104 × 36 days = $3,744. Find the difference between the two: $3,744 − $1,900.44 = $1,843.56.

56. **K.** To calculate the CO_2 level of the lake, divide the amount of dissolved CO_2 of the water by its dissolved CO_2 capacity:

$$\frac{4.7 \text{ mg}}{6.7 \text{ mg}} = 0.7015 \approx 70\%$$

57. **B.** An equilateral triangle has three sides of equal length. First, sketch a diagram:

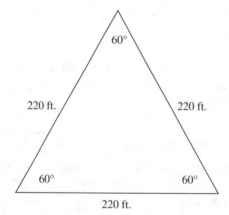

To find the area of a triangle, use the formula $A = \frac{1}{2}bh$. The length of the triangle's base is known (220 feet), but its height is not known. Fortunately, the height can be determined by using the Pythagorean identity and knowledge of the properties of an equilateral triangle. Dividing the triangle in half yields a right triangle with the following dimensions:

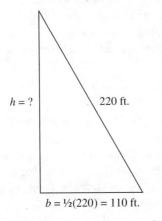

$h = ?$ 220 ft.

$b = \frac{1}{2}(220) = 110$ ft.

Use the Pythagorean identity to solve for the unknown height of the triangle:

$a^2 + b^2 = c^2$

$110^2 + b^2 = 220^2$

$b^2 = 220^2 - 110^2 = 48{,}400 - 12{,}100 = 36{,}300$

$b = \sqrt{36{,}300} \approx 190.52$ feet

Now, calculate the area of the farm plot:

$A = \frac{1}{2}bh$

$A = \frac{1}{2}(220 \text{ feet})(190.52 \text{ feet}) = 20{,}957.2$ square feet

58. **K.** If $y^3 = 216$, $y = \sqrt[3]{216} = 216^{1/3} = 6$. Thus, $y^2 + \sqrt{y} = 6^2 + \sqrt{6} \approx 36 + 2.45 = 38.45$.

59. **B.** The key to solving a probability problem is to divide the number of favorable outcomes by the number of possible outcomes. There are 4 white candies, so the numerator is 4; the total number of candies is $8 + 10 + 4 = 22$, so the denominator is 22. Thus, the probability is $\frac{4}{22}$, which can be reduced to $\frac{2}{11}$.

60. **K.** Multiply each destination's packages by the fraction that will be paid for and add the products:

$(70)(.5) + (50)(.5) + (25)(.28) + (125)(.56) = 35 + 25 + 7 + 70 = 137$

1. **C.** The author doesn't approve of the trickery employed by the "subdividers." It is evident that he regards their sales as a con when he says that "sold" was originally supposed to refer to the lots but came to refer to those who bought them, indicating that the purchasers had been tricked.

2. **F.** The subdividers "had undertaken to put in" these amenities, but before they could, the money disappeared and they weren't able to. The promised amenities were never installed, while the other enticements in the answer choices were employed.

3. **B.** The context of the phrase suggests that Mrs. Groarty is doing something to "support her seven children," meaning that she is making money from the endeavor. Answer choice B fits the context, while none of the other choices make sense.

4. **J.** Because of the recent discovery of oil in their area, the Groarty family expected to have many visitors. Not having clothing "suitable for this present occasion"—that is, their entrance into society—Mrs. Groarty bought a dress that would make her look like a member of high society.

5. **C.** Both the house, with a staircase but no second story, and Mrs. Groarty, who is awkwardly stuffed into an ill-fitting dress that is far more expensive than anyone of her social standing would normally wear, present a façade of luxury that they don't measure up to. Their appearances suggest more grandeur than either Mrs. Groarty or the house possesses.

6. **G.** Although "in the back of the room . . . there was a wooden staircase," the Groarty house "had a flat roof over its entire extent, and at no part was there any second story." While answer choices F and H are true, they are not as odd as a staircase that goes nowhere. Choice J is incorrect.

7. **D.** First, Mrs. Groarty took in washing to support her children, presumably while they were still living at home. Of the more recent events, the first to occur was the oil strike, and as a result of that, Mrs. Groarty bought the satin dress and then the etiquette book.

8. **H.** Although it can be assumed that Mrs. Groarty has worked hard all her life (for example, she took in washing to support her children), her decision to buy the satin evening gown and the etiquette book indicate that she is very eager to become an "oil-queen," having been completely swept away by the prospect.

9. **D.** Although Sinclair doesn't admire the Groarty couple (in fact, he probably regards them as shallow and unintelligent), he does not condemn them or mock them outright. He comments on their activities in a compassionate way, as if he can understand why they are behaving as they do.

10. **G.** Answer choices F and H are incorrect: an oil company does not advertise the lots on Los Robles, and the Groartys use anticipated oil wealth to buy luxury items. Choice J is correct, but it summarizes only the first two paragraphs of the passage and doesn't mention the chief focus of the passage, which is the Groarty family.

11. **C.** Answer choices A, B, and D contain errors or oversimplifications that make them inappropriate summaries of the main idea.

12. **J.** The context of the word "consumption" is that men trade the surplus of what they produce and use themselves. Answer choice J accords with this sense of "use."

13. **A.** In order for a trade to work, each side must want what the other person has in surplus, which didn't always happen. The other answer choices may be plausible, but Smith doesn't discuss them.

14. **H.** Smith's exact words are "a certain quantity of one commodity or the other, such as he imagined few people would be likely to refuse in exchange for the produce of their industry"—meaning that it's a good idea to carry something that almost everyone wants, and thereby increase the likelihood of a trade.

15. **B.** Coins are not mentioned until the final paragraph of the essay. It is important to base your answer on the portion of the passage that the question refers to, and not on the passage in general.

16. **G.** Smith devotes the fifth paragraph to a discussion of metals as the favored medium of commerce, explaining their advantages in detail, so answer choice F can be eliminated. There is no evidence that he feels a "sentimental attachment" to quaint instruments of commerce (choice H), and the issues of weighing and assaying metal bars (choice J) don't negate the advantages of metal, since they can be overcome by using coins.

17. **A.** In both paragraphs, Smith lists the media used without offering an explanation as to why each might have been used in a particular place; this eliminates answer choices B and C. Choice D is incorrect, because the first description explicitly states that each of the media was used in a different region, presumably by a different culture.

18. **J.** This is the point of view of an economist (which Smith was, in fact). In the passage, Smith examined the history of the current economic system; he wasn't writing from the other points of view, none of which matches the writing style or information presented in the passage.

19. **A.** Here are the line numbers at which the items, in order of appearance, can be found: I (8–11), IV (30–42), II (43–54), III (82–90).

Step 7
Review the
ACT practice
exam
....
342

20. **H.** The passage explains how the division of labor resulted in the adoption of commerce, which led to the need for a common medium of commerce, which led to the use of metals, which resulted in the adoption of coins. Answer choice F is incorrect, because everyday life is not discussed in the passage. Choice G is not supported by the passage, which doesn't account for regional differences. Choice J is incorrect, because its focus excludes the transition to a commerce-based economy discussed at the beginning of the passage.

21. **D.** The author agrees that many farmers contribute to the negative stereotype, but he doesn't believe the stereotype to be entirely true, and would thus be likely to disagree with the blanket statement in answer choice D.

22. **G.** In this paragraph, Allen says that farmwork may be rough and unclean, but this does not mean that the farmer doesn't know how to maintain neatness and even elegance in his household. Answer choice J expresses a similar idea, but includes the assertion that farmers are lazy and uncouth, which is certainly not supported by the second paragraph.

23. **A.** A house cannot be fickle (answer choice B). A house can be furnished (choice C), but this is irrelevant in the context of the sentence. The word seems to have a negative connotation, and "fastidious," which means excessively particular about small details, fits the context better than "fancy."

24. **H.** The author uses simile in the form "A is to B as C is to D." He claims that a farmer wearing tattered clothing is to a rundown farmhouse as a farmer wearing fancy, tailored clothing is to a palatial farmhouse—both are absurd and inappropriate to the farmer's occupation.

25. **B.** The paragraph states, "It is an arrangement . . . that costs little or nothing in the attainment . . . and . . . is a source of gratification through life." This directly supports answer choice B. There is no support for choice A or choice D in the fifth paragraph. Allen speaks to the moral obligation of mankind to improve the world (choice C), but this isn't the strongest reason he provides.

26. **J.** Line 64 states that older farmhouses "have been ruled out as antiquated." The other answer choices may be plausible, but none is supported by the passage.

27. **A.** The author establishes a hypothetical situation in the very first sentence; this is not an example from real life. The purpose of the paragraph is to show how a well-meaning farmer can end up doing more harm than good by abandoning traditional ways and adopting new and unnatural architectural methods.

28. **H.** Although the author provides examples of mistakes farmers have made, he generally regards them in a friendly and respectful light, trying to convince the reader that they are not rough and uncouth, as the stereotype suggests. The author would certainly not agree with answer choices F, G, and J, all of which suggest that farmers lack intelligence and culture.

29. **D.** It is important not to confuse the order in which these events appear in the paragraph with the order in which they actually occurred. While the farmer is reported as prosperous before his childhood is mentioned, his childhood occurred before he achieved prosperity. The correct sequence of events is that the farmer was cold as a youth, he finds himself prosperous, he builds an airtight house, and his family gets sick.

30. **G.** Allen's tone throughout the passage is respectful but concerned for farmers. While he understands their motivation for doing what they do, as he illustrates in the final paragraph, he believes that they are often misguided and wants the best for them. In this way, his tone is paternal. He certainly isn't mocking them (answer choice F); in fact, he defends them against negative stereotypes. He isn't condescending (choice H) or reverent (choice J) toward them, since he neither looks down on them nor looks up to them.

31. **C.** This sentence is the best summary of the paragraph's main idea. The other sentences merely provide evidence or examples to support the claim of this topic sentence.

32. **F.** Although the author states that the majority of people use leaf character (shape) to distinguish types of trees, he goes on to explain the flaw of using this method (most trees are leafless for a good part of the year). He would thus be less likely to use this method himself than any of the other characteristics, which he lists as alternatives to leaf shape.

33. **D.** Answer choices A, B, and C are technically correct, but none of them describes a contradiction. Choice D contains a conflict: the author advises against using leaves to tell trees apart in the first paragraph, then does just that in the second paragraph.

34. **J.** Lines 21–22 state that there are only 80 distinct species of pine, although there are over 600 varieties. The other answer choices are correct.

35. **C.** "Character" cannot mean "personality" (answer choice A) in this context. Since "size and character" are specific "characteristics" (choice B) of the needles, replacing "character" with "characteristics" would increase the level of generality. "Length" (choice D) and "size" mean nearly the same thing with regard to pine needles, so "shape" (choice C) is the only satisfactory replacement for "character" in this context.

36. **H.** Lines 53–54 state that "the bark of the white ash is darker in color than the black ash." The other answer choices are false.

37. **B.** Answer choices A, C, and D are described as contributing to the instability of the Carolina poplar. The passage blames its large roots for upsetting sidewalks and preventing the growth of other plants, but not for its instability.

38. **J.** While the passage explains why relying on leaves for tree identification can be troublesome, this is not the purpose of the passage as a whole, so answer choice F can be eliminated. Choice G is not entirely correct, since no information is given about biome or geographical range. Although the passage provides helpful pointers in distinguishing certain types of trees, it is not meant to serve as a quick-reference field guide (choice H)—its organization is not conducive to rapid reading. The purpose of the passage is to introduce the reader to tree identification and provide a variety of examples (choice J).

39. **B.** The author of the passage clearly has an expert's knowledge of tree identification and forestry, which eliminates answer choice A. The passage says nothing about conservation and logging, which eliminates choice C. The passage is not a travelogue, which eliminates choice D.

40. **J.** The tone is characteristic of an academic style, in which the goal is to convey information, not to convince the reader of any particular point of view. No emotion is expressed in the passage, which reads like a detached reporting of facts.

Section 4 Science

1. **B.** Student 1 missed only 3 symbols overall, while Student 2 missed 9 and Student 3 missed 8.

2. **H.** In comparing the number of correct identifications in Experiment 1 to those in Experiment 2, it is clear that each of the students performed better in Experiment 2. The only false statement among the answer choices is "All students accurately identified fewer symbols in Experiment 2 than Experiment 1"—in fact, the opposite is true.

3. **D.** The eye chart contains letters (both vowels and consonants) and numbers, which eliminates answer choices A, B, and C. They are all symbols, however. (Note that the chart elements are referred to as "symbols" in previous questions and in the experiment description.)

4. **H.** To determine the average percentage, divide $(4 + 1 + 2)$ by $(4 + 4 + 4)$; the result is $7 \div 12$, which is 58%.

5. **A.** The students were shown the eye chart up close along with a copy of their responses and were allowed to compare the two; in this way, they could figure out which symbols they misidentified in Experiment 1 and could try to memorize what symbol they needed to guess in Experiment 2. They were still required to stand at a distance from the eye chart, however, and they had not been given an extra incentive.

6. **G.** Although answer choice J is technically correct, it is not the best choice. The mechanism described in choice G is likely to cause a difference in scores, beyond random chance. Choice F is incorrect, because the same subjects benefited from exposure to the results of Experiment 1 in a way that different subjects could not. Choice H is incorrect, since there is no way to assess the eyesight abilities of either group of subjects.

7. **D.** Because the gases are at the same temperature, pressure, and volume, they are in equilibrium and won't move at all. This question requires some knowledge of basic chemistry.

8. **F.** At a higher temperature, the molecules of Gas 1 will be moving more rapidly than those of Gas 2, causing an increase in pressure. Thus, when the valve is opened, the greater pressure of Gas 1 will force it to enter Gas 2's side of the chamber.

9. **C.** An increase in temperature with no possibility of increasing volume will result in an increase in pressure; the two are directly proportional.

10. **F.** Just as an increase in temperature increases pressure, a decrease in temperature decreases pressure. Thus, if Gas 1 is cooled, its pressure will be less than that of Gas 2, and when the valve is opened, Gas 2 will rush into Gas 1's side of the chamber.

11. **D.** Because both the volume of the side of the chamber and the volume of Gas 1 have been doubled, the pressure of the gases will be equal, and the gases will be at equilibrium. If the valve is opened, both gases will remain in their respective sides of the chamber.

12. **F.** The description of Boyle's law at the beginning of the passage states that "the pressure and volume . . . are inversely proportional, provided that the temperature remains unchanged." Thus, temperature must remain constant.

13. **A.** According to Table 1, molasses has the highest viscosity by a large margin. As explained in the paragraph, the higher the viscosity, the more resistant a liquid is to deformation.

14. **G.** The graph shows that the wave height for molasses is greatest, followed by that of cold water, and then by that of hot water. Table 1 shows that molasses is the most viscous, followed by cold water, and then hot water. Thus, as viscosity increases, so does wave height. Answer choice J is clearly not correct, since the wave height for molasses, as shown in the graph, is not 800 times greater than that of hot water.

15. **B.** As water is heated from 40°F to 100°F, the viscosity decreases (from 10 to 8, according to Table 1). Thus, it can reasonably be assumed that the viscosity of molasses would decrease as its temperature increases.

16. **G.** Peak refers to the highest point on the graph; for each of the liquids, this point is the time period from 0.4 to 0.5 seconds. Since 0.5 seconds is not among the answer choices, choice G is correct.

17. **D.** The wave height of both samples of water returns to 0 at 1.0 seconds, but the graph does not show when the wave height of molasses returns to 0. Thus, there is not enough data to answer the question.

18. **F.** The thermal conductivity of glycol is 0.025, compared to 0.025 for nitrogen and 0.026 for air. Hydrogen and helium have much higher thermal conductivities.

19. **A.** Divide the conductivity of mercury by that of water: $8.3 \div 0.67 = 12.4$ times more conductive.

20. **J.** The most conductive material in both tables is clearly diamond, with a conductivity of 1,000–2,500; the material with the next highest conductivity is silver, at 429.

21. **C.** While the thermal conductivities of diamond, gold, and silver are relatively high, the thermal conductivity of ice is very low; the ice would probably melt rapidly when exposed to heat, making it an extremely ineffective insulator.

22. **J.** The size of the salmon run has to do with the number of fish, so only the first graph needs to be examined. The peak was clearly in 2005, when 650 million salmon were counted.

23. **C.** To find the proportion of salmon harvested in a single year, divide the number harvested by the number in the salmon run. Answer choice C has the highest proportion: 148/180, or about 82%. The next highest proportion is 156/200, about 78% (choice A).

24. **H.** The data don't support the group's claim that increasing salmon harvesting has a deleterious effect on the salmon population in the following years. On the contrary, it appears that there is a positive correlation between the size of the harvest and the size of the run in the following years.

25. **D.** There is no data in the second graph for the number harvested in 1945, so the proportion cannot be calculated. Furthermore, the proportion, as stated on the graph, is in terms of the number of fish, while the proportion in answer choices A, B, and C are in terms of the number of tons.

26. **J.** One would ordinarily expect that the size of the harvest would be inversely proportional to the size of the salmon run in the following years, but the opposite appears to be true.

27. **C.** As the temperature increased from 15°C to 25°C, the number of successful germinations went from 5 to 10 to 2, which is an increase followed by a decrease.

28. **F.** Although the highest success rate was for seeds stored at 0°C, this is not one of the answer choices. For seeds stored at the other temperatures, those stored at 5°C had the highest success rate.

29. **A.** In Study 1, the time of storage was varied; in Study 2, the storage temperature was varied. Storage time and germination time shouldn't be confused: germination time is the 30 days that the bean seeds were left in the pots, and that was unchanged in both studies.

30. **J.** Table 1 shows that the least successful storage time was 0 weeks, and Table 2 shows that the least successful storage temperature was 15°C. Combining the two would likely result in no successful sprouts.

31. **C.** In Study 1, the temperature whose results most closely mimicked those presented was 25°C, when only 5 total seeds sprouted. Since 25°C had the lowest number of successful sprouts, there is enough information to draw this conclusion.

32. **G.** Unlike the rest of the variables, which should definitely be held constant to minimize variation in the trials, the person who does the watering is unlikely to have an impact on the plants, as long as the same amount of water is applied by all team members.

33. **C.** Although the success rate of the sprouts increased as storage time increased, it is uncertain whether this pattern will continue indefinitely or there will be a point at which a longer storage time is no longer favorable. Obtaining more data simply to have more data (answer choice D) is not consistent with the principles of science—scientific investigations should always have an objective.

34. **H.** The first sentence of the passage states, "The Big Bang is the leading scientific model of the early development of the universe."

35. **A.** The first paragraph indicates that the term "Big Bang" is used because the universe was "very small and very dense" and "expanded in volume" extremely rapidly.

36. **G.** The answer is found at the end of each paragraph. Scientist 1 states that "other evidence validates the theory just as thoroughly," while Scientist 2 states that "cosmic background radiation is clearly the most compelling evidence to date."

37. **D.** Scientist 2 explains that "Within 25 years, further experiments confirmed that such radiation existed at both the frequency and distribution predicted."

38. **F.** According to Scientist 1, the speed at which a galaxy is moving away from the earth can be determined by Hubble's law ($v = H_0 D$). A distant galaxy would have a higher value for D, and thus a higher velocity.

39. **D.** It is important not to invent support for tempting answer choices. The entire passage must be examined for a definitive reason for the Big Bang, and none is found.

40. **H.** D is defined as comoving distance.

Section 5   Writing

To score your essay, use the guidelines in the box "ACT Writing score sheet" at the beginning of Step 5.

Guide to scoring the ACT exam

There are three types of ACT scores:

◄ The *raw score* is the number of questions that you answered correctly on each of the four multiple-choice sections of the exam.

◄ The *scaled score,* which is calculated from the raw score, is your score for each section of the exam, with a maximum of 36. If you take the optional Writing test, your English scaled score is combined with your Writing score to yield an English/Writing scaled score.

◄ The *composite score* is the average of all of your scaled scores.

Raw scores

You will have four raw scores, one for each of the multiple-choice sections of the exam. To determine your raw score for each section, use the number of questions you answered correctly:

	NO. OF CORRECT ANSWERS	TOTAL POSSIBLE POINTS
English	_____	75
Mathematics	_____	60
Reading	_____	40
Science	_____	40

The total possible points for the Writing test is 12; this number is not included in your raw scores.

Scaled scores

You will have four scaled scores, one for each of the multiple-choice sections of the exam (or if you take the optional Writing test, a combination English/Writing scaled score).

A scaled score is computed by multiplying the raw score for a section by 36, dividing by the total points possible on the section, and adding or subtracting a correction factor. (The correction factor varies by section and is based on the average scores on several recent ACT exams; it is intended to equalize scores across several administrations of the exam. The factors used in the chart below approximate the factors currently applied by the ACT.)

Scaled scores, which range from 1 to 36, are rounded to the nearest whole number; for example, a score of 33.4 is rounded to 33 and a score of 33.5 is rounded to 34.

	RAW SCORE				CORRECTION FACTOR	SCALED SCORE
English	_____ × 36 =	_____ ÷ 75 =	_____	− 2	=	_____
Mathematics	_____ × 36 =	_____ ÷ 60 =	_____	+ 1	=	_____
Reading	_____ × 36 =	_____ ÷ 40 =	_____	+ 2	=	_____
Science	_____ × 36 =	_____ ÷ 40 =	_____	+ 1.5	=	_____

The English/Writing scaled score

The combination of your English scaled score and your Writing test score (out of 12 possible points) yields your English/Writing scaled score. Using the table on the following page, find your English scaled score in the leftmost column and your Writing test score in the top row, then locate the score where the row and column meet; this is your English/Writing scaled score.

Composite score

Your composite score is the average of your scaled scores. It is computed by adding the four scaled scores and dividing by 4. The composite score, which ranges from 1 to 36, is rounded to the nearest whole number; for example, a score of 33.4 is rounded to 33 and a score of 33.5 is rounded to 34.

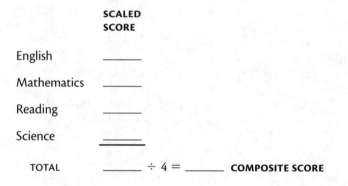

	SCALED SCORE
English	_____
Mathematics	_____
Reading	_____
Science	_____
TOTAL	_____ ÷ 4 = _____ **COMPOSITE SCORE**

Table for ACT English/Writing scaled score

English scaled score	Writing test score										
	2	3	4	5	6	7	8	9	10	11	12
36	26	27	28	29	30	31	32	33	34	35	36
35	26	27	28	29	30	31	31	32	33	34	35
34	25	26	27	28	29	30	31	32	33	34	35
33	24	25	26	27	28	29	30	31	32	33	34
32	24	25	25	26	27	28	29	30	31	32	33
31	23	24	25	26	27	28	29	30	30	31	32
30	22	23	24	25	26	27	28	29	30	31	32
29	21	22	23	24	25	26	27	28	29	30	31
28	21	22	23	24	24	25	26	27	28	29	30
27	20	21	22	23	24	25	26	27	28	28	29
26	19	20	21	22	23	24	25	26	27	28	29
25	18	19	20	21	22	23	24	25	26	27	28
24	18	19	20	21	22	23	23	24	25	26	27
23	17	18	19	20	21	22	23	24	25	26	27
22	16	17	18	19	20	21	22	23	24	25	26
21	16	17	17	18	19	20	21	22	23	24	25
20	15	16	17	18	19	20	21	21	22	23	24
19	14	15	16	17	18	19	20	21	22	23	24
18	13	14	15	16	17	18	19	20	21	22	23
17	13	14	15	16	16	17	18	19	20	21	22
16	12	13	14	15	16	17	18	19	20	20	21
15	11	12	13	14	15	16	17	18	19	20	21
14	10	11	12	13	14	15	16	17	18	19	20
13	10	11	12	13	14	14	15	16	17	18	19
12	9	10	11	12	13	14	15	16	17	18	19
11	8	9	10	11	12	13	14	15	16	17	18
10	8	9	9	10	11	12	13	14	15	16	17
9	7	8	9	10	11	12	13	13	14	15	16
8	6	7	8	9	10	11	12	13	14	15	16
7	5	6	7	8	9	10	11	12	13	14	15
6	5	6	7	7	8	9	10	11	12	13	14
5	4	5	6	7	8	9	10	11	12	12	13
4	3	4	5	6	7	8	9	10	11	12	13
3	2	3	4	5	6	7	8	9	10	11	12
2	2	3	4	5	6	6	7	8	9	10	11
1	1	2	3	4	5	6	7	8	9	10	11

Reminders for exam day

After months of preparation, exam day is near! The day before and the morning of the exam will probably be nerve-wracking.

Your mood and attitude can have a large impact on your score, so—above all—*stay calm*.

Here are some last-minute pointers:

- **Relax the week before the exam.** Don't overwork yourself with too much ACT 36 preparation. You don't have to review every concept and read your 36 Review notebook cover to cover. It's more important that you don't feel burned out on exam day.

- **Eat a healthy dinner, get a full night's sleep, and eat breakfast the next morning.** Food is fuel for the brain, and an empty stomach makes it harder to focus on the exam. Eat healthy natural foods like fruit and whole grains; these will provide sustained energy throughout the exam.

- **Bring a healthy snack and water to the exam.** Staying nourished and hydrated is important for maximizing performance.

- **Don't worry about remembering every ACT 36 strategy in this book.** When a question calls for it, you'll remember what to do.

- **Avoid stimulants.** The excessive caffeine in energy drinks will make you jittery and diminish your focus on the exam.

- **Keep everything in perspective.** Ultimately, it's just one test on one day—you can take it again if you need to. The ACT is not the be-all and end-all of your academic career. Remembering this will help you stay calm and do well.

You've worked hard for this day, and I know you can do well.

Wishing you the best,

Maria Filsinger